Sarah Millican

The Queen of Comedy

Tina Campanella

JOHN BLAKE

Published by John Blake Publishing Ltd,
3 Bramber Court, 2 Bramber Road,
London W14 9PB, England

www.johnblakebooks.com

www.facebook.com/johnblakebooks ▮
twitter.com/jblakebooks ▮

Published in paperback in 2013 as Sarah Millican – The Biography of the
Funniest Woman in Britain
This updated edition published in 2017

ISBN: 978 1 78606 452 3

British Library Cataloguing-in-Publication Data:

A catalogue record for this book is available from the British Library.

Design by www.envydesign.co.uk

Printed in Great Britain by CPI Group (UK) Ltd

1 3 5 7 9 10 8 6 4 2

Papers used b⟨...⟩ ⟨...⟩ ⟨...⟩ ⟨...⟩ ⟨...⟩ ⟨...⟩ ⟨...⟩ade
from wood gro⟨...⟩ ⟨...⟩ ⟨...⟩nform
to th⟨...⟩

Every atten⟨...⟩ ⟨...⟩rs,
but some wer⟨...⟩ ⟨...⟩ople

John ⟨...⟩

Sarah Millican

Thanks to Abi Smith for all her help with this edition –
in her words, while she may not be in the same league as
Sarah, her children think she is pretty amusing!

Contents

CHAPTER 1

The Early Years

'I don't think a lot of the girls I was at school with would have thought for a second that I would be doing this for a living. I see it as a regeneration – you know, like in Doctor Who *– I am a version of that person, but it's a totally different version.'*

Sarah Millican has come a very long way since she first decided to try her hand at stand-up comedy, aged 29. While other comics spend decades performing to small crowds in pubs and clubs, it has taken Sarah just eight whirlwind years to be crowned Britain's new first lady of funnies.

Sarah's brand of comedy could easily be described as defiant. The Geordie comic has certainly had to fight her way through life – elbows out – in order to rise to the top of the UK's crowded list of comedy talent.

But it was her challenging early years that first put her on the path to becoming the queen of filthy humour that she is today. Instead of accepting her lot, she channelled even her toughest breaks into a special brand of Millican fuel – which would quickly ignite her stellar career. And having a tough, caring family was central to her ability to see the humour in the negative.

Not long after her parents, Philip and Valerie, got married, they found themselves sitting on a bus, behind a little girl who was excitedly chattering away non-stop. It was an endearing sight, and one that prompted Philip to say: 'I want one of those…'

And that's exactly what they eventually got – a little chatterbox who they named Sarah. The couple already had a small but perfectly formed family when Valerie fell pregnant with their second child. Their eldest, Victoria, was six when baby Sarah was brought back to the Millican family home in South Shields, on the mouth of the River Tyne, east of Newcastle.

It was May 1975, the same year that saw the birth of American comedian Chelsea Handler, comedy actor Zach Braff and presenting duo Declan Donnelly and Ant McPartlin.

It was also the same year that Charlie Chaplin was knighted by the Queen, the same year that the comedy classic *Monty Python and the Holy Grail* was released, and the first year that unemployment exceeded 1,000,000 in the UK.

Fellow comedians Eric Idle and Steve Furst also hail from the area that Sarah called home – a pretty coastal town that experienced a boom in the 19th century because of its two main industries – shipbuilding and coalmining.

But the last shipbuilder, John Redhead and Sons, closed in

1984, while the last coal pit, Westoe Colliery, stopped mining in 1993 – nearly 10 years after the miners' strike devastated the north east.

Sarah was a small child during that strike, and was heavily affected by the turbulent times. Her father was an electrical engineer for one of the area's many pits, and had already seen strike action before Sarah was born.

Philip was a union branch secretary during the 1972 industrial action – a role that taught him a lot about staring down bullies and coming through tough times. And he went on to instil these values in his daughter, Sarah.

The miners' strike of 1984–85 was an even harsher time in British history – a period that has been immortalised in the film and the theatre hit *Billy Elliot*, in the BAFTA-nominated film *Brassed Off* and in countless books. Tens of thousands of miners went on strike to take a stand against poor pay conditions and the threat of numerous pit closures, under Prime Minister Margaret Thatcher. A staggering 20,000 jobs were lost as Thatcher took on the unions and it was a period of extreme hardship for the dedicated workers and their families.

Philip was one of those who went out on strike with his fellow miners and it inevitably resulted in tough times for Sarah's family.

During the year-long strike the family lived on £2 a week, but luckily Philip had talked the local shops into giving the miners bread and other foods past their sell-by date so they could feed their families.

Even then Sarah could see the funny side of the situation. 'We'd get end-of-day stuff, pies and cream cakes and bashed tins, that sort of thing,' she has since explained. 'And then I remember one of the higher-end supermarkets decided they wanted to help out and they gave us 13 trays of avocados, and all of the miners went, "I don't know what to do with an avocado". We'd literally never seen one before.'

But even with the handouts their finances were stretched to breaking point, and Sarah's uncle would spend hours on the beach collecting driftwood for fuel.

Sarah and Victoria had no money for the bus to school and back. Instead they walked everywhere in tight shoes because the family couldn't afford new ones.

She remembers getting huge blisters on her poor feet, which bled painfully. Sarah suffered in silence, even when her feet were hurting. 'I didn't say anything because I knew we hadn't any money for new ones,' Sarah told the *Sunday Times* in an interview. 'But then Mam went to social services and they said to her: "Hasn't she got wellies?" So I ended up wearing wellies all summer.'

The strike marked the end of lunchtime trips home, as there simply wasn't enough food for the family to have three meals a day. Instead the two sisters ate school dinners for the first time.

'We got free school dinners for a year and the dinner ladies used to give us extra helpings because they knew that was our meal for the day,' she recalled in an interview with the *Observer* in 2011. 'We didn't really know what was going on except that there wasn't much money to spare. My sister still can't look at spaghetti hoops because for ages that was all we had.'

As with all her tales of woe, this recollection is almost Shakespearean in its comedy. Millican's formidable talent lies in her ability to dig deep into her past for almost tragic events that will make her audience howl with laughter. It's a coping mechanism that has helped her get through tough times on countless occasions. It gives her very human brand of comedy a universal appeal.

'I think you have to go through things like that to learn the value of money and to know you can actually survive on very little,' she says.

Through her comedy, Sarah tries to convey a very profound message: we've all been through tough times, but there comes a certain point when we can laugh about the sad things that have happened to us. She takes those times and reminds us of them with style.

Sarah's mother, Valerie, was disabled and used a wheelchair. She'd had polio as a child, leaving her weak and in pain, but also with a dark sense of humour – something she passed on to both her daughters. In fact, Sarah's sister Victoria was herself a funny and feisty child, who now says that the only difference between Sarah and the rest of her family is that Sarah gets paid for being funny.

Sarah loved her childhood, and despite it certainly being tough, insists that she never felt it was a tortured existence. Valerie was the perfect stay-at-home mum and Sarah fondly remembers coming home from school every dinnertime to find soup on the stove and her slippers warming on the pipes round the boiler. She was a protective parent, who wouldn't let her children eat 'space dust', or 'fizz-wizz', the popping candy that was so popular in the eighties – because she thought it was drugs.

At home, Sarah showed her performance skills from an early age, often tap-dancing and performing poetry for her family, who were unfailingly encouraging. But she was also a shy child and admits she was very introverted. When she performed those poetry recitals they were more often than not from behind the lounge curtains. 'I guess I wanted to be heard and not seen,' she has since joked.

Unlike a lot of comedians, it certainly wasn't in the playground where she first honed her funny skills.

'I was the timid, mousy one in the corner, who wasn't popular and was swotty,' she once explained. 'But I did appear on stage at primary school.'

Unfortunately her acting debut didn't go well. 'I was Mary, but I refused to hug the doll as it was nasty and had pen scribbled on its face. After that my acting career was over, so I was chosen as the narrator because I have a clear speaking voice.'

She was a clever child, who wore glasses from the age of six and never learnt to ride a bike. Instead she had an imaginary library, from which she would lend invisible books and hand out fines for late returns. On Monday mornings at school her classmates would write accounts of their weekends. Sarah's would mostly say: 'I played in my bedroom.'

She didn't mix very much with other children. 'I was never really part of a clique at school and was very much an outsider,' she told one Leicester newspaper in 2011. 'But in some ways I think that helps you become a better comedian.'

She admits she wasn't a popular child, but is always philosophical about her early years, saying that kids who do their homework well and on time, 'rarely have many friends'.

Her family wasn't wealthy, and Sarah didn't wear trendy clothes or shoes. At the time she wished that things were different, and looked up to the cool kids, but in hindsight is glad that she wasn't part of their popular crowd. 'That's the kind of thing that makes you a comic – that little bit of resistance,' she says.

Family holidays consisted of long drives through Britain with a campsite at the end. Sarah says that her dad didn't like stopping the car once he'd started, 'so he'd try to drive from Newcastle to Cornwall in one go. My mother would make him a pint of coffee before we left, so he'd be forced to stop and go to the loo, which meant we could go too.'

It's a story that most kids of her generation can identify with, and one that sums up Sarah's early life quite neatly: her childhood was, in the main, fairly normal. An avid book reader, she was an excellent speller, and was very proud of her intellect. She certainly wasn't afraid to correct the mistakes of others.

Her father recalls that one time when he was in hospital, Sarah spent her visiting time intently reading his medical chart. Eventually she looked up at the doctor and said: 'It's a pity you can't spell 'fistula' correctly.'

Everything that Sarah did as a child, she did to the utmost. 'If she had rabbits, she'd learn everything there was to know. When she had guinea pigs, it was the same,' her father told the *Sunday Times* in a 2011 interview. 'She took a book to school once to prove that rabbits don't eat lettuce. To be fair it didn't make her any friends. She was the class geek.'

It was this strength in character and eye for detail that would push her to excel at being a comedian. At early gigs, she would always record her performances and watch them back to monitor the audience's response to each of her jokes.

Her talent for making people laugh may appear effortless, but it is the result of a very intelligent and intense approach to her work: when Sarah does something, she does it well. 'I really believe that hard work pays off and I always try to make sure something's good,' she says of her comedy work.

Sarah was a determined child who desperately wanted to succeed and become the best at something. As a youngster, she used to read the local newspaper and see stories of children her age who had won trophies for tap-dancing, or ballet. 'They had red lipstick and blue eyeshadow on and 14 trophies and I remember saying to my mum, "I'm not good at anything yet!"' she told the *Daily Telegraph* in March 2012. 'I was horrified by the thought that I didn't have any trophies, and I was, like, seven.'

But her father was the sort of man who refused to accept there were things you 'couldn't do', and didn't tolerate laziness. 'He'd say: "The only thing you can't do is stick your bum out the bedroom window and run downstairs and throw stones at it."'

The unfailing love and support she had from her parents meant that she had a happy home life. She idolised her father and still looks up to him today. Philip even has a guest spot on her TV show, where he shares his own style of 'dad advice' with her millions of viewers.

'Irritatingly he's nearly always right,' Sarah says. 'My mam used to say: "I knew he was Mr Right, but I didn't know his first name was 'Always'." He's a good man, my dad. I don't mean a nice man, that's not the same. He's someone you could trust with your life. He's kind, thoughtful, moral and sort of selfless. He just always does the right thing.'

Sarah was mercilessly bullied at school. Although never physically hurt, she endured a lot of upset at the hands of her classmates. 'It wasn't punching or locking me in a cupboard, but it wasn't any less hurtful,' Sarah has said. 'I was a swot. I was good at school and I got on well with the teachers.'

In fact she got on better with her teachers than her fellow classmates, something that her straight-talking mum told her was never going to help her make friends. 'It did make for rubbish parties,' she admits.

She remembers vividly the day when someone pointed out a letter in the problem page of teen bible *Just Seventeen*. The headline was: 'Am I A Boring Square?' Sarah was cruelly asked whether she had herself penned the problem page letter.

Her mum Valerie knew from her own experience of classroom bullying how tough it must be for her daughter. Her advice was to simply ignore the taunts.

'I remember thinking that there must be something more that I can do, a better way to retaliate,' Sarah recalled in an interview, years later. 'But my mam said they'll stop when they're not getting the reaction they want. She was absolutely right.'

Sarah was again defiant in the face of her tormentors. And to this day she still holds a grudge. Now a household name, she often gets friend requests on social networking site Facebook from the very people who used to make her life a misery.

'You get a friend request and it's quite satisfying being able to reject them,' she told one newspaper recently. 'I didn't like you at school, I'm not going to like you now. I hold massive grudges. I'm really good at grudges.'

At the time, her father was her inspiration for coping with the bullies. Sarah acknowledges that she gets a lot of her positivity and drive from the former engineer, who would tackle the bullies who followed his daughter home and constantly encouraged her to work hard, despite the teasing that her tenacious attitude to schoolwork brought her.

Sarah – a chatty and pleasant child at home, so different to her quiet nature at school – tried to hide the bullying from her parents.

One of only two children in her year who wore glasses, she got called names every day, particularly 'Norma No Mates' and 'Speccy Four Eyes'. The name-calling hurts to this day. When one interviewer for the *Guardian* joked last year that he preferred Norma No Mates, because Speccy Four Eyes 'wasn't that personal', Sarah got very defensive.

'Don't tell me what's hurtful when I'm seven. How do you know what's hurtful for me?'

The interviewer tried to diffuse the situation by saying that he'd meant it as a joke, but Sarah didn't take it that way. It's clear that being bullied at school is not something she will ever forget. But it has become a part of what defines her. Sarah is a strong and capable woman, who turns negative experiences into good ones by seeing the funny side of them.

Hers is a very personal kind of comedy, which is why so many of us identify with her stories and jokes. But we all know, deep down, that they are real. And for her to really share these experiences she has to feel them all over again – which must still hurt to some degree.

As a child Sarah quietly ignored the bullies, until her sister couldn't stand to see it any more. Her father recalls: 'It was her sister, Victoria, who told us. There was a girl who'd grab her arm and scrape a playing card down it, till the skin flayed off. What hurt most was that she's the sort of bairn who'd do anything for anyone. But some mistake kindness for softness, and she's not soft. I went through everything that she went through and eventually you learn to stand up for yourself.'

When Philip learned what was happening to his youngest, he took matters into his own hands. At the time Sarah wrote in her diary that her dad had 'put the fear of God' into one particular girl. She was a few years older than Sarah and used to follow her home from school regularly, muttering nasty things under her breath. For the young Sarah it was traumatic and finally she pointed the girl out to her dad. 'He told her it was harassment and that he would ring the police. It worked,' she says.

Philip's actions inspired her to go one step further and stick up for others like herself. He remembers Sarah coming home one day grinning from ear to ear. 'I remember her telling me that the teacher had asked her to pick the netball team, and she picked everyone who'd never been picked before – the fat ones, skinny ones, short-sighted ones... She said: "Dad, we got hammered 26 nil, but it was the best day of our lives."'

When she grew up Sarah wanted to be either a pixie or a stripper – because she thought they'd both be glamorous dancing roles. But her first real ambition was to be a vet, because of her love for animals. As a child she nicknamed herself 'The Hamster Squeezer', because she had a tendency to hug her pets that little bit too hard.

In her teens she went for work experience at a veterinary hospital, where she genuinely thought she would spend her time handing out medicine to sick pets. 'It was horrific,' she has since said. 'I thought you just stroked rabbits, you know, gave them tablets. Then they said, "Do you want to sit in on some operations?"'

Watching someone's treasured pet go under the surgeon's knife put paid to Sarah's veterinary ambitions, as the reality of a vet's job was revealed in all its gory glory.

Sarah was – in her own words – a late developer, and boys weren't a big part of her teenage years. 'I liked boys,' she told the *Scotland Herald* in 2010. 'But they didn't really like me. And the boys who did like me, I didn't like. One boy bit off his wart and showed me it. Somebody leaned over and said: "He loves you". That's apparently why he did it. It had an impact. I'm not sure it was the impact he was looking for.'

And Sarah did her best to throw off any advances that did come her way. 'I'd get asked out for drinks but I thought if a boy buys you a drink you had to have sex with him and I wasn't going to do that, so I made bloody sure I had a drink of my own,' she explains. 'I had a slightly ice maiden quality, which I liked, because I don't think you ever meet anybody you're truly meant to be with in a lairy nightclub when everyone's hammered, you can't hear what anybody's saying and the only thing you've got in common is you're both in the same location.'

It was a wise observation for one so young, but it did mean that her experience of dating was limited – a fact that would bring her heartache in the years to come.

She recalls one disastrous occasion when she brought a boyfriend home to meet the family. The story she tells about that time is teeming with exactly the kind of black comedy that Sarah insists comes from her parents.

'My mam has a picture of Marilyn Monroe dated 1953, and – as if it's the most normal thing to say in this situation – she turns to him and says, "That's the year I got polio."'

The family actually celebrated that anniversary in 2003, with a cake with '50' piped on it. Confused diners at the restaurant they were in thought it was her mum's 50th birthday. As Millican herself says: 'And she wonders where I get my dark humour from…'

In an attempt to bring her shy daughter out of her shell, Sarah's mother got her a Saturday job at the local WH Smith, where she carried out her duties as diligently as her schoolwork. Blossoming into a creative and intelligent woman, Sarah wanted to go to university, but knew that her family's finances wouldn't stretch to such a big expense.

When the strikes were over, Philip had gone back to work at the mines, but the family had continued to struggle financially. Millican didn't complain. 'I knew that the only way they could afford for me to go was if I stayed at home, and I knew part of university was to make beans on toast in a bedsit and have parties. My dad was working seven days a week and I didn't want to put any more pressure on him.'

Sarah saw her family as a close-knit team, and as part of this special group there was no room for selfishness. If something that she wanted would make life difficult for the rest of her family, then she would simply stop wanting it.

From the tender age of 15 Sarah knew that she wanted to work in the media in some way. When someone unhelpfully pointed out that she needed a degree for that kind of career, she just ignored them. So after her A levels, Sarah did a course in film and television production as a way of keeping up her creative interests – but with no thought of putting herself in front of the camera. She tried to get into television production in nearby Newcastle, but there were few jobs, so she was unsuccessful. Then followed a stream of unfulfilling roles in jobs that couldn't even begin to challenge the clever comic-to-be.

She worked in a call centre, and then as a producer for audio books. She is still amused by the title of one Mills and Boon book she recorded in the course of her work: *Once Upon A Mattress*.

'It seemed to happen that we always read sex scenes on a Sunday morning,' she has explained. 'Which seemed so wrong in so many ways.'

When she turned 18, Sarah found work in a local cinema, with people she had never met before. It was a fresh start for the once shy girl, who suddenly found herself popular. She was astonished by how many people liked her and is remembered by her former colleagues as a feisty and funny character.

She continued to fill her spare time with creative projects, taking several night classes each week in subjects like creative writing and film editing. She regularly wrote a film column for her local paper, and made numerous short films with her new friends.

Her subject matter always had a funny angle to it, because that was what she enjoyed. It was obvious that Sarah was bursting with creativity and needed an outlet…

CHAPTER 2

Life Begins
At 29

'Can you imagine if he hadn't left me? I'd still be in a job I hated, watching telly in a damp flat. I had to go really low to come back up.'

When she turned 21, Sarah was still living at home and working in the local cinema. But her spare time was filled to the brim with creative exploits and her ambition was raging.

She wrote plays and poems, edited short films and had even had one of her half-hour plays performed at Newcastle's Live Theatre.

She didn't know exactly what direction she wanted her future to take, but she knew that writing made her feel as if she was going somewhere. It was also an outlet for her vast intellect. In defiance at not being able to go to university, she was giving herself the kind of higher education she craved.

Leaving her school days – and those soul-crushing bullies – behind, she had blossomed into a feisty young woman with numerous friends and talents.

It was at this youthful peak that she met her husband-to-be, Andrew. A colleague at the cinema, he was first a friend, then a loving boyfriend, and a mere two weeks later, Sarah's fiancé. It was, as she herself admits, a whirlwind romance. 'He was my first love, I suppose,' she explained in a recent interview. 'I worked with him. He was funny.'

In her youth, Sarah had a very romantic view of love. She didn't really understand one-night stands and believed that love was for life. Having grown up in such a close family, she had seen her mother and father's strong marriage weather numerous storms and based her own relationship desires on their dedicated devotion.

She was limited in her dating experience and although she'd had boyfriends before, it was the first time she had really been part of a couple. She loved being part of something special.

Having only really just set out on her journey to self-discovery, with Andrew she found herself easily defined – as a wife. 'I was under the impression that once you met someone that's it done, that's sorted,' she told *The Herald* in 2010. 'That's the love life sorted. Let's concentrate on my career. So when I met my ex-husband, that's how I felt.'

Sarah always participates with her audience when she performs her stand-up shows – and regularly asks them personal and probing questions. One of her favourite things to ask on stage is, how do you know when it's love? 'You never know what you're going to hear and it's always unpredictable and funny,' she told *The Liverpool Post*, early in 2013.

Over the years, the answers have been varied. During one show, one woman said: 'A kiss before you go to bed…' Her husband responded to the question by saying: 'If she hasn't changed the locks…' Sarah told the couple, who revealed they'd been married for 30 years, that she loved the power balance between them. She quipped: 'She just wants a kiss – you're worried you're never gonna see her again, or any of your CDs.'

One young man sweetly said of his girlfriend of three months: 'I miss her when she's not here…' Sarah's response was: 'Aw, I can't take the piss out of that – I really want to but I can't.'

Others answered: 'leaving the toilet door open', 'butterflies in your tummy', 'flowers' and 'presents', to which Sarah responded: 'Money-grabbing whore!' One lad even shouted out 'depression', to which she replied: 'You're single, are you? You must be happy then…'

But for Sarah, it was enough just to be in the cosy world of coupledom, and after her wedding in 1997, she quickly settled down to married life. Moving out of her parents' home and into a small flat with her new husband, Sarah was content. 'She loved being married and she loved her little home,' her dad Philip recalled in an interview in 2011.

Andrew was supportive of her writing talents and Sarah has always been keen to point out that he wasn't oppressive or in any way a 'bad' husband. But whereas before she would spend her evenings and weekends scribbling away at some play or another, suddenly she had a new way of occupying her time – spending it with the man she loved. 'He wasn't all "do the dishes, woman", but I was like – "I'd rather play out with you",' she has explained.

But the comfortable routines of marriage eventually took its toll on both Sarah's ambition, and her self-image. She started working at the local job centre and spent her spare time watching the telly and cosying up with her husband.

Sarah spent her working days helping a steady stream of jobseekers to find work. Some parts of the role she found she very much enjoyed – boosting people's confidence and putting them back on the right path. She enjoyed seeing them grow from being, as she describes it, 'quite broken', to getting a job and being back on their feet.

But overall, for Sarah, who admits she's very sensitive under her sweary exterior, it was tough being surrounded by so much fear and sadness.

She would often come home crying, and worried that she would one day become hardened to the work. 'I used to say, "I'm going to write my way out of this shithole",' she said in a 2011 interview with *The Observer*. 'And I didn't mean so much the place I was living or working, just the job I had. I never felt fulfilled, so that's why I wrote, to get that out of my system.'

But, as the years of married life passed, she stopped writing altogether. She said later: 'I just stopped doing it for a bit while I carried on living, having a job and being married and all those sorts of things.'

Slowly her feistiness disappeared, and she became quiet and almost mouse-like again. But she liked being married and was content with the lifestyle she had. For her, the seven married years passed by very happily. She wasn't looking for adventure or thrills – she truly believed she had everything she needed.

The couple bought two cats, and Sarah thought her life was complete – even if somewhere deep down, she knew something was lacking... 'I was too quiet, too meek and mild,' she has since said. 'I'd go out with my sister and her friends but I'd make them go to an Italian and I'd have a margherita pizza. Maybe potato skins as a starter if I was feeling posh.'

Together the couple planned out their future, right down to their retirement plans. Sarah hated her job, but she was counting down to the time when they would both finish their working lives and could just be together, unfettered by responsibility. In reality, she was coasting. But it was only with hindsight that she could see her twenties for what they really were: a life on hold. And sadly that hindsight would come about very painfully.

After seven years, Sarah was used to her married life and still loved her husband dearly. But without her even noticing, the couple were growing apart. One day, without a word of warning, Andrew finally told her the truth: he wasn't in love with her any more.

There was no one else, but he wanted something more from his life and Sarah wasn't making him happy any more. 'I wasn't expecting it at all,' she recalls. 'It came quite out of the blue. And it was emotionally shattering.'

That day was Mothering Sunday, 2004.

As the rest of the country was sleeping soundly, in her small, damp Newcastle flat, Sarah's world was ending. At

2am, Philip received the most heartbreaking phone call of his life. His daughter was sobbing in the street, wandering listlessly outside her once happy home. 'Dad,' she said. 'Can I come home?'

'Anytime you like darling,' he replied. 'You've always got a home here.'

Safe in the bosom of her family, she fell apart.

Her feelings during that time have been much documented, both as part of her stand-up routines and in countless interviews with national newspapers.

'We had plans for the rest of our lives and it's just like somebody has rubbed everything out,' she told one newspaper. 'I was 29 and I had thought my marriage was fine,' she told another. 'So it was an odd time because I'd never been properly broken-hearted before and for a while I didn't want to do anything except cry my eyes out all day.'

For a long time, that's all she did.

Being the ultimate 'home-girl', Sarah felt she'd had everything ripped out from underneath her. After all, she's a woman who still takes a photo from the view of her sofa away on tour with her, and still likes nothing better than to curl up on the sofa, with a blanket across her feet. But now her home was a place of sadness.

'I bullied him into going to Relate, where I paid £70 for a man to tell us he could do nothing for us. They were the most expensive tissues I've ever snotted into,' she recounted on a Radio 4 show in 2008.

Despite her husband's devastating admission, the couple had to remain living together until they could sell the flat that they had once planned to make their family home. Now estranged from her husband, Sarah couldn't bear the thought of going back each night after work. So she turned to a once familiar outlet to occupy her time – writing.

Searching around for something suitable, she enrolled in a new writer programme at her local theatre. 'I would go there straight after work. It got so the staff knew my name. They kind of saved me in a way.'

Flexing her writing muscles once more, the next few months were a mixture of pain and exhilaration. Some days her life felt utterly broken and she thought she would never recover. On others she felt alive again, and free to do as she pleased. 'I had what I call my She-Ra moments,' she has often explained, referencing the popular eighties cartoon figure – a symbol for girl power long before The Spice Girls existed.

'If somebody said, "Climb that mountain", I would go, "Well you'll have to get us the right shoes but I could probably do that." I'd never felt like that before. I had only ever had the middle ground – and to go from so low to so high was exhilarating.' She cut her long hair soon afterwards, an act that many people associate with a break-up.

Sarah stored up her painful memories of that time and retreated into the comfort of her family's arms, as she tried to make sense of what was happening to her life. The house went on the market and eventually sold. Finally the day came when she and her husband had to say their last goodbyes. Packing up the last of her things into a small box, she handed over their cats and shut the door on her once cosy life.

Sarah would have loved to take the pets with her, but her

parents were allergic, and it was to their house that she was now headed.

As she walked away, she was understandably reflective. She had lost her husband, home and feline family and was moving back in with her parents, aged nearly 30. She wandered through the park near their home, crying yet more exhausting tears. Then her phone rang and the simple conversation that followed would prove to be the catalyst for a career change that would soon transform her life.

CHAPTER 3

Laughter As
Therapy

*'Stand-up became my therapy, where I felt valued. The idea of
making strangers laugh… it was a euphoric sensation.'*

Linda Smith was a waspish and beguiling stand-up
comic, who died in 2006 after a three-year battle with
ovarian cancer. Voted the Wittiest Living Person by BBC
Radio 4 in 2004, Linda's extremely popular style was based
around deadpan diatribes about every day irritations – much
like Sarah's would be.

Her earliest stand-up appearances were benefit concerts in
the 1980s, staged in solidarity with the striking British miners.
She was a lifelong socialist, with a no-nonsense attitude.

Sarah Millican had never been to a stand-up comedy
night, but she did enjoy watching comedians at the theatre.
One of those comedians was Linda Smith, and it's easy to see
how the late comic had a huge influence on Sarah's style.

There are other parallels to be drawn between the two. When Linda died, her fans were shocked. She had kept her illness a secret, because she didn't want to be thought of as a victim. Instead she carried on performing and appearing on television, overcoming her fear and suffering – and using comedy as a coping mechanism.

Sarah also used comedy as a coping mechanism, and she used the pain of her divorce as a springboard to success. She took her overwhelming sadness and used other people's laughter to beat it into submission.

The night Sarah and Andrew sold their home, they walked out of the flat in totally different directions, both metaphorically and physically. And bizarrely, on that lonely last walk through the park from her flat, it was Linda Smith who inspired her to begin the long and difficult process of rebuilding her life – though Linda herself would sadly never know.

Linda was performing that night in the Customs House, a popular Newcastle venue, and Sarah, a big fan, had tried to get tickets. Smith was understandably popular in the area, because of her ties to the miners, and sadly all the tickets had sold out. Instead Sarah had been placed on a reserve list.

So when her phone began to ring, and she answered the call through her tears to discover a ticket had become available, Sarah was torn. 'I thought, "I'm not really in the mood for this but perhaps that's exactly why I should go," she has said about that pivotal moment. 'I can't do this, I want to sit in the house and eat cake.'

A few hours later, tears were still streaming down her face – but this time they were tears of laughter. 'I sat on my own and she was wonderful. I came out and my life was just as shit as when I went in, but for an hour and a half I'd forgotten about it.'

It was an inspirational moment. It would be a long time before Sarah would be over the trauma of her divorce, but for that hour and a half Sarah experienced the healing power of a good laugh. 'Laughing is the most important thing,' she often says. 'Laughing can take you out of the life that you have.'

It was the tool she would use to conquer her demons and become that strong feisty woman again – the woman she remembered being, back before her husband broke her heart.

Sarah duly moved back in with her parents, where she would stay for the next two years: 'I turned to my loving family who supported me and helped me put my life back together.'

Back in her old room she must have felt as if she'd gone backwards in her life instead of forwards. She'd been a 'grown up' for years. She'd been married and owned her own flat. Yet now she was sobbing on her old bed like she'd done last as a small child. It can't have helped when her father gently asked her if she wanted her old Philip Schofield posters out of the loft. Sarah had been a big fan of the presenter when she was a child and had pictures of him all over her wall. 'No. I'm not 14, I'm divorced,' she chastised.

Her family cocooned her with love, and her sister in particular was a much-needed source of comfort. She once spent four hours softly stroking Sarah's hair as she mourned her marriage.

Philip made endless clumsy attempts to console his

youngest child. 'He's the most big-hearted, kindly person you could meet but sometimes he doesn't always think through his wording,' Sarah explained diplomatically to *The Shields Gazette* in December 2012.

She recalled how he once sat her down and said: 'Well love, you're bound to be upset. You've lost everything. You've got nothing left.' As Sarah herself admits, they weren't exactly encouraging words, 'but he was coming from a lovely place'. And those words would hold special meaning for Sarah in years to come...

At work, her colleagues knew that she was suffering and did everything they could to help. On days when she felt – in her own words – 'crumpled', she would cry softly at her desk. 'I worked with a guy who asked me if there was anything he could do to help. I said, "I really love pictures of animals and clothes". He saw it as a project. He'd see when I was crying and I'd get an email from him that would have a picture of a pig in slippers. He couldn't change what was happening, but he could make a little glimmer of a smile every now and again.'

It was yet more proof that laughter really was the best therapy.

Over the next few months Sarah took each day as it came. Then, on one of her She-Ra days, she signed up to a new kind of workshop – for people who had written poetry but never performed. And it was at this point that Sarah's journey to national treasure began...

By 2004, Kate Fox had been trying to break into the stand-up comedy circuit for years. She had tried all sorts of performance techniques – characters, audience interaction, wearing glasses, not wearing glasses – but none of them had felt natural. Eventually she added funny poems to her set and finally something clicked. She had found her place – as a performance poet.

Wanting to share her new-found freedom, Kate began running workshops in Newcastle for performers who wanted to try new things. 'At the first one, a woman did a funny monologue about the divorce she was going through,' Kate wrote on her blog four years later. 'Spinning the crap into comedy gold. Pitch perfect punchlines. The audience belly laughed. I said: "You're a stand-up."

That woman, of course, was Sarah Millican.

Sarah had never exactly lacked confidence; her family had been far too supportive for that to be a character issue. But the ending of her marriage had certainly dented her courage. Couple that with her resolute desire to be heard and not seen – to work behind the scenes, writing and producing – and it's hard to see what made her sign up to the course in the first place.

But at the end of the workshop, she performed a monologue which later became the bedrock of her first solo show. 'I was shaking and some of it was crushingly sad. But some of it was hilarious and the audience responded accordingly.'

The sound of the applause was exhilarating. Sarah was overwhelmed by the buzz she felt, and instantly decided it was worth the nerves. Organiser Kate was the first to congratulate her. She could see the beginnings of an outstanding talent and the two became firm friends.

Sarah ran into the ladies toilets and jumped up and down

with excitement. Then, of course, she rang her dad to tell him how it had gone.

For the next six months Sarah continued to write and worked on getting over the split. She read self-help books for inspiration, and was particularly encouraged by *It's Your Life, What Are You Going To Do With It?* by Anthony Grant. 'It was full of exercises that I ignored, but it had a lot of first-hand stories – like, "I was 50 and I got into RADA".'

She decided to see a counsellor, to help her work through her anger and upset. 'I rang the Samaritans at first, who didn't laugh when I told them not to worry – that I was rubbish at tying knots,' she later said on Radio 4.

Before the break-up, Sarah had always thought that counselling was for people who didn't have a loving and understanding family, and countless friends to 'cry at'. But Sarah had those things already – and she quickly realised she needed more. 'I wanted to work through it with someone who could help me fix myself. What I didn't want was to take all this emotional baggage into my next relationship.'

It was a wise decision. But as the words poured out of Sarah at each meeting, her counsellor reached one concrete conclusion: Sarah was a naturally funny woman. 'She kept telling me that what I'd just said was really funny and might make a joke. At the time I was going through this horrible time, but sometimes finding funny things within it,' she told *The Sun* in 2012.

Sarah is now widely known for her jaw-droppingly filthy observations. She has shocked thousands with her tales of broken vibrators, awkward sex and her preoccupation with both male and female genitalia.

But these open and frank admissions on the subject of sex haven't always been a part of her personality. In fact, it wasn't until a post-split trip to Amsterdam that her eyes were opened to the funny side of copulation.

Thinking that Sarah probably needed a bit of cheering up, one of her friends whisked her off to the Dutch capital for a mini break. The resulting few days were a revelation, and would help shape her views on men and women and the things they did 'under the covers'.

Amsterdam is well known for its liberal attitude to sex. A multitude of family-friendly tourist attractions sit side by side with a whirlwind of nude performances, live sex shows, prostitutes plying their trade, and of course, hundreds of sex shops.

She later described the trip in an interview with *The Sunday Times*. 'On the first day, she took me to her favourite sex shop and I remember thinking: "You have a favourite sex shop? I've never even been to one." I just blushed, while she behaved as if she were in a dress store and asked me if I wanted a vibrator to match my coat, but I bought one that didn't. The rest of the shop was full of things that were a complete mystery to me. It was a real eye-opener and quite a good way of coming to terms with divorce.'

The period following her split with Andrew was the toughest period of her life, but also the most revealing. Sarah had been on a steep learning curve and she now knew that it was time to truly change her life. For Sarah, turning her pain into comedy was therapeutic. An idea had begun to form in her brain, and the better she began to feel, the deeper the idea began to root...

Six months after her first performance workshop, she picked up the phone and dialed Kate Fox's number.

'I think I want to try stand-up comedy,' she told her.

'I know,' replied Kate. She had been waiting patiently for the call.

Kate Fox is now a well-respected and highly in-demand stand-up poet and writer. She constantly gigs around the country, in between her stints on Radio 4's *Saturday Live* and BBC2's *Politics Show*. She's also incredibly funny.

She may not have had the fame and fortune that her friend Sarah is currently experiencing – she even openly admits to being a teeny bit jealous – but she is widely credited with being the first person to really send her on her way to stardom. 'I could clearly see her trajectory there and then,' Kate has said about seeing Sarah perform for the first time. And Sarah will always be grateful that she saw something in her.

Kate agreed to find her a stand-up gig and Sarah got off the phone and began to prepare.

When you break a bone in your body, it heals stronger than it was before. The same can be said of broken hearts. She's certainly a stronger woman than she was during her married years and she's no longer 'coasting along in the middle', feeling as if she 'had potential but didn't really know where it was'.

She doesn't blame her ex-husband for the split, despite spending night after night since discussing their divorce on stage. 'He was my first love. He's not a bad man, we just fell out of love. It happens to a lot of people and it's good to be able to handle it. We were very young when we married, but you can't think, "I shouldn't have done it", because if I hadn't, and then got divorced, I wouldn't be here now. We were together for seven years so that's still a long time. I don't regret it at all.'

But she doesn't have anything to do with him either. In fact, she has no idea where he is or what he is doing. 'There was no need to see him again. We cut off ties. I know some people keep in touch with their exes but I think that's weird,' she told *The Mirror* in 2011. 'And he's never contacted me – I guess that makes him a decent person for not coming and knocking once I was famous.'

In some ways, Sarah thinks the whole sad experience was the best thing that could have happened to her – and comedy was definitely the best form of therapy. 'It was definitely therapy for the first six months, no doubt about it. If you take anything hard and someone cracks a joke, as long as it is at the right time, it can be cathartic to be able to laugh. It can be a release valve.

'I think anybody who has been through something relatively traumatic tends to throw themselves into work, or they get drunk a lot or sleep around.

'I just decided to try to be funny for a living, to get good enough so someone would pay me. I knew nobody in the industry, had no contacts, and what I like about it is it just proved you can get on in the industry if you are funny, clearly, and work really hard, and learn from any mistakes you make.

'I worked through a difficult time like anybody does and came out of it with a career. Odd but very, very nice.'

CHAPTER 4

Standing Up

'An audience not laughing is nothing when your husband's just told you he doesn't love you anymore.'

Kate Fox had seen a lot of raw talent when she first watched Sarah Millican perform her two-minute monologue on divorce. She had been an integral part of Newcastle's thriving spoken word and open mic scene for a number of years and was used to seeing people give performance art a go, before giving up.

It's an exciting but difficult world. Any aspiring comedian or poet will tell you that it involves a lot of waiting around, getting nervous and brightly smiling in the face of sparse but critical audiences.

But there was something that lifted Sarah above the rest of that Newcastle scene – a spark that Kate could see had enormous potential – and it was for this reason that she booked her a gig at The Dog and Parrot pub in Newcastle.

It's one thing when others have faith in you, but it's quite another to have faith in yourself. And raw talent will only take you so far – Sarah knew she had a lot of work to do to prepare for her first gig.

She threw herself into it like she had done with every task she performed as a child – diligently. If she was going to do it, she was going to do it the best she could. So she knuckled down and applied her strong work ethic to this new life direction. Delving deep into the pain of her divorce, she began to chart all the darkly funny moments she had experienced since her husband had told her it was over. Then she booked herself into a number of workshops to hone her performance skills.

These workshops took place in low-key and comfortable surroundings. One was at The Bridge Hotel – a hundred-year-old public house, situated next to the historic High Level Bridge and known for its popular live music nights. Another took place at The Cumberland Arms, which was, at the time, just starting to become a haven for the local comedy scene. It was, and still is, home to The Suggestibles, a talented group of award-winning Newcastle improv comedians, who perform on the last Friday of every month.

By day Sarah worked in her civil service job, helping others to get back on their feet by finding them work. By night she helped herself to do the very same thing – by working on her first ever stand-up set.

Finally the big day arrived. Sarah got ready at home, putting on a batwing top, before going downstairs and telling her dad she was off to do a gig. 'I dressed like I was going to a disco,' she has since recalled.

Philip was surprised.

'You? On stage?' he asked, incredulous. 'You cannot be serious. You're the quietest, most reserved person I've ever met!'

His surprised reaction was understandable. But he was also excited and wanted to support his daughter, like he had done throughout her life. Whatever Sarah wanted to do, he wanted be the first person to cheer her on. He asked: 'Can I come?'

'No you can't!' was her swift reply. It was going to be hard enough without having her family in the audience.

She made her way to The Dog and Parrot, and waited nervously for her turn at the open mic event. It had been organised by Kate as part of her New Word Order project, which ran from 2004 to 2010. Kate acted as compere for the regular events, introducing a variety of acts for short five-minute slots. It was a chance to test material out and gauge audience response and was perfect for Sarah's first time on stage.

Located on Newcastle's Clayton Street, close to the main train station, The Dog and Parrot now bills itself as the city's only indie rock and roll bar. It's a cool, relaxed environment, dedicated to good music, and is an avid supporter of the local live singing and comedy scene. It recently won the *Chortle* award for Best Northern Comedy Venue, because of its regular comedy slot *Long Live Comedy*.

Comedians who have performed there include Kai Humphries, former *Byker Grove* actor Phil Harker, and Dan Willis – better known as Harold Bishop from *Neighbours*, who has been performing there in his infamous specs and leather jacket for years.

Sarah had never been to a comedy club before taking to the stage at The Dog and Parrot. 'I'd seen two tours of comedians, in one of the big theatres, but I'd never been in a comedy club,' she has admitted. 'In some way it helped. Some comics see loads of comedy but it means at times they end up emulating people they admire. But because I had not seen anyone like that, it was just all about me. Everything I ever do is personal and entirely factual or based on fact and then exploded for comic effect.'

When Kate announced Sarah's name, she walked out to face the 50 people in the audience. It was the first time that anyone would have seen the timid looking bespectacled brunette ply her new trade. It was the first time anyone would have heard her sweetly soft, high-pitched, lilting tone, delivering her now infamously sarcastic wit.

One of Sarah's early reviews said that she 'looks like a primary-school teacher with the mouth of a biker', which she has always quite liked. 'It's better than being the other way round,' she has since said. The audience must have wondered what this demure looking girl was doing on the stage.

Pale and quiet, she began to speak.

For the first two-and-a-half minutes, arms were folded and not a chuckle was heard in the crowd. One woman who was in the audience that night blogged about what she saw, saying: 'She was quiet and I thought a little aloof (as some talented performers seem to be). I thought her material was funny with a cynical edge; the guy next to me complained.'

Undeterred, Sarah thought back to her family and their clumsy attempts to soothe her broken heart. She began to tell the audience a familiar story... sobbing in a flood of tears and snot, her husband had just told her he was leaving. Doing an impression of her father, she said: 'Well you're bound to be upset.'

Then she paused.

'You've lost everything.'

She paused again.

'You've got nothing left!'

And with those poignant words, the small crowd erupted into fits of laughter. The combination of tone and timing in her impersonation of a practical Geordie man trying to cope with an emotional landslide was instant comedy gold. The audience was finally hers. Enthused, Millican poured out more of the same, and as her confidence grew, the chuckles kept coming.

She has since said of that night: 'It was a tough audience. For two-and-a-half minutes no one laughed and that felt like a lifetime. Then I described how my marriage broke up, how I moved back home with my parents and how my dad tried to comfort me as I was sobbing all day, every day. The room went from silence to a massive laugh and I thought, "Right, that's going at the beginning."'

It's an attitude that led her to begin constantly honing and perfecting her act, something that she still does today. Whenever she puts on a new show, Sarah says she does at least 30 previews at small venues before she even sets foot on a main stage. She tries things out, checking what works and discarding what doesn't.

'I love writing new jokes,' she says. 'I love trying new jokes out. I love the feeling they get when they work. I love the process of shaping a show. It's a bit like gardening – you know that not all your seedlings are going to take, but at the end there's going to be a good tomato plant.'

It's a process that she took very seriously, even at her first gig. 'It's hard work. It's not hard work like being a nurse or being a fireman. But it's hard in that there's no magic formula. You've just got to work your arse off.'

As she finished that first five-minute slot, she bounced off the stage, feeling more alive than she had in months. She was in control of her life again, and it felt good.

After being congratulated on her performance, the first thing she did was pick up the phone and call home. 'Yeee-ss!' she squealed, full of excitement. Her next words were particularly poignant. 'Dad, he may not love us, but there were 50 in there who did,' she enthused. 'It was the best night of my life.'

It was the ultimate therapy for Sarah and it helped put the pain of her husband's rejection into perspective. For the first time, she must have understood that she was starting to heal. As she herself has explained: 'I'd already had the worst kind of rejection. An audience not laughing is nothing when your husband's just told you he doesn't love you anymore. To have one person look at you and go "No"… somehow 50 people in a room going "No" isn't so bad. They're only judging you on 20 minutes of material, not a seven-year marriage.'

Sarah had finally found the direction she wanted to take in life. She wanted to be a stand-up comic. And most of her early material would be inspired by the one thing she loved more than anything: her family. After all, her audience had found the jokes about her dad hilarious.

She threw herself into gigging, supported by her family and friends, Kate Fox, and her civil service work colleagues.

Sarah was focused. Determined. After each performance she would listen to herself on a dictaphone, analysing her performance and the audience's reaction to her jokes. Only a solitary giggle? Out it went. A raucous belly laugh? The joke was moved further up in the running order.

She also worked on perfecting her pre-show routine – a must for any stand-up. There's nothing glamorous about it: no final sweep of blusher, or spritz of perfume. Instead, Sarah's is fundamentally practical. 'I always have a proper last wee,' she says. 'So, like, I might do a few wees but then I'll have to do the big one that'll be the last one. And I also check my nose. I blow my nose and then I check that it's clear because I think if you came out to an audience and they didn't laugh, one of the reasons they didn't laugh shouldn't be that you had something hanging...'

Ever sensible, Sarah kept her day job, filling out forms and tapping away at her computer, while itching to leave the office. Because at night she would get in her car and drive to wherever her next gig was – and she loved every minute of it.

Sitting backstage with other comics, she finally felt truly comfortable. 'I was never very popular at school, but here I was funny and interesting. I could be myself. Comics are a bit messed up, but when you put us all together, we're okay.'

She had found her career and her people. She didn't care how long it took, or how much hard work it would be. She would make this world her own.

CHAPTER 5

On The Road

'To be a stand-up you just have to have the bottle to get on stage. To be a good stand-up, that's something different. You have to be funny and like trains and not mind crying on trains, and you have to be good at showers...'

One of the biggest draws of stand-up comedy is that it looks deceptively easy. You don't need artistic talent or model looks to get up on stage at an open mic night – just the confidence to face the audience and a few sharp observations about life. A laugh here, a laugh there, and the next thing you know you're in showbiz, right?

Sadly it's not that easy. The reality of life as a stand-up comedian is that it is a tough and – ironically – unsociable lifestyle.

American comedian and all-round funny man Will Ferrell calls stand-up comedy 'hard, lonely and vicious'. Many in his field would wholeheartedly agree. For the hundreds of comics who drive around the country to bars and clubs to perform, many would admit that they sometimes feel as if they are paid to travel, not to make people laugh. They spend a lot of time alone, making their way to small gigs, and the hostility they face when they get to their destination can be soul crushing. As a result you have to be tough and fearless to get up on stage.

'Going on stage in front of an audience is nerve-racking,' Sarah admits. 'I have a really good "I'm having a lovely time" face. It's fake. You can fake confidence until you get it. As soon as I have a couple of big laughs under my belt then that confidence is real. There's nothing better than making people laugh. I love it. It's the best job in the world.'

For Sarah, who had already experienced what was – for her – the worst kind of rejection, it was a challenge she enthusiastically faced. Every giggle she elicited from the audience meant one more person who loved her. Every tear of laughter streaming down an audience member's face counteracted one she had shed over her marriage break-up.

So she threw herself into the world of comedy and was determined to make it her own. In any spare moment she had, she worked on her act. 'I think you can break it down into do-able chunks and ultimately get where you want to be,' she says.

She admits she stopped paying attention at work, but her colleagues were still supportive. The flexible timetable of being in the civil service gave her the freedom to gig, while the specific mechanics of the job proved invaluable.

'I worked with them for a long time at the Jobcentre.

Taking people's claims, loads of things like that. I always liked dealing with the public, and I guess that's why, when I talk to the audience in my shows, it's that bit that's a transferable skill. I was good at customer service, always enjoyed that, because it makes each day totally different.'

She was and still is grateful to her colleagues. 'They were very good to me,' she says. 'They said I was a breath of fresh air – that's what they put on my leaving card, which was really nice. I think because I was quite entertaining round the office they just went, "It doesn't matter that she's not very good". My focus was entirely somewhere else.'

As her act became more accomplished, she began to get more and more gigs – further and further away from home. It wasn't unusual for Sarah to leave work, drive for two hours to a pub, perform for 20 minutes, then drive straight back home again. 'Comics tend to travel a long distance to a gig – they live this weird existence, they think nothing of driving for several hours to get somewhere, perform and then drive back through the night. They never see mornings!'

Eventually Sarah got used to her new life. 'This older woman in my office once said: "Where are you off to now, then?" I said I was going to Sheffield, and she said, "On your own?" And I remember thinking, "Yeah! I do a lot of this. I'm actually quite independent. I do a lot of stuff on my own!"'

Soon she was spending more time in her Nissan Micra than anywhere else and was forced to do things she had never expected. Sometimes she would sleep on the sofas of people she hardly knew and became an expert on other people's showers. 'I've thought, this must be what it's like to be promiscuous,' she has joked.

In the car, she listened to BBC Radio 2 and must have wondered whether she would ever hear herself on the radio station. It often has comedians in its studio and even holds the prestigious New Comedy Awards, which Sarah would soon become very familiar with...

Spending so much time in her car didn't however turn her into a mechanic. She would still call for help when she got a flat tyre.

Her most potentially embarrassing moment behind the wheel came in the early hours one morning, when she undid her bra on the way home from a gig before spotting the police, who were randomly pulling people over. 'Luckily they didn't pick the woman with her boobs on her lap,' she says.

She spent a lot of time in service stations, and has clear views on what she'd like to see in them. 'I'd like carveries to open in service stations,' she says. 'If I could get a choice of three meats at 2am that might be me done for life. Comics eat at weird times.'

Slowly she started to get paid for her routines and although it wasn't much – probably barely covering the cost of travel – she was happy to feel like she was making her new career work.

Her civil service job only paid her £9,500 a year, so she didn't feel like she was giving up a huge salary when she finally decided to give up work and be a full-time comic. Her colleagues were as surprised as she was. 'I think my bosses at the time were hoping I'd throw myself into work, but instead, stand-up became my therapy, where I felt valued. The idea of making strangers laugh... it was a euphoric sensation.'

Sarah was blossoming. Carving out a new road for her life

to take was liberating and she enjoyed the thrill of being up on stage. It was cathartic too – most of her early sets consisted of anecdotes about her divorce and how her family helped her deal with it.

Sarah found herself surprisingly relaxed with her audience. Her homely look and string of floral outfits appealed to both men and women and the vulnerability she seems to exude protected her from the worst of the heckling and booing.

It also made the swearing and sex talk all the more shocking – 'like hearing your nan swear', as one fan puts it. 'It was never intentional, this look,' she told *The Independent* in March 2012. 'I never got up on stage and thought, "I'll wear a flowery top so I can talk about dark evil things," but it just so happens that that's the way I dress.'

Kate Fox says that Sarah became a swan the moment she tried stand-up. On stage she makes it seem effortless, but like all the great comedians, that effort is a result of intense practice.

British comic Rudi Lickwood agrees. He says: 'People usually think that Robin Williams used to just get up there and just riff and it was brilliant. This stuff is just coming out. What people didn't realise is that Robin Williams used to go to the theatres and the venues before and he would block where he's going to be, what he's going to do, when he's going to say it, who he's going to say it to, as if the audience was actually there. That is practice. That is rehearsal. Sometimes one word can make all the difference between people getting it and not getting it and the only way that you can be assured of that is by practising.'

The other thing that Sarah knew would help in her new

career, was recognition. And in order to get recognition she began to enter competitions...

Sarah's Top Stand-up Tips

'Being funny is not enough. You have to work hard.'

'Train journeys can be used for napping, writing, plucking rogue hairs (lighting is great) and crying if tired.'

'Travelodges are better than B&Bs.'

'Some budget hotels have takeaway menus at the front desk.'

'Being nice to people – other comics, promoters etc – is the only way.'

'Bitterness and resentment is unhealthy and can slow down or stop your progress. Stop looking at where your peers are and concentrate on your own career.'

'Ask advice from other comics, especially those you respect, but take it all with a pinch of salt.'

'Forums (aside from finding out about gigs) are a waste of your time. Write some jokes instead.'

'You get really good at figuring out people's showers, from sleeping on a lot of sofas.'

'Fizzy sweets do a good job at keeping you awake on long drives.'

'Confidence goes a long way at hard gigs. Even if it's faked.'

'A new joke that works can lift the rest of your set. Some people say it's better than sex. It's not. But both at the same time would be awesome and awkward.'

'Learning to drive means you get to go home more and can

do last-minute gigs. Train ticket prices make the latter almost impossible if you can't drive.'

'If people give you a lift back to London, you'll get dropped off at Trafalgar Square. If people give you a lift back to Manchester, you get dropped off at your door and some will even wait to see you go inside. Manchester is smaller, I know, but still…'

'A notepad is your friend. Your memory is not.'

'Harness every funny thought you have. It makes writing so much easier if you have a starting point.'

'Recording early gigs or those where you're trying new material is invaluable. Your memory will just give you a blanket "It was great" like a dismissive ex. A recording will enable you to say that spontaneous ad-lib again and again.'

'It's not a good idea to churn your set early on. Get a bullet-proof 10 and then extend.'

'A smart man told me to write every day and gig every night. It's good advice.'

'Audience banter skills can be learned.'

'There's no rush to do the Edinburgh Fringe. Do it when you're ready and do as many previews as you can get your hands on. No such thing as too ready for Edinburgh.'

'I'm always impressed by people who keep "parking money" in a compartment of their car.'

'Never ever use someone else's material. If you're told your joke about X is similar to someone else's joke about X, get in touch with the someone else. Often it's dissimilar enough to keep using. If it's the same, you will probably have to drop it. But that's fine, you can write more jokes. Integrity is important.'

'Write your own put-downs. If a heckler gets the better of you, go home and write a suitable put down so if it happens again, you're bloody ready.'

'Don't drink before going on stage. You need to stay sharp. (This may seem a little harsh but I am a little harsh).'

'When writing, put the funny bit at the end of the sentence.'

'Put new material nights in your diary regularly to give you something to write towards. When you're on a bill with your peers, aim to be the best. When you're doing an open spot at a big club, aim to be the best.'

'Always look in a hotel kettle before using it.'

'Keep emergency biscuits and water in your car.'

'Keep small UHT milks (stolen from hotels) in your cupboard at home for cups of tea after long stints away.'

'Watch from the start of the show if you can. You need to get the feel of the room and find out where any problems are.'

'I love an inspirational motto. I used to have: "What have I done today to make me a better comedian?" and: "Just work harder". Might sound a bit wanky but worked for me. I don't believe in coasting it with a good 20 minutes. You should always be getting better, writing more and learning new things.'

'Turn up the volume in the audience, so if something that normally gets a round of applause gets a big laugh, turn up the audience. So a small laugh is a bigger laugh in your head and a bigger laugh is a round of applause.'

'Never comment on a quiet audience or low numbers. Don't piss off the people who came. They don't know they're laughing less at that joke than people did last night unless you tell them. Don't bloody tell them.'

'Ignore chat if you can in a rowdy room but deal with hecklers.'

'Don't shy away from hard gigs and tough rooms. What you learn doing those gigs stays with you and makes you more bullet-proof.'

'If you live and mostly work London, get out and travel the country.'

'Try to see your friends and family.'

'The 11 O'Clock Rule' (Millican's Law) is great for getting over hard gigs. The rule is as follows: If you have a hard gig, quiet, a death, a struggle, whatever, you can only be mad and frustrated and gutted until 11am the next day. Then you must draw a line under it and forget about it. As going into the next gig thinking you are shit will mean you will die.

'Equally, if you nail it, slam it, destroy it, whatever, you can only be smug about it until 11am the next day (in the past, I have set an alarm so I could get up and gloat for an extra half hour) as if you go into the next gig thinking you are God's gift to comedy, you will die.

'That is Millican's Law and it totally works. It means you move on quickly. It has stood me in good stead.'

CHAPTER 6

Firm Friends and First Awards

'My dad said he was going to build a cabinet for my awards, but I didn't let him! You should never have an awards cabinet.'

In her first year on the stand-up circuit, Sarah put herself in the running for four highly competitive awards. The first was Funny Women, a stand-up comedy competition entirely devoted to women. As such, it was the perfect place for Sarah to showcase her post-divorce routine, which although not totally 'anti-men', still heavily appealed to women who had gone through a bad break-up.

Founded by Lynne Parker in 2003, it was a relatively new competition when Sarah entered. It had the sole intention of honouring females in what is generally perceived as a male-dominated profession. Sponsored by Babycham, it also raised funds for various national women's charities and attracted national television and radio coverage.

The competition had three stages, which Sarah flew through. Selected as one of the 20 acts competing in the semi-finals, Sarah gained more confidence in her abilities as she won each heat. That year, the finals were held at The Comedy Store in London – the country's first ever American-inspired comedy venue.

On stage, Sarah was impressive.

But she was narrowly beaten by Debra Jane Appelby, a no-nonsense Yorkshire lass who went on to appear in the BBC's *28 Acts in 28 Minutes* and Paramount Comedy's *The World Stands Up*. She's also appeared numerous times on Radio 5 Live and BBC Radio 4's *Woman's Hour* and has forged a successful career on the UK comedy circuit.

Sarah must have been disappointed to get so close and come second instead of first. But she must have also felt immensely proud of her achievements. Mere months before, she had performed her first five-minute set and now she had come second in a national competition.

Debra-Jane's award proved to be controversial. After the ceremony, it was discovered that she had in fact been born a man, which could have disqualified her from the event. A number of people queried her win, but the organisers held firm. She had undergone a sex change and was legally a woman.

Sarah stayed in second place, following in the footsteps of the previous year's runner-up, Anna Crilly, who played Magda in the BBC sitcom *Lead Balloon*. Close behind Sarah in the 2004 competition, was actress and comedian Ruth Bratt, who came third. Now famous for her appearances in the Kellogg's Nutrigrain adverts, as well as for appearing in

Rob Brydon's *Annually Retentive* on BBC3, Bratt is another distinguished comic who was rising up the ranks at the same time as Millican.

Next, Millican won her way to the final of the 2005 BBC New Comedy Awards, well known for launching comic careers and bringing budding talent to the attention of agents and bookers.

Established in 1995, the awards are considered to have been one of the top UK comedy newcomer awards. During its time, its finals have boasted many well-known names, who have continued to work in comedy to great acclaim. Marcus Brigstocke won in 1996, followed by Josie Long in 1999, Alan Carr in 2001 and Rhod Gilbert in 2003. Other notable finalists include Peter Kay, Lee Mack, Russell Howard, Justin Lee Collins, Nina Conti and Julian Barratt. The list of previous entrants is like a British 'Hall of Fame' of contemporary comedians, all of whom have gone on to have great success. It must have been exciting to be in such great company.

Travelling to Cardiff for the finals, Sarah found herself booked into a Marriott Hotel – a much classier place than the down-to-earth lass was used to staying in. She mingled with the small group of finalists, expecting the usual competitive spirit. But then one contestant piped up: 'Do you think I've got time to ring my mum?'

Sarah laughed and immediately knew she'd get on with the blue-eyed, earnest looking young man, who introduced himself as Tom Allen. While everyone else went and got drunk together, Sarah and Tom spent their time exploring the swanky hotel they were so excited to be staying in. By the end of the evening they knew they would be friends for life…

Now is a good time to point out that Sarah doesn't drink. It's an interesting revelation, as most comedians are notorious boozers… unsurprising, considering the amount of time they spend alone in hotels, or licking their wounds after a tough gig.

Notorious comedy drinkers have included dark poet Bill Hicks, who was described as a 'hard-drinking, chain-smoking ball of angry energy', and *Animal House* bad boy John Belushi, whose manic comic presence many agree was mainly fuelled by his propensity for alcohol.

In 2006 it was widely reported that Robin Williams checked himself into rehab to deal with his addiction to alcohol, which had become all-consuming for the comedian and actor.

American *Saturday Night Live* cast member Tracy Morgan's struggles with alcohol have also been well documented. He was reportedly arrested for drink driving in both California and New York and even had to wear a SCRAM – a Secure Continuous Remote Alcohol Monitoring – device for nearly 150 days to try and save him from the perils of over-boozing. He has been sober since 2009.

Until relatively recently, comedians have been regularly cruelly stereotyped as depressed alcoholics – sad clowns, trying to make people laugh to fend off their own misery. But a wave of new comedians have bucked that trend, with their new and insightful approach to making people laugh. Unlike the dark and brooding comedians of the 80s and 90s, the clean-living lifestyles and down-to-earth attitudes of, for example, Miranda Hart, Michael McIntyre and Tina Fey, have brought comedians up from the proverbial gutter.

Sarah has simply never felt the need to turn to drink for consolation. Instead, she has faced all her problems head on. Plus she's just not very good at drinking. She reacts badly to the stuff, and says: 'My life is so busy, if I do have a day off I don't want to spend it vomiting.' She has, on average, three shandies a year – and feels all the better for it.

Back to the New Comedy Awards…

It was a big deal for Sarah to make it to the final. She performed her piece to the judges and audience and nervously awaited the results. But, yet again, she found herself in second place – this time beaten by her new friend Tom Allen. 'I came second, but I was still quite proud,' Sarah said afterwards.

Tom, Sarah and third-placed Edward Aczel were the last winners of the New Comedy Awards. The following year the competition would take a five-year sabbatical, before being adapted to become a nationwide talent hunt that favours sketch writing and filmed performances over stand-up.

But to come second in the final of its last outing was perfect timing for Sarah, who flourished as a result of the industry buzz that soon arose around her competition routines. She suddenly found herself getting booked for more gigs and appearances, but she still had a long way to go before she had the kind of pull to pack out a 100-day tour…

And as well as a runners-up award, she had forged a fledgling friendship with Tom, which would grow stronger as the years passed.

Tom was just 22 when he won the New Comedy Awards. He has since performed at Just for Laughs in Montreal, London's Soho Theatre, New York's UCB Theatre and he has had his own show at the Edinburgh Fringe Festival for the past three years. His camp Noel Coward-esque performances have led to him being described in 2009 as 'one of the more adorable stand-ups at the Edinburgh Fringe'.

Sarah describes Tom as a 'tonic' and says that she laughs so much when she's with him that she almost wets herself. 'I like my own space but Tom is one of the few friends I can spend a whole day with,' she told *The Independent* in 2011. 'We both like side-stepping the thing a building was made for and going for the secondary function instead. We'll meet at the Curzon Cinema in Soho, for tea and chocolate fudge cake at the café, but we've yet to see a film there. Or at the National Portrait Gallery we'll zip around to get to the gift shop and buy postcards.'

Tom is a big flirt and Sarah loves watching him work his charm, especially on waiters. 'It's not obvious, he just steps it up a notch, there's a bit more banter. He's just a bit funnier and I think, "Why doesn't he do this with me?"'

The two don't make a natural pair, which Sarah readily admits. 'One of our biggest differences has to be our dress sense. Tom has amazing attention to detail, from top to toe. It's quirky and particular. People see me and think I look quite mumsy and accessible.'

But they have been firm friends since that 2005 awards ceremony and it's a friendship she cherishes. 'You want people in your life who you've been friends with when you were starting out. I don't think I'll turn into a dick with the success, but I've seen it happen to others and Tom would tell me if I did.'

The duo have done a few gigs together over the course of their friendship, and not all of them have been major successes. But Sarah insists that the tougher gigs were the ones that actually brought them closer. 'We did one for a room of 40 nurses for National Handwashing Week and it was quite a hard crowd, which is often the case when you perform to a group from a single industry.'

Tom recalls the first moment he met Sarah with equal affection. 'I remember coming her coming up to me and saying, "I like you, I want to be your friend". She's very upfront and open like that, while I find it really difficult to make new friends and could never have done that – it snowballed from there.'

They met again soon after at a swanky BBC party and once more shunned the mingling to sit in the corner and devour the buffet and down cups of juice. Both of them hated the forced conversations that came with the obligatory networking and just wanted to have a good time getting to know each other.

Sarah has also been a helpful sounding board for Tom. 'You feel vulnerable when you first start off in stand-up, but as long as you have someone else saying, "You're going to be OK," it's fine, and Sarah was particularly intuitive about my worries. My favourite advice from her was Millican's Maxim: if you've had a bad gig, forget about it by 11am the following day, and move on.'

Tom loves the fact that Sarah looks so sweet and lovely, but will then come out with something outrageous that will have them both falling around with laughter. Other diners sometimes stare disapprovingly when they're eating out together, but Tom is adamant it's because they're jealous. Or it could be because her laugh sounds like a clown's horn, he isn't sure.

He's also grateful for her honesty and advice, and credits her with helping him use his own tough times to comic effect, just as she herself has done.

'I talk about being gay quite a lot,' Tom explained to *The Independent* in 2011. 'I was on a date and kissing a guy on the street and these lads drove past in the car, with one shouting "You disgusting queers" and another, rather randomly, "– and get a job!" I was on the brink of tears but Sarah inspired me to take those difficult times, as she has, and be honest about my feelings. You're not reducing it, turning it into nothing – you're sharing it and allowing the absurdities to ring out.' It's a very elegant way of describing how Sarah has used her pain and sadness and turned them into a gift for the world.

It's obvious that Sarah and Tom have helped each other navigate the crowded comedy world waters and emerged with a close friendship. But it must have been with a mixture of frustration and happiness that she congratulated Tom on his next award win – because yet again it bumped her into second place.

So You Think You're Funny is an annual stand-up comedy competition for new acts. Founded by Karen Koren in 1988, the prize money now stands at £2,000 and the winner is given the chance to guest present a comedy programme on Paramount, as well as a much-coveted spot on the Best of

British Show at the Montreal Just For Laughs Festival. It is the longest-running best comedy newcomer award in Great Britain and is well-respected by the industry.

When Sarah entered the competition she was following in some very famous footsteps. In 1993, now world-famous Irish comic Dylan Moran won the prestigious competition, and just like Sarah, he had only been performing for less than a year. In 1995 the world was introduced to *Would I Lie To You?* team captain Lee Mack through the Edinburgh-based competition, while in 1997 *Phoenix Nights* star Peter Kay impressed his way to the winning spot.

Sarah competed in the first round of heats, in which three competitors were chosen to go through to the second round. When she was picked as one of those three, she was overjoyed. Firstly, she now had a real chance of recognition, but secondly she was excited about where the second and final rounds would be held. Edinburgh.

Sarah was going to the world-famous Edinburgh Fringe Festival for the first time. She knew that she wanted to one day perform there properly, and so it was a great opportunity to see what kind of audience she would have – and what standard of talent was expected from the comedians. Plus she had her friend Tom Allen with her for company.

But she must have been nervously going over her eight-minute routine as she wandered around the beautiful Scottish city. It was a big opportunity and she wanted to do her absolute best.

After sailing through the second round, the night of the grand final arrived. Walking into the venue, The Gilded

Balloon, would have done nothing to calm Sarah's nerves. A tall, castle-like building, it is now one of the largest and best-known venues at the Fringe Festival, renowned for its innovative programming and for unleashing previously undeveloped potential.

It is a huge venue, comprising of nine performance spaces, three bars, a restaurant, nightclub and a beer garden, and is most famous for its in-house late night comedy line-up show, *Late N' Live* – where 'anything can, and invariably does happen'. Funny, outrageous, and more than a bit sweary, Sarah's brand of comedy must have fitted seamlessly into the line-up.

Many a household name has cut their teeth appearing on the *Late N' Live* stage. Tim Minchin, Russell Brand, Rhona Cameron, Tommy Tierney – the list of its comedy pedigree is endless and, as a result, the So You Think You're Funny competition is widely known as the most influential of its kind in the UK.

For the 2005 competition, Bill Bailey was the MC. So when Sarah walked out on stage to give her eight-minute set it was him who announced her name. She performed well and the audience liked her instantly. As she heard the raucous laughs from the crowd she fell into an easy flow of stories and punchlines, drawn from her already popular material about her family and her break-up.

When she was given the second place award she was still pleased. She knew she had come a long way in a very short space of time and it was an incredible achievement. As previously mentioned, Tom Allen came first and would be heading off to Montreal to be warmly received by a new audience of Canadian fans, while the darkly humoured Joe Wilkinson – who has since supported both Russell Kane and Alan Carr on tour – took the third-place spot.

But Sarah was itching for a win. Never the kind to rest on her laurels, she spent the next few months working and reworking her performance style and content and performing in pubs and other venues as often as she could.

Then, she decided to enter a competition that was in a different league to the three newcomer awards she had so far attempted to win – The Amused Moose Awards. First and foremost a famous comedy club in London, Amused Moose prides itself on its top-billing performances, great value ticket prices and its nurturing of lesser-known talent. It also hosts regular Amused Moose Comedy shows in various London theatres, and they run their comedy awards once a year, before taking the winning talent to the Edinburgh Fringe for their annual Big Value Show.

The club has a large and varied fan base and consistently hosts big household name acts, who use the venue to run through new material before going on tour. And it's not only on stage that famous faces can be found – Paloma Faith, Cate Blanchett and Ricky Gervais are all fans of the comedy venue, so you never know who you'll be rubbing shoulders with in the audience.

The Moose team first began running comedy competitions in 2004, and quickly became known for their keen eye for talent. Award winners have all been previously unknown comics, and have generally become high profile and much sought after following their win. Simon Amstell, Rhod Gilbert, Jimmy Carr and Alex Zane have all been finalists in their competitions, proving the awards to be something of a career launcher.

To enter, Sarah needed to have performed in at least a dozen venues, and to prove that she had been consistently rebooked. As its website states: 'This is not a competition for novices'. It was a big step for Sarah, who by now was getting to grips with life as a gigging comedian and easily met the requirements.

The best of the talent seen throughout the competition would be showcased not only at the Big Value Night in Edinburgh, but also in front of producers, casting directors and agents, as well as journalists and reviewers at London's Bloomsbury Theatre, the following year.

It was a big opportunity. Sarah went ahead and entered.

The closest heat for her to enter was in Leeds, so she travelled to the city for the first round of the competition. She qualified easily and had to travel to London for the quarter-finals in June and then the semi-finals in July at Amused Moose's Camden venue.

After a tense final, Sarah was announced as the Amused Moose 2005 winner. She was understandably thrilled. After less than a year on the comedy circuit she had come second in three competitions and now she had won her first. All the judges agreed she stood out from the other performers, but there was another reason that she was particularly pleased – she had bagged herself a manager.

Chambers Management is led by its founder, Hannah Chambers, and has a client list drawn from the cream of the stand-up comedy circuit. They are a nurturing, boutique agency, that work closely with their selective client list to develop raw stand-up talent into the kind needed for a long-lasting career performing and writing for television, radio and film.

Sarah knew them as the agency that looked after Jimmy Carr, who was fast becoming a rising star in the world of TV and radio. So when they approached her with an offer of representation, she knew that she was well on her way. With an agent on board she would have a steady stream of work and a visible route to the big time. It was celebration time in the Millican household.

The next two years was a flurry of hard work and Sarah found herself travelling to gigs all over the country. Luckily she didn't experience much of the infamous heckling that comedians often fall foul of, and Sarah believes this is because she's not an aggressive performer. In 2009 she told *The Guardian*: 'It's usually men that heckle and I think that there's an ingrained feeling that they've got to be a bit nice to me.'

But even the gentlest of performers can be thrown by a cruel comment, and Sarah had one or two moments in those early years that tested her confidence.

In one early piece of material, which Sarah eventually discarded from her set, she asked the audience what she should do with her wedding dress.

'On one occasion, a bloke shouted out what I thought was "Dye it!",' she revealed to *The Guardian*. 'So I said: "What, you mean lots of different colours?" And he shouted back: "No! D-I-E-T. Diet!"'

At another gig in Oxford she had a similarly cruel audience response. 'A man shouted out: "Wear a bra!" And I was,' she explained. 'It was like being kicked in the crotch. I think I just replied: "It's like being heckled by Trinny and Susannah!"'

Sarah deals with hecklers in the best way possible – by quickly firing back a funny response before saving the moment as a humorous anecdote. It's a mark of her natural comedic talent, and a very good skill to have on stage, where you never know what's going to happen next.

In 2006, Sarah went up to Edinburgh again, this time for The Big Value Show, a 'gang-show' type comedy set, featuring a compilation of performers. It was a low-pressure event, mainly because of the range of acts being showcased. Millican appeared with north eastern shuffling oddball Seymour Mace, as well as Jack O'Kane and Derek Johnson, and was well-received.

She also joined Michael Redmond for his popular *Sunday Service* show, which also featured John Ross, Will Richards, Ricky Sparkles and Dionne Shaw.

A review in *The Herald* described her as 'one of the hottest new things in stand-up' and wrote: 'Sarah Millican is making divorce work. The gently spoken Geordie delivers tender comedy about returning to her parents' house, the truth about curtains and, erm, hating children, rape and killing dogs. It's lovely stuff and won her the Amused Moose new comedy trophy as well as a fistful of bridesmaid gongs, including runner-up spots in 2005's Funny Women, So You Think You're Funny and the BBC New Comedy Awards.'

It was a good opportunity to see how the famous Fringe Festival worked, before she would eventually jump in with both feet two years later. It was also around this time that she began to host her own comedy courses.

In 2006, Stephanie Merritt, a journalist for *The Observer*, went on holiday to Spain, where she stayed in an idyllic country farmhouse to learn how to perform stand-up comedy. Her tutor was Sarah Millican, and after spending a week with the serious teacher, Merritt could see that Sarah was definitely on her way to bigger things.

It's interesting to note at this point that Sarah was confident enough with what she had learnt about the industry so far to feel like she could herself command a comedy class.

Merritt wrote of the experience: 'It was impossible not to warm to this frank, no-nonsense Geordie with her slightly mumsy manner and filthy mouth, but spending a week under her stern tutelage made me realise that comedy was something she took very, very seriously.

'The message she gave us most insistently was that if you want to be good, you have to be prepared to put in the leg work. Write every day, gig every day, travel halfway across the country to perform an open-mic spot if you have to, but always remember that in comedy, you only improve by doing it and learning from your mistakes. I remember thinking at the time that someone so incredibly driven was bound to go far, if only through sheer bloody-minded determination.'

Sarah was picking up confidence and finally gaining recognition. Her name was popping up regularly in local newspaper reviews and the industry was definitely getting excited about her arrival.

Her act was also developing. As well as her earlier material, which was mainly focused on her divorce and coping with its aftermath, she had begun branching out into other areas. She began to include identifiable topics such as home furnishings, families and observations about her childhood, and she had begun to pepper her act with outrageous extras like sex, rape and dog murder.

Significantly, she was also starting to discuss dating and the differences between men and women. Sarah had begun to get out in the dating world again, and it was around this time that she would meet her new boyfriend, Gary Delaney.

CHAPTER 7

When Sarah
Met Gary...

'I'm a whole person. I never want to be part of a couple in that "my other half" sort of way. Without him I am also a person. I love him with all of my heart, but I'm not nothing without him.'

When Sarah first met Gary Delaney, she was intensely focused on bettering her act and gaining widespread recognition. She was still a relative newbie, forging her own path on the comedy circuit, and she was still living with her parents.

It had been a few years since Andrew had broken Sarah's heart, but the effects on her desire for a relationship had been long lasting.

Sarah was wary. Where once she had been a naïve young girl, with a set of highly romanticised ideals of love and marriage, now she was cautious. Although she held no animosity towards Andrew, and would never regret the years she spent married to him, she was determined that she would never let anyone break her heart so completely again. 'I've always, in previous relationships, had a habit of melting into a couple,' she says.

This was not a mistake she would make again. Her success in stand-up had also begun to cement in her the notion that she didn't have to settle for anything. Looking back on her marriage, she saw that for a while she had been a bit of a 'doormat'. Now she was living a very independent life. She was doing exactly what she wanted to do, when she wanted to do it, and it felt liberating.

After her traumatic break-up, one of the things that she feared the most was that she would now have to have sex with someone new.

Sarah had always had a pretty relaxed take on sex. But being dumped felt like she had just been made redundant from a job she loved, and every new sexual encounter that followed felt like a nerve-wracking interview. She told *The Sun* in November 2012: 'I thought, "Oh no, they'll do it differently. It'll be in a different order to normal and he might want to do this first and that last, and I've never done it like that before. It's all going to be new and horrific and I won't know how dark they like it. They might even want to be spontaneous." It was all so terrifying.'

Sarah had entered her marriage with the firm opinion that once she said her vows it was for life, and when that fundamental belief was destroyed she had to re-evaluate her whole definition of love and relationships. She says: 'When you're newly single you start to see sex as having to go for a job interview. You can't just do it anymore. You've got to present the best version of you so that you get the job.'

Throughout her twenties, Sarah was still finding out who she was. Now entering her thirties, she was a changed woman and valued her new, independent lifestyle. There had been a time when she wouldn't have walked into a pub on her own. Now she was entertaining their patrons nightly with her witticisms.

Her sense of adventure had been awakened, but a new relationship was still unchartered territory. Besides, with so much of her set being about the fall-out from a broken relationship, it must have been easy to worry that potential suitors might be quickly frightened off once they saw her show...

But from the very beginning, Sarah could see that Gary Delaney was different.

Gary had been on the comedy circuit for a lot longer than Sarah and was already well-known for his dark one-liners. Born in 1973, he was two years older than Sarah, and first surfaced on the comedy circuit in the mid-nineties – around the same time as Sarah was falling in love with her first husband and settling down to married life.

Gary cut his comedy teeth while working on the sound desk in a London comedy club. As he explained to comedy website *Gigglebeats*: 'That was my apprenticeship. A lot of guys came up from being on the sound desk or being on the door and putting out the chairs and that sort of stuff, then watching a lot of comedy and learning about it. Eventually you start to think you can do better.'

Financial journalist Martin Lewis was also part of the

scene, before he went on to found his popular website www.moneysavingexpert.com – and Gary started his comedy career by writing jokes for him. The pair had gone to university together at the London School of Economics, where Martin was the president of the student union, and Gary was in charge of student entertainment. Gary had founded the university's Chuckle Club, a comedy venue on campus that now draws a huge audience, primarily consisting of non-students.

The pair had remained friends. 'There was a club that he and I used to go to,' Gary recalls. 'And Martin decided to give stand-up a go, so I helped him write his jokes. Then he would deliver them and I'd be at the back of the room thinking "none of you know, but you're laughing at my jokes". That I quite enjoyed.'

Martin describes Gary as one of the naturally funniest people he's ever met and recalls their years at LSE together fondly. 'At uni he was always the funny one,' he wrote on his blog in 2006. 'Yet I was always more confident with a microphone, hence why I did the comedy and he wrote. My "comedy career" was great fun, but by no means my calling, though it did teach me a huge amount. Yet in the end, real talent will out, and Gary put his nerves behind him and has ended up a superb comic.'

In fact, the moment that Gary first ended up on stage was a result of a bet between the two friends. 'I wrote him this joke about nurses, which was how I started,' Gary told *Gigglebeats*. 'I said: "Do this joke, it's the best joke I've ever written, they're going to love it." He did it a couple of times and he told me that the nurses joke wasn't very funny. Then of course, I was like, "you're doing it wrong!" I ended up doing it sort of to prove a point, and it was a bit of a drunken bet as well. He ended up betting me 20 quid I wouldn't have the nerve to do it, and I finally did it. I got up and people laughed and I enjoyed it and carried on, and that was that.'

Gary did his first gig on Valentine's Day 1997, but only did a handful of other gigs throughout the course of that year, before deciding to give it up.

It would be three years before he would get on stage again. 'It took me years to get up the nerve to do my first gig, after that it took as long again to realise it could be a career, rather than just a hobby,' he says.

His was a very different approach to his eventual partner Sarah, who entered the comedy world as if she had been fired out of a cannon. Gary started slowly and eventually discovered that his talent lay in the clever one-liners he was so adept at writing.

Unlike Sarah, Gary never did a comedy course. He learnt by watching live stand-up and admits his first few years were difficult. 'I was kind of deluded and better in my head than I was on stage. That really helped. I was uber deadpan, which is all very well when it's going well, but the lack of flexibility and energy can leave you dying a lot.'

Gary found stand-up a lot more difficult than Sarah did and struggled during his early years gigging. He also experienced the bad side of stand-up a lot more regularly than Sarah ever did and was subjected to a lot of heckling. But Gary's hecklers generally ended up feeling the sharp edge of his wit, and most ended up worse off than him.

For example, at a gig in Sutton Coldfield, Gary broke from his routine and turned his attention to an audience member who'd shouted out 'gay Jew' at him. 'Not only is it woefully inaccurate,' says Gary of that time, 'but the best thing about it is the knuckledragger who shouted it out didn't seem to realise that neither of those two words is actually an insult. I asked him why he thought I was a gay Jew and he said it was because I wore glasses. I then said bad things about his mum. He replied that she was dead. I asked if she died of embarrassment after giving birth to him, and observed that it was good she was dead as that meant she couldn't produce any more versions of him. After that it just got offensive.'

The stand-up stage is a vulnerable place. Much like a wounded animal will attack, comedians will get defensive if audiences try to humiliate them on stage – where they generally feel they're on the verge of humiliating themselves anyway. But there were funny moments during his early years as well, like when a dwarf sneaked behind him on stage and tried to sell the audience earrings. Gary applauded him.

While Gary had got over his stage nerves, he still much preferred writing gags to performing them, so he began to forge a career out of scripting one-liners for famous comedians and TV panel show presenters.

Gary has written for the likes of *8 Out of 10 Cats*, Jason Manford's *Comedy Rocks* and *Russell Howard's Good News*, but he has also appeared on comedy panel shows himself, including *Dave's One Night Stand*, alongside his comedy hero Ardal O'Hanlon and established funny lady Josie Long.

'TV has an incredible demand for gags, usually topical,' he told *Gigglebeats*. 'There tends to be a few of us in a room writing those. Loads of telly shows want gags because usually it's for when the host comes out and does some jokes at the top, or as an opening monologue.'

Gary and Sarah have completely different comedy styles, and both have a deep respect for what the other does. 'I'd rather be able to write a good gag than act everyday things out in a likeable manner to a full stadium,' he says, describing exactly the style that Sarah has become so accomplished at.

But they have the same views on making it as a comedian, and the same work ethic. 'I like acts that work really hard. My main advice is always work hard. Write every day. Gig every night. You will get better. Most comics are lazy. Every day you are working harder than them you are pulling ahead of them. I started out with many people more talented than me. Most are gone now. The 10 or so open mikers who I started out with who worked the hardest are the ones who made a living out of it, not the most naturally talented 10.'

They also have the same dirty and dark sense of humour. One of Gary's best-known gags is: 'I filled my Escort with diesel. She died.' It's one you can definitely imagine Sarah laughing at.

I myself was lucky enough to see Gary Delaney perform a set for the Monkey Business Comedy Club in north London, in January 2013. The venue was an upstairs room in the famous Belsize Park pub the Sir Richard Steeles, and Gary was the headlining comedian.

He arrived late in the evening, but just in time to see the tail end of the very odd act that preceded him. Standing at the back of the darkened room, he could hear the audience's hushed disappointment. After four very funny performances, this act was bombing, badly, which was not good news for Gary, who would have to follow them.

A comedy sketch involving a woman riding her 'son' like a horse, it was sadly not liked by the crowd – and as a result the room was cold when Gary's name was announced. He bounded onto the stage and in a matter of seconds, proved to everyone why he is such a well-respected, constantly in-demand comedian.

'I hate it when you watch the act before you and you realise they're doing exactly what you planned to do for your set,' he said cheekily. 'I'll have to miss out that bit I guess,' he added. The audience erupted into fits of laughter and all at once he had them on his side and ready to laugh at his jokes.

He was commanding but refreshingly down-to-earth. As he delivered a steady stream of expertly crafted gags, he frequently paused to laugh at his own jokes, many of which were at his own expense. His bespectacled presence was similar to Sarah's – calm and encouraging. People were laughing with him, not at him, and it was clear he was a seasoned pro, despite his misgivings about his live performances.

The half-hour set passed in a flash and spiky-haired Gary sauntered off stage, leaving the audience – which numbered approximately 70 – wiping their eyes and clapping appreciatively.

Gary believes that the comedy circuit is a lot more professional now than it was when he first began plying his comic trade, and on the whole he's glad that this is the case.

He claims that audiences are less patient, and harder to please than in the nineties 'when they laughed at any old crap really', but that standards are a lot higher now and comedians command more respect.

It was against this background that Sarah and Gary met, discovered a mutual professional respect, and eventually fell in love.

But Sarah was nervous about their relationship. Gary was a regular on the comedy circuit while Sarah was just beginning to make a name for herself. In her mind, dating a fellow comedian – and a talented one at that – could have been fatal for her career. So for a long time they kept their fledgling relationship under wraps.

'When we started going out we didn't tell anybody for ages,' she told *The Guardian* in October 2012. 'Because I didn't want anybody to think he was writing my jokes, because he wasn't. I was doing it all myself.'

Sarah had worked so hard to hone her set and her material, but most importantly she was proud of her independence, and was not about to lose this by having herself defined as one half of a comedy couple.

So is it competitive, being in the same line of work as the one you love? Sarah is adamant that it isn't, although she has clearly had the more mainstream success of the pair. 'It's just like having a funny friend. It's never competitive. It's like, would two people who work in shops come home and say: "I sold more handbags than you"? No they wouldn't, because they get in from work and say: "Oh I'm so glad I've finished work. Let's put the telly on and get the tea going".'

Starting to share her life with another man did impact on

her material. Comedians largely rely on life experiences for their inspiration and sharing a life might mean sharing the spoils of a life lived together. But Sarah insists there are no arguments over their 'funny bits'. She says: 'He does one-liners, his is all based on wordplay, so if anything funny happens between us, I get it!'

So while Sarah used aspects of her boyfriend's personality and quirks in her sets, Gary didn't at all. 'He's never told anything on stage that is based on his life,' she says.

As time passed, they grew closer, despite the physical distance between them. Gary lived in Birmingham, while Sarah lived 80 miles away on her own in Manchester – and although they'd been together for over six years, it was an arrangement she was happy with.

After such a whirlwind first marriage swallowed her identity whole and left her something of a broken woman, she didn't want to let that happen again. 'It feels important now to retain my sense of self,' she says. 'I'm a pretty normal well-rounded person and so is he and we happen to go out and we're in love. But we're not the same thing. I think part of the reason my marriage melted away was because I changed from being feisty to being dowdy, and I lost my passion.'

Sarah's fans will know that Gary features regularly in her performances, even though she never names him. Instead she initially referred to him as 'the boyfriend', and has charted their relationship journey through her on stage material. For example, she has discussed the problems they face when it comes to present buying for each other, and has even shown her audience some jewellery he'd accidentally bought her from teen shop Claire's Accessories, instead of her favourite Accessorize.

'The only time we ever argue is Christmas, birthdays, present-buying times,' she said during one gig. 'He really likes surprises and I really hate... surprises.'

Another on-stage swipe at her partner came at the end of a sweet little story about their holidays together... 'We've both got busy lives and when we go on holiday we like to go somewhere relaxing – we like to look at pretty scenery and read books. My boyfriend doesn't like to fly so we tend to stay within the UK. So, because we don't have to pay for expensive flights we sometimes treat ourselves to a posh hotel, and the last posh hotel we stayed in had two baths, either side of each other.

'I thought: "Ooh, we're going to be able to have really romantic baths together, without having to stare at hairy toes..." They're not horrific, they're just, you know, feet. Nails are a bit long, toes are a bit hairy – there's crusty bits on the bottom, you know, that sort of thing. It looks like he could pick up mice with them. They have a certain sort of owl-like quality to them.'

Sarah may often lampoon him on stage, but Gary is supportive of Sarah's work – ever eager to point her in the direction of the mistakes he makes, so that she can use it in her shows.

Sarah cites him as a major influence on her work ethic. 'If something funny happens when we get intimate, he's the first to go, "Write that down before you forget". He comes to my shows and laughs the loudest when it's stuff about him. He's thrilled when I talk about him. He actually turned round to someone at a gig once and said, "you know, everything she says is true". He loves it because I might be talking about how he says really inappropriate things sometimes, but he also comes across as absolutely hilarious. Who doesn't want to be thought of as funny?'

When Sarah comes off stage, many of her fans want to shake Gary's hand too. It's obvious they are a very caring, relaxed couple, who support and love each other equally.

But an echo of pain from her divorce was ever-present – Sarah was still cynical about love. 'We're having a lovely time, but I don't believe in forever,' she said on *Live at the Apollo* in 2011. 'I don't believe in blokes, or songs, that say "I'm gonna love you forever". No you're not. You're gonna love us for a little while and then you're gonna leave us and you don't really know why.'

On the word 'really' her voice rose slightly and she began fanning her eyes, as if to fend off tears. The audience murmured, sympathetically, before Sarah grinned and said: 'No, I'm fine, really. He was an arse.'

It's at moments like these that you realise Sarah is a lot more complicated than she appears on stage. As John Walsh wrote in *The Independent*: 'It's not every comedian who can hit an audience's funny bone with observational gags about the sex war and potty-mouth confessions about bottoms and vaginas one minute, then enlist their emotional support for her tales of abandonment the next. But Sarah Millican isn't any comedian. She uses sorrow and regret as the springboard for her extremely funny act.'

Sarah's relationship with Gary proved just how much she had changed from the 29-year-old divorcee who felt her life had ended. She had grown since that marriage break-up, and the lessons she learnt along the way weren't ones she was willing to ignore.

She was blissfully happy with Gary, but said she didn't want to jeopardise that happiness by doing something silly – like living under the same roof. And for a comedian used to travelling to gigs, 80 miles wasn't a great distance. 'It's not a long way when you travel 50,000 miles a year,' she saids. 'It works out really well. When you live with your partner, there are times when you think, "I wish you'd just go out". That never happens to me. Ever. We never do housework with each other, so I'm never ironing or cleaning. It's lovely.'

It's something that a psychiatrist might say developed as a backlash to her failed marriage. Believing that a typical 'couply' existence was responsible for the death of her relationship, Sarah removed the banality of everyday life from the equation, so that she was left with only the 'good bits' of a relationship.

Every week they'd spend a few days together, before leaving to return to their separate homes. 'When I don't see him I miss him,' she told *The Mirror* in March 2012. 'So when he does come round I'm always genuinely pleased to see him. I don't think that happens when you live together. This has all the benefits of a long-term relationship, without the niggly bits.'

It was a point she once again made clear during an interview with *Woman and Home*, in December 2012. 'I think you've just got to make sure that you don't slip into complacency. So I never iron or hoover when he's there, so that when we're together we go for lunch or nice walks. And there's no routine, so you can't get bored of no routine, can you? It gives us both breathing space, and we see each other a lot more than we would if we lived together because we plan ahead. He's still the most important person to me. But I think I am also important.'

On stage she discussed the subject with more candour. At one of her live shows she admitted: 'When we're apart, and I get to sleep in my own bed, on my own, I fucking love it. Starfish! I love it. We all love our partners but when we're trying to get to sleep they all do niggly things, don't they? Like… breathing.'

It was a modern and somewhat refreshing arrangement – one that even Sarah admitted others found unconventional. But then, they aren't a conventional couple. In 2008, at which point the couple had been together for two years, *The Metro* reported: 'In the town where they live, they are affectionately known as Mr and Mrs Rape…'

It went on to quote Sarah as saying: 'I can talk about how happy I am with him, but I still can't do forever with him, even though I love him. We've decided on 19 years and then an appraisal.'

Four years later, her views hadn't changed. 'I don't know if we'll ever move in together. It's weird how everybody thinks that what we're doing is odd, whereas I think we've nailed it. Everybody else is doing it wrong.'

But though strong and independent, and definitely flying the flag for women in comedy, Sarah was no militant feminist. When Gary once stayed in her flat while she was away, Sarah was horrified to discover upon her return that he had broken something electrical. 'Because I'm a feminist, I rang my dad, so he could tell me what to do,' she explained in a 2009 web interview. 'But as I was chatting to him, Gary fixed it. And although I'm capable, sometimes it's nice having someone do something for you and it's nice for them too. Often I'll let Gary open a stiff jar because it makes him feel all puffed up and masculine, even though I could have done it myself.'

It was obvious that Gary and Sarah shared a fun-filled, loving relationship, but what about the possibility of children? Was that something she would have considered changing their current arrangement for?

In short, the answer was no. Sarah didn't see any baby Millicans in her future – with Gary or anyone else.

During a 2010 interview with *thisisleicestershire.co.uk*, she joked. 'A friend recently had a test for polycystic ovaries and it turns out she has it and is pleased,' she told the reporter. A condition that is caused by an imbalance in female hormones, polycystic ovaries causes the sufferer to grow unsightly facial hair and leaves them with difficulties in conceiving a child. 'Now... I don't want kids and neither does she, so I called her a lucky cow,' Sarah said. 'Come on, there's a reason why she has a beard and a belly...'

In 2011, she took the subject of not wanting offspring more seriously, when she told *The Guardian*: 'I have no intentions of having children. I have no responsibilities apart from myself. Even in my relationship we're very much two individuals who are in love rather than being "a couple", and that's a massive distinction in my mind.'

A year later she hadn't changed her opinion. In an interview with *The Mirror*, she explained: 'I don't have kids and I've never wanted them. They ask a lot of questions and I'm not good at answers. I'm not massively knowledgeable on a wide range of topics and I think to be a parent you have to know why the sky's blue at least.'

Gary has definitely broadened Sarah's horizons – if not to the point of entertaining the idea of children, then at least in the world of food. She had never been out for a curry, or a Chinese, before hooking up with the comic – two cuisines she now enjoys frequently. 'I can't believe how adventurous I've become,' she says.

And while unconventional, the pair are known as the Terry and June – or George and Mildred – on Twitter, because of their cyberspace exchanges. Both of them are huge fans of the social networking site, and tweet regularly to their followers. As of January 2013, Sarah's followers numbered an incredible 705,000, while Gary's count was at a respectable 38,000, and included Jamie Theakston, Dara O'Briain and Charlie Brooker among his followers.

As well as their comedy exchanges, they also tweet about each other's TV and live appearances, to support each other's work.

With her on-stage jokes about Gary, Sarah can sometimes go straight for the jugular. 'I saw my boyfriend in a suit and I must admit I was a little bit turned on,' she said in one routine. 'I don't mind telling you – I think it was the prospect of a regular income.'

But despite their living apart and despite the effect her marriage break-up had on her view of love, there was a beautiful romance about the pair. Maybe she had just become a more realistic romantic.

In 2009 she gave an interview to an Australian newspaper and told them about her most recent birthday. 'My boyfriend took me to Blackpool... to see an Elvis impersonator,' she revealed. They'd had fish and chips, and normally teetotal Sarah even pushed the boat out with a half pint of shandy. She said: 'That was me done for the night. Brilliant.'

But the most telling sign of her devotion to Gary came when she chose him over her other great love – cake. Sarah famously loves sweet treats and talks about them often in her routines. She has a section on her website dedicated to pictures of her favourite confectionary, and many of her fans bring cupcakes to her show for her.

But in a 2010 interview with *The Herald*, she was asked to choose between cake or sex, and after a lot of thought, said: 'Oh, there's a question... Well, they're not mutually exclusive. You do know that? I'm going to go out on a limb and say cakes are better than sex because I can't have sex in here now with you watching. Well, I could but it would be awkward. Whereas I could have that...' – she indicated a calorific strawberry construction in front of her – '...on a train. I could have that on the passenger seat while I'm driving. I think maybe cakes are better than casual sex, but sex in a relationship with someone you love is better than cakes. But if someone loves you they buy you cake, so it's win-win really.'

'All you do is write what you think is funny – you don't know if people are going to come, like it, if reviewers are going to come, if they're going to like it, and all I've got to go on is what I find funny...'

CHAPTER 8

Sarah Millican's Not Nice

By 2008, Sarah had been successfully gigging for four years. She had won The Amused Moose Award and been runner up in three other highly regarded competitions. She now had an agent, a new boyfriend, and was getting repeat gigs in a variety of venues up and down the country.

Life was good.

She had also finally moved out from her family home and into a smart rented flat in Manchester – it was the first time Sarah had ever lived alone, and she told *Woman and Home* magazine: 'I had no idea how awesome it is and I don't know if I ever want to go back. It's just the freedom. There's no compromise necessary. It's a sort of healthy selfishness and it also means that I'm not selfish when I'm with my boyfriend.'

Sarah chose Manchester for a number of reasons, the most important of which being its location. 'Manchester is so much easier for gigs,' she told *The Manchester Evening News* in 2010. 'There are so many places just an hour or two away, so you can come back and be in your own bed a lot.'

She now refers to Manchester as her adopted city, and likens coming into the main train station as how it used to feel when she came across the Tyne Bridge – like she was coming home. 'I loved it and I loved the people and the feeling I got when I came here,' she said in the article, which joked that she had been appointed an ambassador for 'Marketing Manchester'.

The flat-hunting process had been another funny experience, made so by her unintentionally comedic parents. Neither of them could understand why Sarah would want to live on her own. Her mum told her: 'People only live on their own if they've got no friends', while her dad made her look up the word 'hermit' in the dictionary.

When she first started looking for her new home, Philip helpfully suggested not looking at any with a balcony – in case she was tempted to throw herself off. 'He wasn't being funny, or cruel – just practical, which is the position me dad comes at everything from,' she says.

But soon she was happily settled in her new place, where she could enjoy the simple pleasures of living alone – like walking around naked and decorating in whatever style she liked. 'Suddenly there were no restrictions, no compromise,' she has said of the time. 'You don't have to say, "are you alright with those blue curtains because I quite like the red ones, but you like the blue ones". Now I can have red curtains. If I want no curtains, or curtains made from children's ears, I'm going to have them.'

Living on her own also meant she could turn her flat into a sauna, without anyone complaining it was too hot. 'I love to be warm,' she told *The Radio Times* in 2012. 'When my friends come round they tell me they always have to wear short sleeves as my flat is always "Nana hot". We bought onesies last Christmas, but with the heating on we were close to collapse. I never want to be rushed to A&E in head-to-toe fleece.'

Happily settled in her new life, it was time for Sarah to step it up a notch – by going solo at The Edinburgh Fringe Festival. Sarah had performed at the festival before, but never alone. Instead, she had done what many other comedians choose to do when they are first starting out: she shared a show. She had previously dipped her toe into the Fringe waters by performing as part of an ensemble cast, like for example, at the Big Value Show in 2006.

Comedian Ian Fox says there are benefits to choosing this approach, and that often, many comedians will come together to produce a compilation show. In his online blog, entitled *How to Produce a Free Festival Show*, the seasoned Edinburgh show producer gives the following advice to new comedians:

'If you're a new comedian and you regularly do 10-minute slots, don't sign up for a full hour slot thinking that you can set yourself the challenge of having an hour's material by August. Over the last few years I've seen loads of new acts try and fail at this. Mainly because putting together an hour is extremely difficult; 40 minutes is hard enough but it's that last 20 where it all goes wrong. Instead, best thing to do is find some other comics in a similar position and put on a showcase where you do 10-15 minutes each and rotate as headline and compere.

'There are enormous advantages to doing this. Firstly you get all the benefits of performing every day, such as increased confidence and becoming more relaxed and loose on stage, without the downside of having to endure the painful sight of audience members getting up and walking out on you. Plus you don't get a mauling from whatever press turns up to see you. It's also much cheaper, as you split the costs between you. Any press reviews you pick up will be likely to be positive – unless you're completely rubbish – and you'll come out of it with one or two decent quotes for your CV.'

The other great benefit, as Sarah was to discover, is that doing compilation shows means that in the future you can still be eligible for the prestigious festival's Best Newcomer Award, as the rules state you have to be doing your first solo show, 50 minutes or more in length, to enter.

Sarah was obviously setting herself a real challenge when in January 2008 she booked herself in for a one-hour slot at The Pleasance Courtyard – a well-known Edinburgh Festival comedy venue. She titled her show *Sarah Millican's Not Nice*, and began counting down the months to the August spectacular.

Sarah knew that her material had to be of a very high quality – there would be reviewers and journalists in the audience, as well as people who had paid good money to see her. It was also a considerable financial gamble for Sarah, as performers have to pay registration fees, venue hire and accommodation costs. Unsurprisingly, very few shows even break even. The 2008 festival registration fee alone was a hefty £289.05.

No one new to the world of comedy goes to the Fringe to make money. They either go for the networking opportunities, they simply treat it as a training ground, or they see it as a springboard for career advancement.

It was, and still is, a very competitive environment. Essentially all the best comics are performing at the same time, in the same city. Sarah didn't want to disappoint the people who had chosen to see her over anyone else.

She spent the next few months revising her material, and practicing her 'I'm having a lovely time' face. Then, when the time came, Sarah packed her bags and moved into a little flat in Marchmont, Edinburgh, which she was sharing with another comedian. The festival lasts for nearly a month, so most comics share together to keep costs down.

When they opened the door to what would be their temporary home, Sarah finally had a taste of the university-style experience she had missed out on. The place was filthy. Hence the first thing she did, upon arriving at the Fringe for her debut solo show, was to go to the shops and buy a stash of cleaning products. Pulling up their rubber gloves, the two comics blitzed the place before rewarding themselves with a feast at local eaterie, Monster Mash.

Later, while leafing through the Fringe brochure, she circled a massive 50 shows that she wanted to go and see. No matter how her show was received, it was going to be an incredible month and she didn't want it to be all hard work and no play.

Sarah was pleased to be booked into the Pleasance

Courtyard for her show's run. With over 500,000 visitors each year, 16 venues, and every kind of entertainment imaginable on the billing, it's fondly known as the heart of the festival.

But then disaster struck...

Back in 1990, because of the huge array of acts performing at the Fringe, its organisers had installed a special computerised booking system, which allowed show tickets to be bought from a number of locations around the city. With the advent of the Internet, in 2000 the Fringe launched its own official website, allowing tickets to be bought online for the first time.

It was a huge boost to Fringe earnings – by 2005, over half a million tickets had been sold online. Following this success, the Fringe decided to design a festival-wide ticketing system, to try and consolidate its sales. It has also since been suggested that the move was borne out of the discovery that several major venues in Edinburgh were launching their own independent ticketing system, taking income away from the Fringe organisers.

In March 2008, a company was hired to design and install the new system. But they had never done anything like it before, and only had 14 weeks to install and test it.

The system failed spectacularly.

It happened on an overcast day in June – the first day of advance Fringe ticket sales, and a notoriously busy day for festival ticket buying. Some shows had a very limited number of seats and were in high demand – getting tickets early was the only way to guarantee you would see your favourite act.

Chaos followed. Thousands of people tried, and failed to buy advance tickets, and despite repeated attempts to fix the problem, it soon became apparent that it wouldn't be possible.

The failure was described as the biggest crisis in Fringe history, and led to a bill of around £300,000 for the Fringe organisers. But worst of all, sales suffered. After so many acts had paid a fee to perform, many wondered if they would end up in debt because of the poor sales.

In fact, sales were down 10 per cent from the year before, when 1.7 million tickets had been sold. It was a huge loss, although it was partly blamed on poor weather, the Beijing Olympics, and the economy.

But for the acts due to appear at the festival, it was a huge blow and for Sarah, it must have been frightening. She still had no idea how many people would be in her audience each night. It was her first year as a solo stand-up artist, so she couldn't quote sell-outs from previous gigs on her promotional material and posters.

And despite her recent wins, a lot of people had never heard of her. But the only way to get fans was to perform. So on the first night Sarah went onto the small stage and tried not to let her face fall when she looked out over the audience.

There were just five people.

Sarah tried not to be downhearted as she went through her routine, wearing her specs and something flowery from her wardrobe. On stage, she was slender and delicate looking, with plain brown locks falling to her shoulders. She looked more like a nursery school teacher than a sweary comedian who was about to talk an awful lot about sex.

But her routine must have been a pleasant shock for the

five-strong crowd, because the next night Sarah saw more people in the audience. The night after that she saw even more. And her audience kept growing...

Four days later, when she described the night in a novice's account of her first week at the Fringe, it was obvious she was pleased at how things had gone so far. She told *The Guardian*: 'On the first night I had an audience of five. The fact that they had bought tickets without knowing who I was felt like a massive compliment. Out of five shows so far, three went brilliantly and two weren't so good. But I'm notoriously hard on myself. I had a reviewer in on one of my bad nights, and they gave me four stars.'

In the frank and honest diary-style piece she was ultimately philosophical about how her first week had gone. 'Every time I've had a good show I treat myself by eating chocolate or going to see some comedy,' she wrote. 'So far I've seen Josie Long, Andrew Laurence and Jon Richardson. They were all great.'

Sarah also mused a little on her competition. 'The standard is really high,' she admitted. 'You get people in the audience who've just seen Mark Watson or Tim Minchin, which means the pressure's on. But I don't feel threatened. I can't do what they do, but they can't do what I do either.'

They certainly couldn't. Because Sarah's routine was a culmination of all the pain and sorrow she had felt, all the lessons she had learned, and all the experiences she had grown through since her husband had left her four years before.

She addressed questions that resonated with everyone from divorcees, to happily married couples, and even to the single and willing. What if I'm rubbish at sex? Why did I marry the first man who liked me? What if no one ever fancies me again?

Sarah's audience quickly began to fill out, thanks to the power of word of mouth. Soon everybody wanted to see the potty-mouthed northerner who was causing such a stir in the courtyard.

Comedy critic and art writer Brian Logan was one of the first to review Sarah's show. 'Breaking up is hard to do,' he wrote in *The Guardian*. 'But if you launch a stand-up career on the back of it, well that's got to take the edge off... It sounds like therapy masquerading as entertainment, but you'd be hard pushed to find a jollier set on the Fringe. Millican establishes a real atmosphere of bonhomie, which is no mean feat when your subject is heartbreak and you're probing couples in the front row for their sexual peccadillos.'

Logan found Sarah refreshing. He admitted it wasn't an unfamiliar stand-up style – there have been plenty of female comics who combine a lovable demeanour with a foul mouth. Nor, he said, was it an especially appealing range of material – her subject matter rarely delved further than smut, sex and relationships.

'But there's no denying that Millican applies the formula with brio and (not withstanding her self-proclaimed cynicism) a big heart, and the jokes feel fresh and true,' he said.

The jokes, in fact, had people howling with laughter. And there were plenty of them. From the one about having sex with men in their thirties – 'generally much better, but you've got to rub their legs afterwards for cramp', to the one about administering hand relief on a bus – Driver: 'Are you ever going to get off?' Sarah: 'Tell me about it, my wrists are f***ing knackered.'

But it wasn't just her expertly crafted jokes that began to fill her seats, night after night, it was her delivery too – a delivery that she certainly had a natural talent for, but that she had also honed over the years. As Logan summed up: 'Sometimes the funniest pay-offs need no words: Millican's face is priceless. The marriage failed, but the comedy career is unlikely to.'

It was a stunning review, but it wouldn't be the last. By the end of the Fringe, every journalist was talking about Sarah Millican.

But even as the buzz was growing around her, Sarah sometimes found the experience a tough one. After one particularly hard show, it was up to Gary to cheer her up, by taking her to a chip shop and buying her a bag of the potato treats along with two bars of dairy milk.

Another wobble came when she went home to Newcastle, to celebrate her father's birthday. Spending the whole day travelling, she missed her afternoon nap and felt tired and probably a bit grouchy. Seeing her mum and dad also highlighted how much she was missing her family. But she soon got herself back on track and facing her packed little Pleasance Courtyard hut with her usual gusto.

Sarah settled into a routine. Every afternoon at 5pm, she went back to her little flat in Marchmont – next to Edinburgh's grand public park, The Meadows – and performed a little ritual. She had a power nap, put her face on, and walked back through The Meadows chanting the order of her show under her breath. Luckily the only other people around were performers, who were mostly doing the same thing.

She also tried to make sure she had snacks in her bag, as it is hard to do an hour-long show when your energy levels are flagging.

After her shows had finished she would go with friends to various late night eateries. One of her favourites was the appropriately named Favorit, which opened till the very early hours.

At 2am one morning, one of Sarah's friends ordered muesli with sliced bananas. The staff member was apologetic and said they'd run out of the fruit, but Sarah was remarkably prepared and said: 'Bring a knife, I've got one in my bag!'

Sarah is, as she herself says, 'annoyingly maternal', for someone who so loathes the thought of having children. She made friends quickly at the festival, and often behaved like a surrogate mum to them. 'I once bumped into my flatmate in the Pleasance Courtyard and asked her if she had eaten yet,' she recalled in *The Independent* a year later. 'She said she'd had a hotdog and a gin and tonic. She seemed to think that was adequate. I plied her with microwaveable dinners.'

Some viewers were left confused by the title of Sarah's show – why was Sarah Millican 'Not Nice'? Steve Bennett, writing for the comedy website *Chortle*, tackled the answer in his review of the show: 'Sarah Millican may look quite sweet and she certainly sounds that way… but as this show's title gives away, that's an utterly deceptive image. She's not nice in two ways: because she is, in her own words, 'a bit of a cow', and because her material can be utterly filthy. Her lilting north east accent sugar-coats everything from sex toys to coprophilia, giving an illusion of gentle charm to the crudest of material.'

It was a succinctly accurate description of the 33-year-old, and one that whetted the appetites of many a Fringe-goer.

'The vivid pictures she paints of a pain, unsalved by her father's casual doom-mongering, bring a hefty dose of reality to her jokes,' added Bennett. 'And my, has she got jokes. Tim Vine aside she surely has one of the highest gags-per-minute count on the Fringe, with punchlines arriving every few beats with unwavering punctuality. The effect of such an onslaught is irresistible and laughs come thick and fast.'

Sarah ordered her show very cleverly. She didn't just instantly bring out the sex and swearing – instead she gradually built up to it, initially talking through her divorce like a sad bedtime story. 'They said time is a healer, as if someone had died. Rubbish. If he'd died I'd have had my mortgage paid and danced on his grave,' Sarah told her shocked audiences.

With the laughter flowing freely, Sarah then headed to her most comfortable ground – below the belt – where she remained for the remainder of the hour. Her material verged on the masculine, with non-stop references to bad sex and masturbation. But viewers were impressed when she steered clear of the penis jokes and clichés and, as Bennett put it, 'refreshed the genre'.

'Although she has a generally unromantic view of relationships... a note of optimism – albeit pragmatic optimism – does emerge at the end, as she concedes that she is happy in her new relationship. It all adds to the feeling that her stand-up is based on real experiences, not contrived for the sake of a gig. It's how she avoids clichés, and stays likeable, all contributing to what is an impressive, and consistently funny, festival debut.'

What Bennett was voicing was the honesty that is an integral part of Sarah's charm. People generally don't like to be lied to, even for the sake of a gag. An obviously faked moment or emotion can separate a viewer from the journey they've been undertaking with the comedian and leave them feeling like they have woken up from a hazy laughter spell.

The same goes for comedians who try too hard. Audiences don't want to feel uncomfortable or embarrassed for the entertainer they've paid money to see.

At her Fringe debut, with her frank and self-effacing manner, Millican made the ever-growing crowd in her audience feel like they were part of her world. She asked them questions about their sex lives – 'Do you use food in the bedroom, flower?' Or: 'Do you dress up for your partner, pet?'

She was greeted with both shy reticence and an avalanche of volunteered information. She coped equally well with either. During one show, Sarah asked one man in the audience whether he had ever had a shower with a partner.

His girlfriend was sitting next to him when he replied that yes, he had. Sarah was just about to ask him for more details, when a voice from the back shouted: 'Ask him what happened in Magaluf!'

There was an awkward moment of silence. His girlfriend looked puzzled and he just looked very uncomfortable.

Sarah quickly understood that the guy at the back obviously knew the red-faced man and was trying his best to embarrass him. The poor guy was squirming in his seat, trying to figure out how best to dodge the answer.

Sarah was kind and immediately diffused the situation. She gently asked: 'Do you want to tell us something that your girlfriend clearly doesn't know about, which happened in Magaluf?' When the man said that no, he really didn't, she led the audience in a round of applause and swiftly moved on.

Millican rolled effortlessly with what was thrown at her, making it seem like the audience were at a good friend's Ann Summers party, rather than a comedy show led by a stranger. Most impressively, she never let the show go off track, which can often happen when you interact with the audience. It was a combination of all of these things that led more and more people to her show, which soon sold out, and more and more reviewers to sit in on the action.

Her promotional poster was soon covered over with star rating stickers – so many, that by the end of the festival her face was almost obscured with the praise.

Sarah's show also proved something else that cheered the hearts of her reviewers: you don't need to be cool to be funny. Sarah happily gave a large number of interviews throughout her first Fringe run, and didn't try to make herself out to be anything she wasn't.

She told reporters that her favourite song was Cliff Richard's *Wired For Sound*. She spoke about how proud she was to be compared to a young Thora Hird – in contrast to many of the other comics, who would have preferred edgier comparisons, like Bill Hicks or Lenny Bruce. She even joked about the benefits of being 'a square' during an interview with the *Daily Record*. 'If another comic asks for a lift home from a gig, I have no shame about putting Take That's *Greatest Hits* on the car stereo. They never ask for a lift again.'

Sarah was overwhelmed with the positive reviews she was getting, and began to hear her name touted as a possible festival award winner. When she was interviewed by *The Metro*, she acknowledged her huge delight at how well she was being received, but countered it with her typical self-effacing attitude. 'I appreciate this isn't a typical Edinburgh,' she said. 'I'm expecting next year to be completely rubbish. If I get nominated, that's great, but even if I don't, people will go: "Oh my God, you should have been nominated!" I win either way.'

The remaining festival days passed quickly, and the town buzzed with talk of the deceptively sweet and paradoxically filthy newcomer.

Seasoned festival reviewer Jay Richardson reviewed her show for newspaper *The Scotsman*, and wrote: 'Throughout the show, you're persuaded of a talent – and indeed sexual confidence – belatedly enjoying its fullest expression. Millican's "not nice" feelings have developed from being a source of shame, through her post-marriage insecurity, to unabashed pride, her sadistically delivered lines on masturbation and crap sex technique offset by a pragmatic affection for her current beau, exemplified by their rollercoaster non-engagement. So much of herself and her audience's intimacies and indiscretions are packed into this hour that it's totally devoid of filler, yet absolutely brimming over with muck.'

In hindsight it was inevitable: Sarah soon received word from on high that she had indeed been nominated for a festival award.

Celebrated at a prestigious evening ceremony at the end of August, the .if comedy awards were attended by a wide swathe of the UK's media and presented by a host of comedy stars. They consisted of a main prizewinner and a best newcomer award – which Sarah had been nominated for. The best newcomer award recognised the talent of festival virgins, and acknowledged the promise of their career in the world of comedy.

Sarah was nervous and excited. Two years before, Oxford-educated funny lady Josie Long had walked away with the award, after her debut show *Kindness and Exuberance* was a landslide success. In 2007, Cambridge University's Tom Basden – member of the four-man sketch group Cowards – snatched the title, with his show, *Tom Basden Won't Say Anything*.

Sarah knew that the Best Newcomer Award would be an incredible achievement. Out of the hundreds of new and talented performers who had bravely tackled the festival that year, standards had been notably high.

And she hadn't been to any university, let alone the country's two greatest learning institutions, as both her predecessors had done. Both universities have a long-held association with comedy as entertainment, and regularly produce highly talented comics and performers from behind their ancient stone walls.

For example, since 2003, Oxford University has been home to The Oxford Imps, an improvisational comedy troupe who perform every week during term time. They have been described by Fringe festival magazine *Three Weeks* as the best show they ever had the pleasure to witness, and count an armful of comedy award recipients among their number. These include Ivo Graham, winner of the 2009 So You Think You're Funny? competition, and Chris Turner, finalist at the 2011 BBC New Comedy Awards. Many alumni of the Imps have continued their passion for improv after their time at the university, founding a number of successful groups around the world including Chicago, New York and Sydney.

The ever-changing group thus has a rich tradition of comedy performances to draw from, giving wave after wave of new university students the chance to learn about the techniques and skills needed in both stand-up and improvisational comedy.

Cambridge University has an even more prestigious history of fine comedy. Founded in 1883, the Cambridge University Footlights Dramatic Club – commonly referred to simply as the Footlights – has been run by university students ever since.

The club has established a tradition of performing at the Fringe festival, and for decades has dominated the British world of comedy – spawning groups such as Monty Python and The Goodies. Their 1981 revue heralded the arrival of Fry and Laurie, and won the inaugural Perrier Award at the Fringe. A large number of its former members have gone on to win BAFTAS, Oscars and countless other awards, and have enjoyed long and successful careers in the entertainment and media industry.

Today, Footlights is seen as an unofficial finishing school for many of Britain's most well-known comics and entertainers, and cast members have included Morwenna Banks, Clive Anderson, David Baddiel, Alexander Armstrong and David Armand.

Following in the footsteps of such impressive comedy credentials must have seemed nigh on impossible for Sarah, the daughter of a miner from South Shields, who only started performing in her late twenties. But then again, impossible was a word that her father had told her didn't exist.

At the awards party, Sarah mingled with the other nominees and waited for the winners to be announced. She even got starstruck, when she bumped into Clive James. As she told *The Huffington Post* in November 2012, 'I was so nervous, I just jabbered and he had no idea who I was.'

She was busy munching a carton of noodles when she heard her name announced over the loud speaker: because she had won the Best Newcomer Award.

Astonished, she went on stage to collect it. Her noodles were left to go cold as she was whisked away to be interviewed by a steady stream of journalists. 'I'll use the prize money to pay off my car loan,' she told them in a haze of happiness.

It had been a whirlwind month in Edinburgh. From the initial disappointment of her first show, success had snowballed for the once shy schoolgirl. She had well and truly blossomed into a startlingly funny comic. But even at this seemingly high point in her career, greater things were yet to come…

CHAPTER 9

Lights, Camera, Action!

S arah's first experience of the world of television came the night she won the Best Newcomer Award at the Edinburgh Fringe Festival in 2008.

Suddenly everyone wanted to see and speak to Sarah and every journalist and presenter wanted to be the first to interview her. But it was multi-talented media personality Lauren Laverne who managed to get the first television interview with the award-winning comic.

At the time Laverne was presenting *The Culture Show*, BBC2's arts magazine programme, which focuses on the best of the week's arts and culture news. It had been on air for four years, and had weathered some early criticism to establish itself as one of the longest-running arts magazine shows in the history of BBC television. The interview was an exciting prospect and would bring Millican to the attention of a whole new audience.

Sarah looked demure as she shared a sofa with Laverne, wearing a flowery shirt and a green cardigan. She was beaming as the presenter introduced her as the winner of the .if newcomer award, and her fresh complexion was rosy with happiness.

She didn't seem nervous at all, which was remarkable considering it was her first TV appearance. It may have helped that Lauren is from Sunderland, a mere five miles away from Sarah's native South Shields. But whatever the reason, the pair quickly fell into an easy conversational patter.

'How did it feel at the envelope-opening moment?' asked Lauren. 'I felt really sick,' Sarah laughed. 'Clive James announced the winner and I had a friend with us to make sure they did say my name. Because I have this fear – what if they've said somebody else's name and I get up and somebody's going to pull me back?'

Lauren chuckled and asked whether Sarah had made any attempt to thank her ex-husband when she accepted her award, but she shook her head. 'I made a point of not thanking him,' she said, before telling Laverne her story. 'I had never thought of doing stand-up till I got divorced,' she explained. 'I'm not sure it's what everyone would do when they got divorced, but it was certainly something I fancied doing. And I think it's about the questions you ask yourself when you split up from somebody, and I think everybody's split up with somebody, so everyone can identify with it.'

Lauren agreed, and even said that for a lot of comedians their bad times must end up as great fodder for their shows.

She pointed out that she had recently interviewed the grand dame of comedy, Joan Rivers, who had told her that she simply wasn't funny when she was happy.

'Maybe it's all going to go, now I have an award,' Sarah said. 'But I still think I'm funny when I'm happy. Funny things happen in a new relationship because it's quite scary being in a new relationship after you've been with the same bloke for seven years.'

Lauren asked about Sarah's preoccupation with sex – was it something she talked about quite a lot in general? To the viewers at home – those who hadn't seen Sarah perform – it must have seemed an odd question: what would this gentle-looking, softly spoken young woman have to say on the matter?

'Well, you're supposed to talk about what you know,' Sarah said delicately. 'I don't know if that means I know a lot about it, or I'm just really inquisitive. I just write about what makes me laugh, and you know, certain things are a little bit wrong in the bedroom.'

Sarah giggled a little, before Lauren returned to talking about the award she had just won. 'It's been amazing,' Sarah gushed, her face an open book. In her smile it was clear to see she had been having the time of her life, and was overwhelmed by the response to her show. 'All I've got to go on is what I find funny, and it started off really well and I got reviewers in straight away. I got really good reviews, so that helped sell out the rest of the run, so it's been ridiculous.'

It was a heart-warming interview, which showed Sarah to be full of television potential. It wouldn't be long before the calls to guest on a multitude of TV shows would come rolling in.

After the Fringe, Sarah packed up her things in the little Marchmont flat that had been her home for the previous month, and went back to Manchester. She gave herself a well-deserved holiday, flying off to a quiet sunny spot just outside of popular tourist destination Benidorm, in Spain. Sarah didn't have a definite plan when she returned, but in the meantime she went straight back to gigging. She spent any spare time she had formulating her next show, which she planned to take to the Fringe the following year.

In September, Sarah began devising brand new content and steering clear of any new jokes about her divorce. That time in her life had served her well, but she had mined the sad experience as much as she could, and wanted to show growth in her next show.

She didn't, however, want to tackle a subject that she knew nothing about, so she decided on a variation on her last theme – the differences between men and women…

It would be an ambitious subject to tackle. Generally perceived as one of the hardest areas to do well at in stand-up, many have tried and failed to step outside of the realm of clichés and sexism, and into genuinely funny territory. The fact is, no matter which point you start from, you're always in danger of alienating half your audience.

But Sarah was unperturbed and thought, 'let's get it sorted once and for all…' She came up with a plan that she thought would help her approach the subject fairly – she began sending out hundreds of questionnaires, asking men and women to answer questions about their perception of their sex. She was careful to make it a representative study, reaching out to both people that she knew, and people she didn't.

When the completed questionnaires began coming back in, Sarah studied them carefully and began to base her show around the answers. It was a goldmine of material, all she had to do was figure out the best way to use it.

The 2009 Fringe was a long way off, but by late autumn, Sarah was well on her way to formulating her new hour-long show. It may have seemed to those around her that she was starting a little early, but Sarah had always liked to be prepared.

She was teetering on the brink of fame, but deep down she hadn't changed at all – she would always be the studious girl who started her homework early, worked diligently to overcome every challenge she faced, and was always fully prepared for exams. 'I hate it when a comedian says, "that show, oh, I just wrote that on the train, it took me a few hours",' Sarah told one Leicestershire reporter. 'People do that so they look cool, because it takes me nine months!'

But whilst wading through her new joke ideas in early October, Sarah was interrupted by a very exciting invitation: 8 Out of 10 Cats wanted her to do a guest spot on one of their episodes. It was a huge indication of her burgeoning fame. The Channel 4 show only features the cream of comedy talent, and if they wanted Sarah they must have been very impressed with what they had seen of her.

At the time that Sarah was invited to make her first appearance, the show was already in its seventh season. A panel show in format, it is based on statistics and opinion polls mainly carried out by the company Harris Poll. Hosted by Jimmy Carr, the show features two teams, each consisting of a regular team captain and two celebrity guests.

Dour comic Sean Lock has been a team captain since the show's inception, and over the years a wealth of comedy talent has graced its stage including Johnny Vegas, Stephen Mangan, Jason Manford, Simon Amstell and David Walliams. It was a chance for Millican to enter the mainstream and she was hungry for the opportunity.

Arriving at the BBC Television Centre, where the show is recorded, she was pleased to discover who her fellow guests would be. Joining Sarah for episode six of the series were Salford comic Jason Manford, singer Peter Andre, *Inbetweeners* star Greg Davies and *Cold Feet* actor John Thomson.

On the show, the teams chatted about the recent Tory party conference, Ant and Dec nearly getting blown up in Afghanistan, and the film *E.T.* Sarah joined in the panel discussions, offering up nuggets of her dry wit for the audience. When Jimmy Carr gently ribbed her about her hometown she took it all in good spirits. Talking about their recent trip to Afghanistan, Jimmy said: 'Ant and Dec were appalled by the violence, poverty and mistreatment of women. So they left Newcastle and went to Afghanistan.'

The audience laughed at the gag, and Sarah, dressed in a pretty black top, hung her head in pretend shame. Jason Manford pretended to comfort her by gently placing a hand on her arm.

Two days later Sarah was still in London – but this time it wasn't to appear in front of a small television audience. Instead she would be performing at the hallowed Royal Albert Hall…

A vast concert hall situated in Kensington, West London, the Royal Albert Hall is nearly 150 years old. Since it was opened by Queen Victoria in 1871, it has played host to the world's leading artists and performers and is now one of the UK's most treasured buildings. Each year it hosts more than 350 events, including classical concerts, rock and pop performances, ballets and operas, charity performances, award ceremonies and banquets.

One of these events was the Secret Policeman's Ball, and it was as part of this amazing yearly occasion that Sarah would be appearing on stage.

It was a huge deal. Five and a half thousand guests would be packed into the famous venue, including members of the Royal Family and a host of other famous and influential people. It was by far the biggest audience Sarah had ever performed to. She was used to a few hundred folk in the crowd – how would she cope with such a vast sea of faces staring at her?

A televised benefit gala, staged primarily to raise funds for the human rights organisation Amnesty International, the Ball was first held in the mid-seventies where it initially took the form of a series of comedy galas featuring famous British comics.

Comedy legend John Cleese had been approached by Amnesty International and agreed to round up a few friends to perform a series of three gigs for charity. His 'friends' included his Monty Python co-stars, The Goodies, and a number of other brilliant Oxbridge comedians. Tickets were only available through *Private Eye* and sold out within four days.

The event evolved into a yearly extravaganza, featuring not only comedians but also live music and other entertainment. It starred the very best of the British performing world. Joining Sarah on stage in 2008 were Frank Skinner, Alan Carr, Graham Norton, Sean Lock, Mitchell and Webb, Shappi Khorsandi, Russell Howard, Katy Brand, Tim Minchin, Meera Syal, Sharon Horgan, Gok Wan and TV's best-loved impressionist Jon Culshaw. Indie band Razorlight provided the music, while Canadian comic Russell Peters appeared via videolink.

It was an epic, star-studded event and Sarah must have felt honoured to be included along with such well-respected entertainers. But it was a mark of how far she had come in the short four years since she first performed at Newcastle's The Dog and Parrot.

Pictures taken backstage at the event show Sarah clearly enjoying herself. Wearing a huge grin, she larked about with fellow comic and kindred spirit Shappi Khorsandi, who like Sarah has also cited Jo Brand as a major influence on her work.

It was a long night. The three-hour event was filmed for a 95-minute television special to be broadcast the following day. A unique 'cinecast' was also broadcast – where the event was shown live in 35 cinemas in major British cities, four cities in Australia and one in Canada.

The Cineplex cinema chain made the film available on 50 of its 1,317 screens and ticket sales were high. It was major exposure for Sarah and the subsequent reviews were great.

The Guardian said that the audience couldn't have been unhappy about the line-up, and wrote: 'Nor did many of the junior performers let this vast televised occasion down. Mitchell and Webb's self-doubting Nazis were much improved by the subtraction of canned laughter, while Sarah Millican's tales of sex and domesticity got the laughs they deserved.'

UK comedy website *Chortle* was equally impressed with Sarah's performance. 'Sarah Millican was the epitome of cool on this night. She may have been largely unknown, but her tetchy and pragmatic observations on sex and relationships will have won her plenty of new fans and she loaded the short set with an enviable number of rock solid punchlines.'

Understandably, the following day Sarah's name was all over the Internet. But interestingly, it was on Tim Minchin's official fan site *Angry Feet* where she was praised most highly. Minchin's most die-hard fans had travelled from all over the UK to either go to the Royal Albert Hall or get tickets to one of the live cinecasts – and hadn't been disappointed with his performance. But on his forum they discussed Sarah's performance in detail, raving about the new girl in comedy town. 'Sarah Millican ruled, go the north,' wrote one Minchin fan. 'I really liked Sarah Millican; think I'll book for her solo show after seeing her tonight,' said another.

Sarah's appeal was widening and her name was becoming more and more well-known. On that night – 4th October 2008 – she had taken one more step towards becoming Britain's new darling of the north.

Sarah had enjoyed the star-studded event immensely. But she knew she had to continue working on her next show, so she returned to Manchester, enthused by her recent run of success. There she began gigging again in earnest, often accompanied by her boyfriend.

In November she and Gary travelled to Nottingham, to play at The Grove Pub in Lenton. It was the kind of venue she had been used to before her big break in Edinburgh, and Sarah felt right at home in the cosy pub.

The gig was part of the popular local Funhouse Comedy Club nights, which always drew large crowds to its venues. But with Sarah headlining, the audience that night was packed with people hoping to experience her award-winning brand of comedy. Local club promoter Spiky Mike was excited about her presence in the line-up. 'This could be the last chance to catch her before she moves up to theatres,' he told *The Nottingham Evening Post*, excitedly.

He had no idea how right he was. Despite now spending most of her time back in the pubs of the north east, it wasn't long before Sarah was back in London. News satire programme, *Have I Got News For You*, had got in touch, asking Sarah to appear on one of their forthcoming episodes.

Often cited as the first comedy panel show to dominate ratings, its first series aired in 1990 and it has been a staple of British comedy ever since. Many of the highest flyers in the comedy, acting and political world have guested on the show, including Bill Bailey, Janet Street-Porter, Jo Brand, Ken Livingstone and even Germaine Greer.

It was a huge accolade to be part of the BBC show, and Sarah didn't disappoint. Not only did she guest on the main show, but she also starred in an extra feature. The programme had just begun a special series of 'webisodes', designed for, as David Mitchell put it, 'people who can't be bothered to turn their televisions on'. It was called *The Inevitable Internet Spin Off*, and was broadcast online between 2007 and 2009 – encompassing series 33 through to 38.

On 5 December 2008, the British public was treated to Sarah's debut on the show. Presented by Mitchell, Sarah was on Ian Hislop's team, while comedy writer Andy Hamilton joined Paul Merton. Sarah had gone down to the London Studios, former home of London Weekend Television, the day before, in order to film the episode. She laughed along as Mitchell struggled with his opening lines, before getting her first chance to speak.

In her typically revealing style, she immediately started telling the audience about her train journey – and more specifically what she ate on it. 'I came down on the train today and had soup, and a smoothie,' she told them earnestly as they cheered her presence. Her face changed to one of concern. 'That's a lot of liquid,' she added. 'I feel a little bit sick – just so you know.'

It may have been an unusual topic of conversation, but what the audience didn't realise was that they were getting an early glimpse of Millican's unique and infectious comedy style. She is always very personal, almost to the point of over exposing herself. It's interesting to note that even on such a highbrow comedy show she didn't try to be anything other than herself.

The other panellists gently teased the newbie. Ian Hislop leaned over conspiratorially and told her in a slightly condescending manner: 'The main thing is, don't go to the toilet in the middle of the show…' Sarah was unfazed.

She pointed to her chair and shot back: 'But can I do it here though?'

The audience chuckled, as Ian began to tell a story about one infamous panellist who had left the studio during filming – to go to the toilet. 'We had Russell Brand on...'

'...Never mind,' Sarah cut in, making the crowd laugh once more.

Next, they discussed the police force's response to burglary and once again Sarah had a tale to tell. She'd had the unpleasant experience of being burgled and told the rest of the panel that at the time she couldn't get an officer to come and take her statement.

'Not even one?' asked Ian.

'No,' she said deadpan. 'It's true.'

She was silent for a moment – a deliberate pause designed to make the audience feel sorry for her, before she added: 'I left my door open, so, it's not really technically burglary. It's just somebody trying doors.'

Andy Hamilton tried to get some sense out of the funny story, by asking: 'So what offence did they say it was, Sarah, if it wasn't burglary, because someone stole your stuff, presumably?'

'Yeah but it was mostly rubbish,' she quipped. 'And the insurance still went through – hurray!'

She told the story with a wide-eyed innocence, and everyone listened intently before bursting into laughter. It was another example of her comedy technique – eliciting sympathy from the audience with a sorry story, before ending on a gag.

But David Mitchell pushed her further: 'So you left your

door open, and all the rubbish went?' 'Yes,' Sarah laughed. 'It was obviously just the bin men, wasn't it…'

Sarah was a welcome female antidote to the otherwise all-male panellist line-up, and she gave a great account of herself on the show. She even found herself on the winning team.

After a well-earned Christmas break, Sarah could reflect on 2008 as being a very good year. Being awarded Best Newcomer at Edinburgh, live TV appearances and guest spots on some of Britain's most popular panel shows – she could never have imagined the exciting direction her new hobby would take her when she first signed up to that small Newcastle comedy workshop in 2004.

But now she was planning to return to Edinburgh as an established comedian – would her second show be as popular as her first?

CHAPTER 10

Sarah Goes
Down Under

'People always ask if work has taken me to places I'd not otherwise have visited, and I say, "Yes, I would not otherwise have been to Lincoln or Nottingham". It's taken me to Australia, too, somewhere I'd always wanted to go, but felt was too far to visit without a mission. My mission was the Melbourne Comedy Festival.'

By the time 2009 arrived, Sarah's schedule was jam-packed. She had spent months working on the material for her new show, which she was looking forward to performing during her 25 new Fringe dates in August.

She wanted her second show to be more mature, and to show a definite development in her work. To that end, she had avoided most of the references to her failed marriage that had dominated her debut, and instead was concentrating on the differences between the sexes. She was at home with the new content, in which she had decided to attempt to rebrand what people see as 'typical' male and female traits.

It was an ambitious project and very culturally relevant. As a newly successful female in what is still perceived as a very male-dominated area, she now had a voice and she wanted to use it.

But the main point of the show was that it had to be funny, so Sarah began to road test her new show – literally. Over the next few months she did an incredible 27 preview shows all over the country. She analysed her audience's response closely, and discarded any bits that she felt they didn't particularly like. She moved her jokes around and chose which ones she wanted to start and finish with. It was a huge amount of work but she undertook it with her usual diligence and focus.

Then, in April she flew to Australia. She had been invited to perform at the Melbourne International Comedy Festival – one of the three largest comedy gatherings in the world, alongside the Edinburgh Fringe and Canada's Just For Laughs.

News of her Fringe success had travelled across the world and the Aussies were keen to experience the sweet-voiced Geordie's award-winning brand of mumsie filth. It was also the perfect opportunity to test out her new material on a completely different audience.

She wasn't the only Brit on the roster, and as a result was in good company for the long trip. Sarah found herself staying in the same hotel as Tim Vine, Josie Long and Sadie Hasler – and hung out with them during her Down Under down time.

Sarah had arrived a few days before the festival was due to start and was almost immediately whisked away to her very first movie premiere – for the comedy *The Boat That Rocked*. She got ready in her hotel room with Sadie and Josie, and put her iTunes on shuffle so that the girls could have a bit of music while they glammed themselves up.

Sarah was worried about what embarrassing music was hiding in her collection, so she positioned herself close to the laptop so she could skip any cheesy tracks. But… 'As soon as I had popped into the bedroom to put my dress on, Josie was all over it and Beyonce's *Single Ladies* kicked in,' she wrote on her blog. 'I hate everything it stands for but damn, it's catchy.'

Sarah was having fun with her girly pals, and was excited about being in Australia. But she had never been to a red carpet event before and despite the hype, she found it boring. 'The paparazzi were surprisingly uninterested apart from a tiny boy who interviewed us… about the festival. The next hour-and-a-half were like a socially awkward version of getting to the pictures too early. You can't get the popcorn yet as you will have eaten it, you can't go for a wee as you'll just need another. The canapes were all a bit posh for me and as I don't drink, I got increasingly more bored. But luckily so did everyone else.'

It was refreshing to read that Sarah's new fame hadn't changed her one bit. Going to posh dos and standing around for the paps wasn't something she had ever aspired to – and she wasn't a big fan of it now that it was being thrust upon her.

The next day, Sarah did the obligatory promotional

rounds, going on radio shows and speaking to journalists to drum up interest in her shows. She also did some shopping and made a list of the comics she planned to see while she was at the festival. She ate out at a fancy restaurant, where she chose food from a menu she barely understood. 'And it was in English,' she moaned. 'What's the matter with sausage and mash?'

She couldn't shake a headache that had been brewing all day, which she put down to the worry she was feeling about her first Melbourne gig, taking place the following day.

She had grown pensive about her appearance, and decided to get her hair cut. The shorter style suited her, but the effect on her appearance apparently wasn't enough and she began to think about dyeing her hair too, amongst other possible changes. 'I am currently unhappy with my physical appearance,' she wrote. 'A haircut has sorted out my head and when I get home exercise and less cake will hopefully sort out the rest.'

It was only natural that being so far away from her family and friends she would grow a little insecure and thoughtful, especially since she was growing more nervous about her forthcoming shows. Plus, she admitted she'd watched an episode of *The Biggest Loser* and had been amazed at the contestants' transformations – a guaranteed way to make yourself feel a little less confident about your appearance...

The next day Sarah got on stage in front of her first Australian audience – totalling 24 paying guests. She was a little disappointed overall, but tried not to dwell on it. 'First show, settling in, good but not great,' she wrote. 'New reference tweaks seemed to work, a few jokes just didn't work and I think they found me a bit rude.'

The next day she chatted to some of her fellow comics and found they'd had a similar experience. She felt a little more confident, especially when she found her audience had tripled for the night. 'Went in with renewed vigour and, largely due to a brilliant chat with an hilarious man in the front row, the show really took off. Loved it. A man confessed to once eating a raw egg off his girlfriend's bellybutton.'

It was at this stage that Sarah began the practice of counting badges to ascertain her popularity. At the end of her Edinburgh shows, Sarah had handed out promo badges to her fans at a rate of around 50 per night. 'I think it's a good sign if a lot of people take badges as I don't think I'd take a badge for a show I didn't like,' she wrote. That night in Australia she handed out 89 badges and was rightly pleased.

Then came press night – the night when all the reviewers and journalists came to see the show for their articles and blogs. Sarah knew she would have to be on top form and heaved a huge sigh of relief when she began to hear the huge guffaws from the audience. 'Went really well,' she wrote. 'Will keep my fingers crossed for a nice review from someone which will help sell tickets. Enjoyed the show very much. 88 badges taken. Cool.'

After the show had finished, Sarah decided to treat herself to a comedy show. But when she got outside she found herself overwhelmed by the huge numbers of festival goers (ironically, she's not good in crowds) and so she went to the cinema instead. It was a good choice and boosted her spirits. 'I saw *Monsters vs Aliens*, complete with 3D glasses and popcorn. I felt like a Normal. Normals go to the cinema on a Saturday don't they? The film was ace and is genuinely funny.'

Sarah needn't have worried about press night — the reviews were great. Comedy critic Lisa Clark highly recommended the show, and wrote: 'It was like spending an hour with your favourite filthy aunty. She appears so homely, sweet and non-threatening... There was actually very little innuendo in the show, because Sarah is not afraid to call a spade, a huge dildo. In fact one of the topics she covered was the names we use to refer to our "privates". She did require some audience participation, but she was very nice about it. She was so open and down-to-earth, she actually made you feel comfortable about the sexual nature of most of her material.'

It was a long stint down under – 26 days – and as well as performing herself, Sarah saw a lot of excellent comedians. 'Tonight I saw Mary and Max and it was lovely and made me happy,' she wrote on her blog. 'Last night I saw Adam Hills's show *Inflatable* and it "inflated" me. I want to tell Janeane Garofalo how ace I think her show is without sounding like a weirdo.'

She also spent more time with comedian Tim Vine, who she described as a legend. 'We were talking about what you should and shouldn't eat on Good Friday. And Tim stood up and said, "I think you'll find our Lord prefers something Savioury" and sat back down...'

But she also watched a lot of television – 'I watched a bit

of *Pink Panther* with Steve Martin… and it made me want to cut out my eyes' – and had a lot of time to think. She grew more reflective and shared her thoughts with her fans.

'I've discovered the following things,' she wrote. 'Drinking loads of water is a better cure for my headaches than Nurofen ever was. I have no fears. Around a table with six other comics the other night, we all started to talk about our fears and I realised I don't have any. It was quite a surprise. I used to be scared of spiders, enclosed spaces, dentists, loads of things. I don't think I have any irrational fear. I still can't quite believe it. Australians love a bloody badge. I am running low. My new material for my new show is working (thank God). I am broody. For a tiny baby koala of my own.'

Sarah loved Melbourne but she really missed her family and her boyfriend. She kept in touch via Skype but sometimes it wasn't enough and she found herself feeling very down.

During one Skype session, she said to Gary, sadly: 'You're too far away…'

Her boyfriend misunderstood and moved the webcam closer to his face. It made Sarah laugh and she immediately saved the moment in her memory – it was great comedy material.

But despite the difficulties of being apart from her loved ones, her first Australian festival was a success. 'Shows are going well,' she wrote half way through the month. 'Of course, there's the odd hard one but that only makes me normal. Tickets are selling well, selling out most nights.'

When she flew home at the end of the stint, Sarah must

have been very proud of herself – she had sold out her show most nights, got some brilliant reviews and eventually been nominated for the festival's Barry Award.

Australia loved her so much that she was invited back the next year. Sarah was on a roll.

CHAPTER 11

Preparing For Typical Woman

'My nickname is the cake pigeon. Whenever I press myself against a cake shop, I go: "Oooh".'

Sarah was glad to be back home after her epic overseas adventure. She still had a lot of work to do on her new show and just a few short months to prepare for her second Edinburgh Fringe.

But on her birthday in May, Sarah found herself travelling again – this time to Ireland, for the Kilkenny Comedy Festival. It was another chance to test out her new show material, and local reporters were keen to find out how she was feeling about the upcoming Fringe. 'Having got divorced for the last one, I can't really generate a massive life trauma again,' she told them, before joking: 'I'll just have an abortion this time, it'll be fine.'

Sarah was also asked what she thought about the

perceived notion that it is tougher for women to succeed in comedy and made her thoughts very clear on the matter. 'There are a million reasons why I might not do well at a gig. But none of them are because I'm a woman. In a way, it's slightly easier for girls because we stand out. I'm doing a gig tonight with three blokes and they've all got to establish themselves as 'the guy that does one-liners', 'the guy that does surreal stuff', whereas I can just be a woman and I'm automatically different.'

It was a thoughtful answer to a very interesting question. And it wouldn't be the last time Sarah was asked her thoughts on the subject…

When the summer months arrived, Sarah was ready for Edinburgh. But first she had another exciting TV project to work on – with Britain's top-earning comic Michael McIntyre.

Like Sarah, McIntyre had also won a Fringe Best Newcomer Award – five years earlier than her, in 2003. But unlike Sarah, Michael had a solid background in comedy. His father, Ray Cameron, was one of the late Kenny Everett's scriptwriters, while his mother Kati used to dance on his self-titled show.

Despite his Edinburgh win, it had taken years for McIntyre to climb to the top of the British comedy scene – years in which he struggled to make ends meet by doing small improv gigs all over the country.

Sadly, his early shows weren't as well-received as Sarah's. 'In the early days, I'd travel miles to a show, then stand up telling unscripted off-the-cuff jokes in front of people who didn't get them. Life doesn't get much worse than being humiliated like that,' he told *The Daily Mail* in November 2012. 'I'd drive home, thinking: "I stand there talking rubbish, people think it's rubbish, I have no qualifications, but this is all I've got." It was 2003 and I had absolutely nothing else.'

His career stalling, McIntyre had fallen heavily into debt – a common trap for performers who have no other income. He knew something had to change. But much like when Sarah's husband left her, there had to be a trigger.

Eventually he found the extra drive he needed, inspired by his wife Kitty and the birth of their first son, Lucas. 'I worried his first words would be: "You are in how much debt? Couldn't you have just waited before having me?" So I went nuts sorting out my mess before he got big enough to tell me off. I used to get paid £160 a gig and I'd squeeze in as many of those as possible. I even worked when Kitty was so sick that I really should have stayed by her side, except I couldn't stop thinking: "I've got to make another £160."

In hindsight, the most importance difference came when McIntyre began to employ the same work ethic that Sarah had practiced from the very beginning of her career – gig, gig, and gig some more. Also like Sarah, he started heavily scripting his performances.

It worked. By 2009 McIntyre was performing to a staggering 500,000 people on his first record-breaking tour of the UK – which included six nights at Wembley Stadium and four at The O2 Centre.

The BBC had watched his rise with interest and offered him a Saturday night slot for a new series – *The Michael McIntyre Comedy Roadshow*. It was on this show that

Sarah was invited to perform. Hosted by Michael, the show took the form of a travelling comedy roadshow, broadcast from different venues around the United Kingdom and Ireland. Each episode featured a classic routine from Michael, followed by three other comedians and a final headlining act.

The series aimed to bring new comedy acts to a BBC One Saturday night audience and would give Sarah more huge exposure – even though she was told she would have to tone her act down for the performance. It would mean less of her ruder content, and a complete halt on the prolific swearing. (Sarah loves to swear.) And with her episode being filmed at the Manchester Apollo, for once she didn't have far to travel either.

Sarah joined John Bishop, Mick Ferry and headliner Jason Manford at the well-known venue. Once again she was surrounded by some of Britain's most talented comics, and once again she didn't disappoint.

Dressed in a frilly red dress over baggy jeans, she was announced by McIntyre and gave a huge smile as she sauntered on stage. She was her usual self-deprecating self… 'I had a bit of a new year's resolution this year,' she confided in the audience. I decided that I was gonna start watching my weight. My downfall is cakes and puddings. I don't really drink an awful lot and I was going to say I don't do drugs, but I did have a space cake once – I just heard the word "cake". But I just found it really dry… I might not know drugs but I do know cake, and I think a bit of buttercream wouldn't have gone astray. It's almost like they hadn't thought about the cake part at all…'

Sarah instantly had the audience on her side with her chatty and down-to-earth style and they were soon crying with laughter.

'In a moment of confidence I did recently toy with the idea of getting some thigh-high boots,' she told them. 'Fishing for compliments I asked my sister, "Where would I get thigh-high boots that would fit my thighs?" And she said: "Well trannies must get them from somewhere…"'

The difference from her earlier stand-up work was obvious. Millican had started to focus on very different areas of her life, leaving her painful divorce behind. And with people still laughing, she was proving to herself that she was no one-hit wonder. She was in fact a very talented comedian – one that audiences both loved and admired.

The day after the show was aired, Sarah's mailing list had a huge surge in numbers. And her email went crazy with women asking where she had bought the bright red dress she had worn to perform in.

The roadshow had been very good for her career. Pulling in viewing figures well into the millions, when it comes to building up a fanbase, that kind of showcase is the equivalent to years of touring for a comedian.

John Bishop and Kevin Bridges both saw their careers skyrocket after appearing on the show, and Sarah agreed it was a positive move. 'It's a quicker way of doing it than working your way round every comedy club where most people there are already fans,' she told one journalist. 'Some people think that comedy on telly kills the live scene but I disagree – I think it feeds into it. A lot of my audience say that my show was their first live comedy experience. People will watch something on TV and then they'll try and get tickets to see that comic next time they're in their town.'

Sarah had definitely proved popular with television audiences and she was soon back on our screens – this time with Charlie Brooker, for his new show, *You Have Been Watching*.

It was right up Sarah's street – a panel show quiz about what's on the television. Filmed at London's Riverside Studios in July 2009, Sarah was asked to watch various programmes before going on the show, where she would be asked to suggest hypothetical improvements on their format and critically assess them. She would also have to answer a series of fun quiz questions about what she had watched.

Sarah is a big fan of watching TV so it was no hardship for her to do this piece of pre-filming homework. Joining her were Frankie Boyle and Reece Shearsmith, who eventually beat Sarah to win the quiz.

After a whirlwind few months, Sarah now had every reason to look forward to Edinburgh, which was by now less than a month away. The promotional poster she had printed for the Fringe reflected her boost in confidence. With sleeves rolled up, Sarah recreated the iconic pose of Rosie The Riveter, the bicep-flexing lass who inspired factory-working women during World War II.

With her newly-highlighted brown locks tucked away under a headscarf, her look of steely resolve concealed the burden of expectation critics felt she must have been carrying after such an impressive debut the year before. It was the perfect look for Sarah – a brassy girl who speaks her mind about everything.

Unlike for her previous show, the poster was littered with reviews: 'British comedy needs a new female star and might just have got one…' – *The Herald*.

'Wonderfully wrong... Incredibly funny…' – *Metro*. 'Her set is as neatly constructed as her individual, triple-punchline jokes…' – *The Daily Telegraph*.

It neatly summed up Sarah's identity and attracted a lot of Fringe-goers to her show, which once again took place at the Pleasance Courtyard. Tickets went on sale priced at £11.50 and her entire run sold out in a matter of days.

Everyone wanted to see whether the darling of Edinburgh 2008 could prove successful in 2009 – including the army of Fringe reviewers and journalists. One by one they came to experience Sarah's new show – *Typical Woman*. And one by one they raved about it. 'Sarah Millican might be playing the same thimble-sized hut as at last year's Fringe, but she has come a long way in 12 months,' wrote *The Evening Standard*. 'A panel-show regular who can hold her own in television's testosterone-fuelled bearpit, this deceptively soft-spoken Geordie excels at being smart, risqué and witty, a marketable package indeed.'

Everyone could see that Sarah had moved on from her post-divorce tales and rocked with laughter at *Typical Woman*, which covered everything from sex manuals, rape fantasies, the joys of eating cake and why she thought she would make a terrible lesbian.

Even highbrow newspaper *The Independent*, which was slightly more subdued in its praise, singled her out as a formidable talent: 'One of the things that I enjoyed most about Sarah Millican's if.comedy newcomer award-winning show last year was its earthy and bawdy tone as well as the canny pacing of proceedings. Following up a winning show is never easy and while this one reinforces the natural ability of Millican for comedy, it is muted by comparison. Many new to Millican will still walk away impressed by her, recognising that she is up there with the big boys, breaking down the stigma that suggests that women just aren't funny. One minute feisty, the next almost tender, Millican doesn't go for the jugular as much as she did last year and it's down to individual tastes as to whether that is a good ploy.'

As with the year before, Sarah got the audience involved in the act, as each night she attempted to work out whether she was more male than female. Asking the crowd to shout out typical male and female traits, she jotted them all down before ticking off which ones she felt best described her. Whichever she had the most of, would decide if she was more a typical male or typical female.

She proved a worthy opponent for a group of male students when they told her that loving *Star Wars* was a male trait – her knowledge of the trilogy was formidable. Although she did nearly come undone when she asked: 'Which one was the one with all the teddies in it again?'

'Playing in the mud', was another male response, along with 'football' and 'urinating standing up'. Sarah had them with that one – 'Ah, but I've bought a She-Wee', she said proudly, talking about a new device that women can use to wee standing up.

A surprising number of men were envious of what they perceived was the female's blissful bathing ritual, while an entirely predictable number said that if they were female they would spend a lot of time playing with their own breasts.

It was a clever piece of theatre and one that got her more than a few laughs. And as each night was different, each show appeared fresh and off-the-cuff. 'We are all a bit man and a bit woman,' she explained to the *Scottish Sunday Express*. 'Someone is perhaps really masculine, or really feminine, but we are all the same.'

Another reporter quoted her as saying: 'You can't generalise that this is what men do, this is what women do… All of my stuff is based on personal stories to back up my arguments.'

The Evening Standard's reviewer found the show culturally fascinating, as well as funny, saying: 'Her new show, *Typical Woman*, dabs a thin coat of high-concept gloss on comedy's ubiquitous gender debate template. Millican is the kind of thoroughly modern complex feminist who gets offended when a man admires her breasts but is quietly flattered that he has admired them. She hates being categorised as a "typical woman", while confessing she cannot nail a mirror onto the wall.'

It went on: 'Instead she puts a mirror up to her fans' lives, spinning out saucy stories about her own boyfriend that everyone relates to and reels in the audience with intimate front-row chat. Though the latter might be harder in the future when she is inevitably playing big theatres. If the terrain occasionally feels well-trampled, Millican's expert gift of the gab lifts it way above the norm.'

Sarah had succeeded in taking a tired comedy concept – the difference between men and women – and reinventing it in her own inimitable way. 'It's all very well to be a feminist, but it's nice to know you've got good knockers,' she quipped, before talking about the time she was flattered to be mistaken for a prostitute. 'I recently walked past a prostitute and she gave me a look that said, "Get off my patch…" I was thrilled. She thought I could sell this,' she said excitedly, pointing to herself.

She went a step beyond comfortable when she revealed that she and her boyfriend had 'indulged' in a little rape role-play – 'I genuinely don't think he expected me to be armed…' And it was all delivered in a sweet voice that one reviewer described as 'a Geordie Minnie Mouse'.

Critic Brian Logan wrote in *The Guardian*: 'The difference between men and women is the hoariest subject in comedy. But it's not what Sarah Millican's show is about. Oh no. Millican's *Typical Woman*, which consolidates the success she had last year as the winner of an if.comedy best newcomer award, contends that those differences are overstated, and we're all a mix of male and female characteristics. A nice theory – which in practice legitimates lots of jokes about the, er, different characteristics peculiar to men and women…'

The sold-out show was an instant success. Each night, a diverse audience left the Pleasance hut and walked away still laughing from her one-hour routine. One woman even came up to Millican after the show and told her she'd had chest pains during the show because she had laughed so much.

Sarah was pleased to see a lot of men in the crowd too. 'No comic likes a single sex audience,' she told one festival reporter. 'You want a mix of ages and backgrounds, couples and groups. Still, I love it when I see tables of blokes howling at my stuff, because I often think "you never thought you'd laugh tonight".'

But after a solid week of successful performances, she was still cautious. 'Everything is going okay,' she told the *Scottish Sunday Express*. 'If you're not prepared now, you never will be. It's a bit like with an exam and it's the last moment of revision. You know that way, how the night before you think you're ready so you go off and put the telly on. My hope really is that the audience goes away having had a brilliant hour, that's the main thing. Sell-out shows, good reviews and nominations for awards are good – as are the plaudits placed on you by other people – but the main thing is just to try to make the audience laugh. It's not about changing the world.'

Reviewers confidently predicted her chances at the Fringe Awards, and when her run ended they were proved right. It wasn't a major accolade like the year before, but Sarah was given the recognition she deserved when she placed third in the annual funniest joke competition.

Gagster Dan Antopolski walked away with the £1,000 first place prize, leading the 27-joke shortlist picked by nine comedy critics for TV channel Dave. Taken from his *Silent But Deadly* show, his quip was: 'Hedgehogs – why can't they just share the hedge?'

Paddy Lennox came second, with: 'I was watching the London Marathon and saw one runner dressed as a chicken and another runner dressed as an egg. I thought, "This could be interesting".

Sarah's third place spot was given for her boob joke: 'I had my boobs measured and bought a new bra. Now I call them Jennifer Warnes and Joe Cocker because they're up where they belong.'

It had been a long run – one that had been ultimately successful for the South Shields lass. Through hard work, hours of revision and practice and a lot of determination, Sarah had once more conquered the Fringe. But when the main awards were announced, Sarah wasn't on the list. Neither were any other female comedians – it was an entirely male shortlist. Was sexism rearing its ugly head?

The Guardian asked Sarah to give her opinion on the matter, and her response was suitably scathing. 'Upon hearing about the six nominees for best comedy show at the Edinburgh Comedy Awards, and the five for best newcomer, the thought never crossed my mind. The following thoughts did: "Ah, brilliant, Kevin Bridges is there". And: "Bugger, I'm not – I'm going to buy myself a 'not on the shortlist' top". That's how it works.

'Of course, one of the questions implied is whether women are funny, and I can't be bothered to answer that again. It's a question I get so bored of and refuse to fuel the fire of a debate that shouldn't – and mostly doesn't – exist.'

She went on to say that she was confident that the reason she wasn't selected was nothing to do with her gender. Nor was it because her show wasn't good – the glowing reviews she had received were testament to her popularity.

'It's that it wasn't what the judges were looking for this year,' she said. 'Last year, when I was nominated alongside Pippa Evans and Mike Wozniak for the best newcomer award, no one wondered why there was only one man. Is it that men just aren't very good at writing their first show? No, it's because the shows that Pippa, Mike and I wrote were popular among a group of people who happened to be judges.'

If she had ever thought she had made it onto a shortlist because of some kind of box-ticking tokenism, Sarah would be outraged. 'I would have wanted to be removed from the list,' she explained, before adding: 'The other question is whether it's harder for women. No, it's not. It's hard for all of us. And we all (nominees included) are tired and want to go home now, please.' But history has a long record of sexism in comedy. Did *The Guardian* have a point?

CHAPTER 12

Women in Comedy

'I am not female: I am a comedian. I want to be judged alongside other comedians on merit, not on gender.'

Let's fast forward for a moment. In December of 2011, sales of Sarah's debut DVD *Chatterbox* passed the 150,000 mark. It was an astonishing achievement, making her not only the highest selling female comedienne since French and Saunders, but the biggest female British comic of all time. It was an appropriate milestone and many in the media said it was the beginning of a new era – one in which women were seen as real rivals to men in the industry, rather than merely support acts, which many had accused them of being up until that point.

Much was made of how not just the changing world around her had brought about this situation, but also about how Sarah's comedy itself was responsible for what she had achieved.

By employing her lewd and bawdy style, with its assaults on expectations of decency and some would say 'masculine' content, she was taking on the male comedians at their own game. People who said women were not capable of being as funny as men, suddenly had to rethink what they had believed for years. Here was a woman who was matching men, gag for gag. Was it that women weren't as funny? Or was it the material they had traditionally used?

But, in many ways, what Sarah was doing was picking up a comic tradition that had been around for generations. Only, it was a tradition that had been lying dormant for nearly a century.

Not long before he died, the revered left-wing writer and critic Christopher Hitchens famously said of female comedians: 'It's a tragedy that the two things men prize most – women and humour – should be so antithetical.'

It wasn't a new point of view. It was one that had been said repeatedly in the previous century. It was hardly surprising. In the late 20th and early 21st century, the vast majority of the comedians that received critical or popular success were men. There had to be a reason why.

Even as recently as 2009, such esteemed feminists as Germaine Greer have stated on record that they believe women are not as funny as men, despite being equally intelligent. She put it down to sex, in that, men end up being more effective at comedy so that they can have more sex. Women don't need to be so funny as they don't need to try so hard.

Greer said in *The Guardian* in 2009: 'Can it be that women are programmed to laugh at men's jokes, as they are not to the jokes of their sisters? Comedian Arthur Smith once said, "Women don't get shags after gigs. Men do." This may be more revealing than Smith knows. Women comedians are probably not looking for shags in any case; if they were, they probably couldn't say so.'

But the accusation that women can never be as funny as men goes back a long way. And the explanations for it are many and varied.

As early as the turn of the 20th century, philosophers and psychoanalysts had written off women as being incapable of creating anything new or anything that might interest people. Sigmund Freud, in a 1925 paper on the *Anatomic Distinction Between the Sexes* claimed that, 'Women oppose change, receive passively and add nothing of their own.'

In saying this he was developing his theory of male envy by saying that because women had started out wanting to be men but were never able to be so, they became so insecure that they ended up being afraid to contribute in case it made them hysterical. He believed that women who tried to act like men ended up suffering from hysteria – the result of trying to be what they were unable to be. He claimed several of his case studies showed women who demonstrated male tendencies like fantasising about sex, ended up suffering from hysteria. Hysteria often resulted in women being sent to asylums. As a result, women who were being sensible, avoided adding something 'of their own, and acted 'passively.'

He was writing at a time when the role of women was more defined than it had ever been in history. During the Victorian era and into the 20th century, the world of work had fractured so that men were increasingly required to do the manual or intellectually challenging jobs, which tended to pay much more, whereas women ended up doing more menial work like dress making or domestic service. Women were expected to know their place in case they thought they should be doing the sort of work that would allow them to earn as much as a man.

What people saw on stage was a reflection of what was happening in society. From the early 20th century onwards, women were increasingly only given supporting roles in the theatre, as chorus girls or dancers in the musicals. They would occasionally be given romantic roles as leading ladies, but the parts they were allowed to play were nearly always as objects of desire by men. In every case they played second fiddle to the male lead, who had the best songs and the best lines.

The early 20th century saw many developments in theatre, with bigger and bigger theatres allowing for more and more lavish productions. In these new expensive theatres, impresarios couldn't take the risk that an act might bomb – he wanted to know in advance that the act was going to be a success. As a result, increasing numbers of productions were written and rehearsed well in advance of the performance appearing on stage. The age of risqué acts, which had a chance to build up a profile over time, had long since disappeared.

It was an age in which only musicals were able to rival the cinema. If people didn't go to either of these, they went to see well-known comedians who had sharpened their skills in the music halls of the Edwardian era. In the 1920s or 1930s, there were very few women performing their own acts in the theatre.

The same could not be said of the men. The comedians who broke through into film and later television after the war were dominating the theatre and seaside venues between the wars. George Formby, Norman Wisdom, Max Miller, Stanley Hollway, Arthur Askey and Max Bygraves were just a few of the men who dominated in the pre-and post-war period, who later moved on to film or television.

The only exception, being a successful woman, was Gracie Fields who, like Sarah, was a sassy northern working class woman whose dramatic persona was usually as a character who overcame her roots to make good at the end. But, Fields was only able to succeed in a man's world because she softened her comedy with song. In the string of films she made in the pre-World War Two years, Fields most often played characters from the tough urban north who brought everyone together, amid hard times, with a song. In *Sing As We Go*, in 1932, her whole town is thrown out of work when the local mill closes down, but Gracie cheers everyone up on a holiday in Blackpool.

Gracie Fields, for all her northernness and working-class charm, was streets away from the modern-day female comedians like Sarah, with their ability to make comedy out of the most intimate of subjects and match male comics with their rapier wit.

It would be years before female comedians and performers would be able to offer the same sort of material as their male counterparts and would take a sea change of social values and expectations before they could do so.

In Britain, things only began to change in the late 1970s. It started with a movement that later came to be known as alternative comedy. Starting in The Comedy Store in London's Soho, alternative comedy rejected the tired, hackneyed jokes and repertoires of the performers that had been on the scene for years, many of who were still appearing on TV years after they had come up with their routines.

The biggest reaction was against the performers who appeared in mainly northern clubs who were known for aiming their jokes at the ethnic minorities or women. What the founders of 'alternative comedy' felt they were doing was overturning a status quo that had existed for years in which it appeared to be acceptable to poke fun at people from a different race or gender.

Others used 1979's victory for the Conservative Party in the General Election as a mandate to make material out of politics, something that had only been rarely seen up until that point on TV revue shows like *That Was The Week That Was* or in student unions.

Early performers at The Comedy Store included Rik Mayall, Adrian Edmondson, Alexei Sayle and Ben Elton. Two others who were later to go on to huge TV success were Dawn French and Jennifer Saunders. The Comedy Store performers attempted to copy a new style of comedy that had been performed in the United States for a couple of years which made jokes, not out of someone's colour or sex, but out of their politics or out of what people found embarrassing.

For many years before 1979, people who had hoped to have a laugh had had the choice of two types of joke teller. There was the northern club performer, like Bernard

Manning, who had white, mainly working-class audiences rolling in the aisles with their one-liners about immigrants or mothers in law.

For those who found Manning and his ilk a bit bawdy, there was always the other option; the ageing has-beens left over from the fading glory days of theatre variety in the 1950s and 60s, who had become the mainstay of light entertainment on TV. While Morecambe and Wise are one of the few acts that still stand out from that era, there were many on TV in the 1970s that have long since been forgotten due to their routines failing to stand the passage of time.

Within months of The Comedy Store opening, its regular performers burst on to Britain's TV screens, battering down the door of the comedy establishment to shout out loudly, 'We are here, and we're not going away.'

Popularity of the TV show *The Young Ones*, particularly among students and young people, who had long since failed to identify with the older generation of comedians, ensured that alternative comedy was here to stay. Soon, The Comedy Store was not the only venue where so-called alternative comedy was being seen and heard.

The Comedy Store wasn't completely revolutionary. Student comedy had been around for years. The Edinburgh Fringe had been set up in 1947 and, together with the Cambridge Footlights, had acted as a venue for student theatre for many years before. But, like the Footlights, the Fringe only had a relatively limited middle-class audience and it tended to use the format of revue and sketch shows rather than the traditional format of standing up telling jokes.

Stand-up as we understand it today had begun in America in the vaudeville theatres between the wars, and then quickly moved on to television as the number of sets exploded in the 1950s. Bob Hope was among those who took their act from performing in front of audiences for radio shows in the 30s, to gigs in front of troops in the war, to performing on TV after the war. But, stand-up of that style didn't move across the Atlantic until the late 1960s and early 1970s.

What the opening of The Comedy Store did, as it grew in popularity, was show that standing up, telling jokes on a small stage, in front of an audience that was often intimately involved with what was going on, could be successful in Britain too.

At first, the number of female 'alternative comedians' was very small. French and Saunders went on to appear on *The Young Ones* and also on *The Comic Strip Presents* a few years later, but they were initially almost the only women on the circuit. When they appeared, they made sure they left their mark. Jennifer Saunders left audiences aghast when she appeared on stage wearing tampons in her ears. It was something that people in Britain just hadn't seen before.

Almost the only other woman on the stand-up circuit, who came from a slightly different background, was Victoria Wood. Wood had won a talent show called *New Faces* in 1974, but didn't start appearing in front of audiences telling comic stories until the early 1980s.

Having written a series of sketch-based TV segments, shows and plays, she was allowed a shot at her own stand-up and sketch show in 1984 with *Victoria Wood As Seen On TV*. In many ways though, Wood's show was more in the style of the comedians of the 1970s, with its light-hearted observation humour and reliance on pastiche. While her musical numbers frequently referred to sex, they often held back from the frankness and honesty later successful comediennes would be known for.

Meanwhile, in the United States, several women were also championing a new type of comic material – born out of the new feminist ideas heard in magazines like *Cosmopolitan*.

Joan Rivers had been fashioning her routines for years, so in the 1970s and early 1980s, she felt able to let rip in a way that female comedians had never done so before. She had started in the early 1960s in the small, in-your-face, comedy clubs of Chicago and New York's Greenwich Village. By the middle of that decade, her irreverent style caught the revolutionary mood of the time, and she began to appear on TV, with slots on *The Tonight Show* and the *Ed Sullivan Show*.

Roseanne Barr, who started later, at the end of the 1970s, probably did more to make the idea that women could be funny and popular acceptable than anyone. By taking on men directly, using her lightning wit in a way that women were just not supposed to do, she made half the audience suddenly sit up and think 'I wish I could say things like that!'

When Roseanne's eponymous show, which was modelled on her real life and children, became one of the most watched shows of the 1980s, those who booked comedy started to finally believe that women could be funny.

It had taken nearly a century to re-establish something that audiences in Victorian times had taken for granted.

Before the First World War, women had been nearly as

important to stage audiences as men. Artists like Marie Lloyd, Jenny Hill, Bessie Bellwood and Vesta Tilley were in every way regarded as equals to the male comedians of their time. Many could command huge audiences in the Victorian music halls. The massive demand for tickets to see them drove the development of music hall theatre into larger and larger venues.

Marie Lloyd (1870-1922) broke all taboos by making a career out of a mix of comic songs like *My Old Man Said Follow The Van* and comedy routines packed full of innuendo and double-entendre, at a time when women were not supposed to talk about sex, let alone enjoy it.

Jenny Hill (1868-1893), like Sarah, used the breakdown of her marriage as inspiration to take to the stage where she openly subverted what was expected of women by dressing as a man to comic effect. Another female comic, Vesta Tilley did the same, appearing regularly as a male impersonator. She ended up on the bill of the first Royal Variety Performance in 1912.

Meanwhile, Bessie Bellwood (1856-1896) developed a saucy stage persona which was often thought highly abrasive – she would often argue down hecklers until they couldn't come back at her – but always remained loveable, using a style that many of today's top female comics would identify with.

All these artists were accepted by Victorian audiences, despite going against all the conventions of their age, because they were hugely entertaining – mostly because they ignored what was expected of them to make people laugh as much as possible.

As the Edwardian age dawned after 1901, society began to change and women were increasingly expected to 'know their place'. Any challenge to that orthodoxy, like women appearing confidently on stage, had the potential to upset the established view. Theatre impresarios began booking acts which upheld the mainstream way of thinking, and female comedians of the sort like those mentioned above gradually faded from sight.

With no women around to prove otherwise, it was no wonder that people were left asking the question: 'Are women as funny as men?'

It took not just French and Saunders and Victoria Wood to open the way, but other even bolder performers like Jo Brand to pave the road for more women to attempt to stand-up and make jokes on stage alongside the many men already doing so. A former psychiatric nurse, Jo Brand took up comedy as she approached 30 – the same age as Sarah – after feeling her life was wasting away. *The Independent*, in 2009, said that at her first gig, a male heckler started shouting 'F*** off, you fat cow' and kept up his tirade throughout her entire performance. It ended without applause.

She decided to call herself *The Sea Monster*, to pre-empt the inevitable abuse about her weight, but still faced, during her early appearances on the alternative comedy circuit, having a pint of beer thrown at her, having her face slapped and being pelted with food.

Despite that, she persevered and by the late 1980s, had a regular slot on Channel 4's *Saturday Night Live*, which had been started a few years earlier as a springboard on to TV for alternative comedians. She then went on to have her own show, *Through The Cakehole*, and thereafter made regular appearances on panel shows through the 1990s and into the noughties.

The fact that Jo, a large woman with a laid-back laconic style, could survive in the quick-fire world of male-dominated comedy, proved a spur for many woman who looked at her and said to themselves, 'If she can do it, maybe I can too'.

Jo's success, as well as that of the other early female comedians, opened the way for others to come after. Stand-up night organisers, as well as TV producers, began realising there were audiences out there who wanted to hear what female comedians had to say.

In the late 1980s and 1990s, a slow trickle began to turn into a stream of talented women coming through. Helen Lederer, Morwenna Banks, Caroline Aherne, Mrs Merton, Jenny Eclair, Rhona Cameron, Donna McPhail and Mel and Sue all broke through to feature on TV programmes that showed off their talents. But they still only represented a fraction of the number of men on the circuit.

In the last decade, there have not only been repeated calls for more to be done to put more female comics on the stage, but efforts have been made to provide forums to allow give them the chance to do so. Initiatives like Funny Women, a competition which has been criticised for charging an entrance fee, have championed all-women line ups, highlighting talent that might not have emerged had the contest not existed.

Despite what Sarah told *The Guardian* after her second Fringe run, she admits that although things are much easier now than they have ever been for comedians like her, the nature of what stand-up requires, will always be a barrier that prevents as many women taking part as men.

In 2011, Sarah told *The Observer*: 'When I look at my audiences, it's 50-50 and that's not all women who've brought their boyfriends – often it's the other way round. If you talk about funny things that happen during sex, blokes can identify just as much. Maybe it's just that women don't get their side of the story told as much at comedy clubs.

'I think, if you're funny, you get on. If you're not, you don't. Gender doesn't come into it. And it's too easy to use it as an excuse. If I don't do well at a gig, I could come off and go, well, it's because they don't like women. But it's more likely to be because you're jokes weren't good enough. Or you didn't have the confidence. Or it's just a hard gig. There's a million reasons why an audience might not like you and it's almost never to do with gender.

'The reason why there's not so many women doing it, is because of the lifestyle. It's quite solitary. There's a lot of driving around, at the beginning, staying in not very nice hotels or on sofas. Maybe it's not a life women are as suited to. Some women do it and have families. I'm in awe of them.'

In *The Guardian* a year later she added another point that suggested it could just be about the practicalities of booking acts. She said: 'Bookers will spread you out. Maybe, because there's only about 10 to 12 [women] at [a particular] level. A bit like, they might spread out the one-liner guys. You're kind of in a bracket of your own – which is fine. I understand that people want variety on a bill. It's also positive discrimination in a way. They may like to have women on the bill.'

So, if women can be as funny as men, if more of them can put up with conditions on the road, there could be a fantastic queue of them waiting to step up to the mic and impress everyone with their wit and timing.

But, it is important to remember those who came before. Sarah said the comic who went before her who she is most to be grateful to is Jo Brand. When asked by *The Guardian* whether Brand inspired her, she said: 'Absolutely. She's our queen. I can't imagine what it must have been like for her to do stand-up on stage when she was such a rarity. But I'm grateful that she did, because it has made my life so much easier and it's definitely paving the way for the next lot. Who's to say? Maybe at some point in the not too distant future, there'll be no paving that needs to be done. It will be entirely paved.'

Maybe Sarah doesn't realise just how responsible she herself has been for some of that paving. In 2011, fellow comic and pal Jimmy Carr told *The Sun* that Sarah was remarkable precisely because she isn't seen purely as a female comic. 'If anyone's reading this as a female thinking, 'I want to get into comedy', you're pushing at an open door… I think Sarah Millican will do extraordinarily well. She's a funny comic. She isn't a funny "female comic". She's just a really funny comic.'

Above left: In 2008 Sarah took to the stage for one of her first high-profile gigs at the Royal Albert Hall as part of Amnesty International's Secret Policeman ball.

© *Ian West/PA Archive/PA Images*

Above right: Sarah's show 'Not Nice' was a huge success at the Edinburgh Festival in 2008, winning her a nomination for The Intelligent Finance Best Newcomer Award. She would return to the Festival a number of times.

© *Geraint Lewis/REX/Shutterstock*

Below: Sarah teaming up with David Mitchell and comedy legend Ronnie Corbett on *Would I Lie To You?* in 2010.   © *Endemol UK/REX/Shutterstock*

Above: Sarah during her hilarious appearance on *The Graham Norton Show* in 2011 alongside actor Vince Vaughan and P Diddy, during which she amused (and shocked) her American fellow guests with her candid stories.

Below left: With her 'Sarah' mug on the set of *Loose Women*.

Below right: Sarah with her then-boyfriend, fellow comedian Gary Delaney, in 2012. The couple got married in a small ceremony at the end of 2013.

Above: In an indication of just how popular she had become, Sarah was given her own BBC chat show, *The Sarah Millican Programme*, in 2012.

© *Martin Rickett/PA Archive/PA Images*

Below: Sarah in a singalong with Barry Manilow, James McAvoy and her beloved Phillip Schofield on *The Jonathan Ross Show* at the end of 2014.

© *Brian J Ritchie/Hotsauce/REX/Shutterstock*

Above left: Chatting with the Duchess of Cambridge after performing at the Royal Variety Performance in 2014.

Above right: Sarah during a visit to *This Morning* in 2016.

Below: Sarah appearing on-stage during Sandi Toksvig's 'Mirth Control' show at the Women of the World Festival in London in 2015. One of Sarah's biggest projects in recent years has been Standard Issue, the online magazine (and now podcast) aimed at all types of women.

CHAPTER 13

A Walk On The Wild Side

'Meet Chief Brody, who is settling in nicely. Though my slippers appear to be the enemy…'

By summer 2009 Sarah already had a wide and growing fan base. Not all of them could travel to Edinburgh to see her second Fringe run, *Typical Woman*, so they must have been pleased to hear a familiar voice on the television half way through August.

The busy comedian had somehow found the time to fit yet another TV appearance into her busy schedule. And it's safe to say this one would be remembered as one of her favourites – as it involved things that were small and furry…

Sarah had always been a pet lover and often talked about her encounters with the animal kingdom on stage. 'I sometimes get lonely, and I think I could do with an animal – a pet would be nice,' she mused in one show. 'If I could have any animal I would probably have a cat, but I can't have a cat because my boyfriend's allergic.' She paused and her face fell in mock sadness...

It was a stage move Sarah had truly perfected, and she often employed it to great effect in her performances. Fresh-faced and innocent looking, you couldn't help but feel for her in those silent moments. The audience was duly sympathetic...

'So I can't have a cat till we split up,' Sarah continued, instantly brightening. 'Most people don't have something to look forward to at the end of a relationship – I can't wait till he starts f***ing other women: "I'm off to the pet shop, sod off..."'

Once the audience had finally stopped laughing, she went on to tell them about how being one of her childhood pets could at times be a little bit dangerous. 'I always loved them a little bit too much,' she said menacingly. 'There's a name for people like me – it's hamster squeezer.'

'I love them so much,' she said, wrinkling her face up. 'Have you ever stroked a dog so much you can see the whites of its eyes? And then when you stroke along its back, its little back legs buckle under the pressure? I do worry about my boyfriend... Because I love him so much...'

Along the same lines, she has also admitted to quite a peculiar fetish – gorilla fancying. In an interview with Brighton magazine *L7*, she said: 'I did see a gorilla at Chester Zoo that I quite fancied. I like a hairy man! It just gave me a look and I thought: "It's been a long time since anybody's looked at me like that." I went back recently and it was still there. Not married yet. No ring on its finger!'

It wasn't the only time she has talked about her passion for gorillas – or hairy men either, for that matter. Her love for the jungle beasts pops up from time to time in her current stand-up routines even now.

I've already mentioned that when Sarah was freshly divorced, one of her colleagues regularly sent her funny animal pics to make her laugh. Fast-forward seven years and nothing has changed – she still loves to ogle cute creatures in clothes. The only difference is that now she receives the pics from her fans, and she has her own website to display them all on.

The best photos in her collection come from the author Neil Gaiman, who has a friend who works in a zoo. 'Occasionally he'll stick a hat on an animal that he shouldn't and take a quick photo and send it to me,' she says. So what's the most exotically dressed animal she has on film? The answer is a rhino in a panama hat. Amazing.

When she was in Australia in 2009, she described her favourite day out as being a trip to the aquarium, where she met a Pomeranian dog. 'We saw pot-bellied sea horses,' she wrote on her myspace blog. 'The blurb said the males have bellies to attract the women. What a lovely world to live in. We also saw divers feed massive stingrays and elbowed some kids out of the way too. We paid more than they did.

'Then we bought giant burgers and ate them by the sea. A woman came along with a tiny fluffy dog, which we played with for 45 minutes. Every time a woman walked past or sat down, she was immediately captivated by the little dog and oohed and aaahed along with us. It made me think, if only wars were instigated by women... Peace would easily be restored by a six-week-old Pomeranian with a chew toy.'

So when the opportunity came up to join the cast of a brand new animal-based comedy show, it's easy to see why Sarah was happy to say yes.

Walk on the Wild Side has been described as a reinvention of Johnny Morris's classic show *Animal Magic* – but it's a lot cheekier, and therefore a lot funnier. Combining the beauty of raw natural history footage with the talents of some of Britain's best entertainers, the innovative show was set to be an instant hit.

Essentially a comedy sketch show, it dubbed comedy voiceovers to classic footage of some of our favourite furry and scaly friends. If you've ever trawled YouTube looking for talking animals (come on, admit it) this would definitely be the programme for you. A world of penguins with the *X Factor* and meerkats auditioning for *The Apprentice*, the show was written by comics Jason Manford, Isy Suttie, Jon Richardson, Steve Edge and Gavin Webster, while the filming was provided by the BBC's Natural History Unit.

It gave a humorous voice to all manner of members of the animal kingdom, and imaginatively conjured up the banality of their day-to-day lives. Highlights included a group of acapella sharks entertaining submarine pilots, a teenage polar bear losing her phone and a cockney fruit-selling peacock.

'I just do my accent in everything,' she laughed in a special behind the scenes feature. 'There are some other members of the cast who are amazing and do loads of different accents, and I've got, er, this voice, and I've got a quite good Joanna Lumley voice. It doesn't even sound like her, it's just posh. And I can do the noise of a horn honking. That's my repertoire. So when I go in and they say, "You're gonna be a Geordie pigeon", that's what I am. I can't do many accents…'

Despite her (arguably) limited skills, Sarah played a variety of characters. In one episode she played a trapped starfish, being rescued by the CRCRs – the coral reef crustacean rescue. In another she played a bored and yawning hippo – 'Ooh, sorry, I am listening, tell me more about your kids?'

Amongst others, she's been a timid owl, frightened of her scary new neighbour, and one half of a British bird couple on holiday in Spain – complaining about everything, including the Germans and their towels. Sarah enjoyed the experience, which involved working in a London sound studio with the other comedians and was a welcome dose of good fun.

She was half way through her *Typical Woman* show in Edinburgh when *Walk on the Wild Side* began to air on BBC One. So along with the rave reviews she was getting at the Fringe, Sarah could claim a host of extra plaudits for her work on the animal show.

'It shouldn't work but it does,' wrote the *Radio Times*. 'You take natural history films, put silly voices over the animals and edit it into sketches. With input from the likes of Jason Manford, the result is the kind of thoroughly, joyously daft comedy that is custom-made for adults and children to enjoy together, *TV Burp* style, on a Saturday evening.'

'Critics may claim it's another example of lowest-common-denominator humour, in the manner of ITV1's *Animals Do the Funniest Things*, yet it's hard not to smile at the sight of a weight-obsessed panda and a hip hop-loving badger,' said *The Daily Telegraph*.

But all that animal madness didn't begin to quench her desire for a pet of her own. Appearing on *Room 101* with Frank Skinner three years later, she tried to send 'cats who ignore me' into the infamous room of no return. 'I'd really like to have a pet but I don't have that sort of lifestyle so I can't have an animal, so I have to rely on other people's animals,' she said. 'Stroking strangers' cats, that sort of thing. I'll be driving along and if I see a bonnie looking cat I will pull in and go and try and find the cat. But they can be little buggers in that they just hide or they ignore me or they go right underneath a car. Not my car, it wouldn't be so bad if they did that. I'd get a hatch fitted so I could just drag them straight in. But they hide right in the centre where your arm can't reach. You go all the way round and your arm can't reach.'

Six months after *Room 101*, Sarah finally got herself a pet of her own – and no, Gary didn't have to break up with her first! Her new housemate was an adorable small ginger kitten. Sarah named him Chief Brody after the character in *Jaws*, and began posting his exploits on Twitter and her own webpage almost instantly.

'I used to spend a lot of time looking at cat videos on the Internet,' she told *Female First*, soon after welcoming the Chief to his new home. 'It's like YouTube have sent me an email asking if I'm alright because I haven't been on in ages. I just love him so much and I put one picture up and it got re-tweeted about 500 times and I was there saying "Oh my God, loads of my followers love cats too!"'

Chief Brody has fast become famous in his own right, and now has his own Twitter hashtag. Sarah even gets complaints if the flow of Brody pics ever stops.

Sarah is not alone in her public display of love for her cat. Presenter Dawn Porter has a beautiful Siamese cat called Lilu, who goes everywhere with her – even on international flights. Fearne Cotton regularly posts videos of her cats Keloy and Tallulah on her official website and Twitter feed – including one where she does an amusing Discovery Channel impression to try and hunt them down.

Ricky Gervais was given his cat, Ollie, by best pal Jonathan Ross, and openly admits to absolutely adoring him. (The cat, not Jonathan. Well, maybe Jonathan too…) Ollie gets a lot of camera time and is always posing for pics, which Gervais shares with his fans. But heartthrob Tom Fletcher from the band McFly definitely claims the title of top celeb feline enthusiast – he has three cats, Marvin, Leia and Aurora and has even written a song about them: *The Sleepy Cats Song*.

I wonder if Sarah can sing…

CHAPTER 14

Your Favourite
Aunty

*'I would like help with my style but nobody seems willing to take
me on…'*

When Sarah returned home from her second Fringe
run, she immediately fell into what had by now become
her yearly routine. She took some time off to rest, and then
began to work on her material for the following year's
festival.

But in December she was invited to perform on BBC
One's *Live at the Apollo* with Jack Dee. Filmed at the
enormous Hammersmith Apollo, in west London, the
stand-up extravaganza is famous for showcasing a wide
variety of new comedy talent.

Sarah had already shown she could command a large
audience when she had joined Michael McIntyre earlier in
the year for his *Comedy Roadshow*. And although she has

admitted she struggled with nerves in her early days – 'I used to be so nervous I couldn't eat for four or five hours before a gig' – there was no trace of nerves when she walked on stage at the Apollo, wearing a pretty dress and boots.

'Hello,' she said, smiling confidently. 'How exciting is this?' She was obviously excited herself, and it soon proved infectious for the audience.

But showing off a shorter haircut than ever before, Sarah was clearly undergoing something of an image transformation. Gone were the girl-next-door flowing locks and baggy jeans that had marked her early years on the circuit.

Back then she had performed solely at small venues, where she relied on a certain level of intimacy with the audience to make her show work. Part of that intimacy came from her non-threatening appearance, and in fact, it was well thought out. 'One reason I would never want to be attractive on stage, is that women have a tendency to judge you a bit more than men,' she has said. 'I wear dresses over jeans because I want to look feminine but not too girly and certainly not too vulnerable. I'm all about the empowerment of women, but you've got to be really careful in comedy. You can't just shove the word feminism out there, because then everybody goes "oh no, she's going to burn her bra!"'

Her down-to-earth look had certainly made her style of comedy even more shocking. She had frequently been described as one of the bluest female comics around, and delighted in the accolade. 'People don't expect it because I'm not coming out in a basque and a whip, I'm coming out in a flowery dress – not that it was ever my intention to go

"I'll dress in a flowery dress, they won't expect me to talk about rape!"'

Whether intentional or not, her 'look' has worked well for her. But now that she was appearing more and more on larger stages and on television, she began to make subtle changes to her clothes and hair. It was a natural development, which had begun in Australia, where she had walked the red carpet and attended her first wave of star-studded events.

As much as she would never change herself to fit in with anyone's preconceptions of a 'typical woman', she must have wanted to appear stronger and more polished to reflect her blossoming position as a headlining act. And although comedians have never been judged on their looks, whether subconsciously or not, she began dressing the part. Over the next six months she would go from brown hair to striking blonde, resulting in a much bolder look. Her clothes would get brighter in colour, replacing the simple black tops she usually wore for her television appearances.

Sarah now says that she sees herself as a kind of role model for women overlooked because they're not super-skinny, glamorous or young. 'There is something liberating and defiant about going on stage and saying you are 36 and 13 stone,' she said in a 2012 *Radio Times* interview. 'I feel like it's my responsibility not to lose weight, to be honest. I'm a bright, successful woman who isn't stick thin. It's like the old films that say marriage and babies are the happy ending. A lot of people think that being skinny is the happy ending, and it's not. Being happy is the happy ending.'

In one of her 2010 shows she recounted a story she had

recently read in the news about a celebrity who had 'ballooned' to a size 12. 'Ballooned? I'd give my right arm to be a size 12. In fact, my right arm might be a size 12!'

It's a way of asserting her 'one-of-us' credentials. Complaining about her weight and her appetite, as she so often does on stage, makes her reassuringly normal to her audience – and proud of it.

'I'm just me,' she told Dominic Cavendish for *The Independent* in 2010. 'A polished version of me, of course, I have to make sure to write jokes, I'm not an idiot. What people identify with is that I'm a bit like your sister, or your mam, or your auntie. I'm just normal. I fly so many flags. I fly a flag for women. For the working class. For those who didn't go to university. For the north east and the north in general. And for women of a certain age. If one person starts to follow their dream at 29 because they've seen it's possible, then that's ace.'

It's a lot of pressure to put on herself. It's almost as if she feels that if she stops being that person – if she follows the standard celebrity route of weight loss, stylist and wardrobe overhaul – she'll be letting people down.

She wouldn't be able to crack the self-deprecating true-life jokes we all relate to – about the time she had to be cut out of a dress in Monsoon for example, or when the supermarket self-checkout tried to weigh her stomach when it was resting on the scales. 'My muffin top is now a muffin shelf,' she has famously quipped.

She has definitely moved on in confidence since she bemoaned her weight in her Australian diary in 2009. When Veronica Lee interviewed her for the *Arts Desk* in 2011, she wrote: 'When she mentions in passing she's a size 16 she makes it clear she's happy about it.'

But Sarah still feels odd about becoming something of a sex symbol for men. 'I get people saying I'm "weirdly sexy",' she told *TV Magazine* in 2011. 'Or: "You're my secret crush." Why secret? Though it's nice when blokes fancy me – it means they actually fancy a normal looking woman. I look a similar shape to somebody you'd bump into in Asda. Other women off the telly look hungry and cold – whereas I am full and warm.'

Yet again, Sarah wasn't doing herself justice. Because when Janice Turner interviewed her in 2012, she commented: 'Off-stage in jeans, boots and beanie hat, Millican looks younger and trendier.'

But despite now being happy with her weight, it's clear she still feels somewhat insecure about her image – perhaps reinforcing further that fact that she is, after all, a typical woman. Wearing a bright red patterned dress, she appeared on *The Jonathan Ross Show* in 2012, along with fellow guest and celebrity stylist Gok Wan. When she walked on stage she was wolf-whistled and gave a little giggle. But when Ross jokingly asked her if she would like some style tips from Gok Wan, she suddenly turned shy. 'I would like some help with my style but nobody seems willing to take me on,' she told him.

'What's wrong with you?' Jonathan said, obviously surprised. 'That's a nice outfit, I like that with the leggings under the top, it's nice.'

What Sarah said next was very revealing. 'I describe it as funky nana, because if you saw a nana dressed like this you'd think oh, she looks pretty good. But maybe on a 36-year-old it's not so good.'

Jonathan laughed and instantly lightened the conversation. 'That's perfectly good, that's given me an idea – you should bring out a clothing line called Funky Nana!'

'Do you think?' she smiled. 'Just loadsa cardies and slippers and nothing in-between, just let the air get round.'

It seemed that even when her career was going so well, she still saw herself as a work in progress. 'I think I need to upgrade a little bit, like I don't go to designer shops and things like that,' she told Ross. 'Instead of going, like maybe in the past I would have gone into Dorothy Perkins and bought one top, now maybe I might buy two and some earrings to match.'

Sarah also admitted she still felt intimidated by what she called 'posh shops'. But she has still made a conscious effort to work on her style, however uncomfortable it made her.

And the first sign that this transformation was taking place was on stage in 2009 at The Hammersmith Apollo. She looked pretty and youthful, yet still ultimately approachable. She made the audience laugh with tales of her parents' helpful approach to flat hunting, and how she prefers living alone to sharing with a boyfriend – 'The sex is better – I don't bother with foreplay.'

She mused on why she could never find any Valentine cards to reflect her relationship status. 'Even though I'm in a relationship I think of myself as independent… They're all one extreme or the other – they're either sex buddy or soulmate, there's no in-between. Where are the cards for the practical woman in love? Something that says, 'I love you, we're having a great time, but if we split up, I'll probably be okay.'

And she made everyone feel a little bit uncomfortable with a story about sharing self-portraits of her lady bits with a friend…

For the next half an hour she had the audience in the palm of her hand. She returned to Manchester happy with how the night had gone.

Christmas was approaching, and soon after, a brand new year would start – bringing with it more opportunities for awards and accolades. So instead of cosying up with her favourite hot water bottle and slippers over the festive break, she knuckled down to her writing. Because as well as writing her new stand-up show, she was working hard on another project…

CHAPTER 15

Sarah Millican's Support Group

'My theory is that together we can solve each other's problems…'

In January 2010 Sarah celebrated the beginning of a new year along with a brand new phase of her career – because it was the month that she first moved into the world of radio.

First, she was a guest on a brand new radio show on 5 Live called *7 Day Sunday*. Broadcast for an hour in the 11am to 12pm slot, the show was presented by Mancunian Chris Addison, the gangly-limbled, baby-faced comic best known for his portrayal of Ollie in political comedy satire *The Thick of It*.

When the show was first announced, it was pitched as a topical news series aiming to 'pull apart the week's big news stories and see what makes them tick'. But Addison cheekily described it as 'four relatively ill-informed idiots fail to take the news seriously for an hour'. Taking an irreverent look at the news stories of the previous seven days, it featured special guest stars including Pub Landlord Al Murray, who eventually took over hosting duties from Addison a year later.

But despite Millican's sharp wit, it was not a critical success. After the first show, Jane Thynne from *The Independent* was perturbed by the lack of variety – it covered mainly the season's heavy snowfall and featured little political content. She found it odd, considering Addison had made his name in a politics-based programme. She called Addison witty, but ultimately reserved judgment on the show overall, recommending he slow down the pace and stop his 'nervous giggling'.

The Times was less positive. Chris Campling described the first episode as a duplicate of the 'dismal, desperate show it had replaced – *The Christian O'Connell Solution.*' He gave it another chance by listening in on the second episode, but said it had no chemistry and 'none of the News Quiz-esque scoring of laughter points, where clever people fall over themselves in their desperation to be funnier than the last'.

Elisabeth Mahoney, from *The Guardian*, found the show quite funny, but hit the nail on the head when she said that the listener had to stay very focused, as the four-way dialogue could be confusing because it covered a comprehensive sweep of topics. It was a rocky start, but Sarah's presence as a regular guest during series one and two certainly lifted it.

However, Sarah's dulcet tones were about to dominate the

airwaves in a completely different show – one she was infinitely more suited to. Occasional guest spots would now become a side-project for Sarah, because she had been given her own Radio 4 slot. *Sarah Millican's Support Group* was born.

It wasn't the first time Sarah had written for Radio 4. In 2008, after her first Fringe Show had been so well-received, Millican had penned a one-off special for the station, called *Keeping Your Chins Up*.

It was essentially a version of *Sarah Millican's Not Nice* in which she explained, in story form, how she had reacted to her husband leaving her. But this time, Radio 4 were giving Sarah her own show, not just a one-off slot. *Support Group* was a perfect vehicle for Millican's cosy, aunt-like persona, and featured Sarah in the role of a modern-day agony aunt dealing with a variety of often ridiculous and pointless woes.

'Hello, I'm Sarah Millican,' read the BBC promo material. 'My new series for the wireless, *Sarah Millican's Support Group*, is starting on Radio 4 and we're inviting you to join us. We all have problems. Sometimes you just need cream from Boots. Sometimes you need advice. For the latter, come to us. For the former you're on your own. There's no membership fee and all are welcome. Particularly those in pyjamas, like me.'

Just as Sarah was coaxing her audience to confide in her during her live shows, her soothing voice would now invite the 'public' – in reality a series of excellent actors – to share their private conundrums. Pretending to be an agony aunt, she would offer advice and consolation.

'Often my friends come to me with their problems,' she said in a promotional video for the BBC's website. 'I used to think it was because I'm sensible and logical and good at sorting things out. But I've got a feeling that it might actually just be because I've got loads of problems. I'm just like you – well, some of you. Not the posh ones, obviously.'

The show was actually piloted in November of the previous year, and immediately tested positively. It was recorded on 2 December 2009, and 7, 14 and 27 January 2010, at The Drill Hall in London – which now houses the RADA studios. The series first aired a month later on Radio 4, on Thursdays at 11pm. The late slot was decided on because of the adult content of the show, which was largely scripted but did feature some fairly blue improvisation. A host of fine actors played the various roles of Sarah's guest callers – divulging their most personal of problems in front of the live audience.

Sarah's solutions usually involved a combination of cake, tea and hugs, the kind of homely comfort that she had experienced her whole life from her parents. A blend of fiction and live audience interaction, it was a novel concept, and it gave Sarah the chance to freewheel into the funny little comedy asides she was so good at.

The first problem Sarah and her 'support group' tackled, was the issue of dating outside of your class. 'Should you, why would you, and will it work,' asked Sarah, introducing the topic. 'I consider myself working class,' she explained to the audience. 'I choose *The Simpsons* over the news any day. Once in London I stayed with a wonderful friend of mine who had dimmer switches. I had no idea how they worked. I was 29. I've never dated outside of my class. Posh blokes don't work for me. I like proper blokes, who normally go to

ASDA but sometimes treat themselves to Tesco's. Blokes who wear the creases out of a shirt.'

After her comedy preamble, the show's first problem caller was invited into the studio. Played by an actress, a very posh 'Carol' explained her issue, which involved falling for a working class plumber. She was worried about what her friends and family might think.

What followed was a back-and-forth comedy duet on the issue, littered with some truly excellent plumbing euphemisms, on which the audience was invited to offer their own opinions. It was an interesting format, made exceptional by both the performing skills of her acting co-stars, and Sarah's witty and quick-fire interactions with the audience. The 'problems' were all well-written and sparked a landslide of great material for Sarah to deliver gags from.

'I can't get hair to grow on my head, but my nostrils, ears and back are lush with new growth. Any way to change this direction?' 'This is quite a common problem among men in their mid-thirties,' Sarah replied with authority. 'I think maybe you could just try sleeping upside down? If that doesn't work, then you need to accept the fact that you're going bald, pet. It's fine, you'll be all right – it's quite attractive really. Big, bushy nostrils? Not so sexy. Maybe you should get your girlfriend to pluck them – they love that.'

'I took up the guitar to make girls like me. It didn't work, so I took up the ukelele. Is this a step backwards? Because I've not had any interest for over two years now.' Sarah replied: 'If there's one thing I know about women, it's that if we don't respond to a big instrument, we're not going to respond to a small one. Talk to women. Be nice.'

'I've honed my skills with women by researching Dear Deirdre columns, religiously. It's still not working. Where am I going wrong?' 'That's weird, because women bone up on men by reading *Viz* and that always works. Maybe *Dear Deirdre* only works if you think all women only solve their problems by overacting in bikinis?' Cue massive guffaws.

Her co-star, Simon Daye, also regularly received some big laughs. His character, Terry, was billed as a random member of the audience, giving his own opinion on the problems discussed. In one episode, when faced with the knowledge that escorts get free dinners – a revelation that Sarah was very interested in – he shouted out: 'I can eat dinner at home, I can't see the point of that at all.' Talking about his fictional ex-girlfriend in another episode, he said: 'I picked her up in Aldi. Literally. She was standing in front of the beans and I moved her away from the beans.'

A 'man of the people' cabbie, on the show Sarah described Terry as 'ill-informed but from the heart'. He sounds remarkably like Sarah's dad, Philip, who many believe is the inspiration for the hugely funny character.

Also joining Sarah in the show was Ruth Bratt, who played self-qualified counsellor Marion. 'Although I have A levels in French, German and Media Studies, and an NVQ in life, I still thought it best to bring in a proper expert,' Sarah told the audience by way of introduction. 'Someone who has written essays on "feelings"…'

Bratt's Marion was a very clever caricature of the classic self-help guru – one who is only really interested in hearing herself talk. Using a huge number of superfluous similes and pointless analogies to summarise their guests' problems, she came across as unwittingly condescending – and most of her words of encouragement were actually just thinly veiled snobbishness. 'Should you feel that you deserve another bite of the relationship cherry,' she told one bereaved 'guest', 'then might I suggest that you first you plant the seed – the seed of yourself. At the moment you are a dry, harsh soil with bits of grit in it. Why don't you water yourself with hobbies and pastimes? Soon you will be worth spending time with.'

The show was a huge success and was immediately commissioned for a second series. For Sarah's fans it was great to see her fronting her own show, instead of simply guesting on somebody else's. It was great timing too. After hearing so much about this new comedian, the British public must have been gagging for a larger showcase of her work to be aired. They were well satisfied with what Sarah delivered.

Critics were equally impressed. 'It rather reminded me of Mrs Merton at times, but that's no bad thing,' said Jane Anderson in the *Radio Times*. 'The scripted "problems" are tightly written with jokes fired at high velocity, but it's her instant responses to members of the audience who dare to pipe up that prove her worth as a razor-sharp-witted woman.'

After her divorce and subsequent counseling sessions, it's interesting to note that Sarah was obviously still fascinated by the concept of laughter as therapy. And as many of the issues divulged on the show were relationship–related, you could be forgiven for thinking she was still somewhat preoccupied with the demise of her marriage.

'I haven't always been so clever,' she said, after introducing the first show. 'I have been known to eat a pound and a half of mint imperials while trudging my way through *My Guy Monthly* wondering where "the one" is. I've also sat on a friend's living room floor with a bottle of £1.49 wine and cried and shouted until it was time for Vienetta…'

Making light of serious issues is just one of the weapons in Sarah's comedy arsenal. But it is one that she employs to great effect, and it made *Sarah Millican's Support Group* – her first big solo venture – a very popular radio show.

Another reason that it proved so successful, was the channel it was aired on. BBC Radio 4 is the second most popular British radio station in the country (after Radio 2), and over 10 million people regularly tune in to enjoy its diverse and thought-provoking content. It has a strong reputation for showcasing comic talent, including both experimental and alternative comedy – and a huge number of our most successful comedians and comedy shows first aired on the station.

In 1964 – when Radio 4 was called the BBC Home Service – the station was responsible for broadcasting the classic improvisational comedy show, *I'm Sorry, I'll Read That Again*. Originating from the Cambridge University Footlights revue *Cambridge Circus*, it soon developed a devoted youth following, with its attendees describing its live recordings as being more like rock concerts that comedy shows.

And it was no wonder – because it had a cast who would go on to become rock stars of the comedy world. Cast members Tim Brooke-Taylor, Graeme Gardner and Bill Oddie went on to become The Goodies, while co-writer John Cleese's journey from Radio 4 took him to Monty Python and far beyond. In hindsight, the programme clearly shows Monty Python's roots, as Graham Chapman and Eric Idle also contributed regularly to its script.

Its influence on the comedy genre in general was huge. Much more improvised and fast-paced than anything that had been heard on the radio before, it helped listeners to prepare for a new brand of modern comedy that was heading for their television screens – exemplified by *At Last The 1948 Show*, Spike Milligan's *Q* series, and *Monty Python's Flying Circus*, to name but a few.

It also led to the 1972 spin-off radio series *I'm Sorry I Haven't A Clue*, which outlived it by decades, and is still broadcast on Radio 4 to this day. Currently hosted by Jack Dee, Tim Brooke-Taylor still stars in the show.

The world was first introduced to the character of hapless Englishman Arthur Dent on the station in 1978 – an intergalactic traveler whose friend, Ford Prefect, wrote for *The Hitchhiker's Guide to the Galaxy*. Later adapted into the best-selling book, Hitchhikers began as a science-fiction comedy radio series, which came into existence after Douglas Adams was asked to pitch a radio sitcom to the station in February 1977. Adams said in an interview that when he discovered the producers wanted a sci-fi theme, he 'fell off [his] chair, because it was what I'd been fighting for all these years'.

It was certainly innovative in its content, but it was also the first radio comedy programme to be produced in stereo, and was unique in its use of music and sound effects, winning a number of awards.

In 1988, Radio 4 became the first home of the classic improvisation show *Whose Line Is It Anyway*, which featured a young Clive Anderson as host and John Sessions and Stephen Fry as regular guests. Created by Dan Patterson and Mark Leveson, the radio series consisted of six episodes, and had such wide appeal that it was instantly snapped up by Channel 4 to be made into the hugely successful television show version.

In more recent times, the station also launched the career of Steve Coogan, when it first broadcast the current affairs parody show *On the Hour* in 1991. Written by a host of talented comedians, including Chris Morris, Richard Herring and Armando Iannucci, it starred Morris as an overzealous and self-important news anchor, accompanied by a regular cast that included Patrick Marber, Doon Mackichan, David Schneider, Coogan and the fabulous female comic Rebecca Front.

Frequently surreal and highly satirical, the spoof show perfectly demonstrated Radio 4's attitude to alternative and often groundbreaking comedy. The nonsensical content – 'Borrowed dog finds Scotland', and 'Where now for man raised by puffins?', for example – was delivered in the same serious manner as real news presenters, as it was Morris's intention to show how the public would believe anything if it was delivered to them with a straight-face. It fooled many listeners, who sometimes rang in to complain about how the anchor was treating his guests.

It was as part of *On the Hour* that Coogan first portrayed the insecure and narcissistic buffoon, Alan Partridge. A socially awkward and deeply insensitive character, Partridge was such a hit on the show that Radio 4 commissioned the six part series *Knowing Me Knowing You with Alan Partridge*, which was picked up by BBC 2 for a television series in 1994. Partridge is now a celebrity in his own right...

Another slightly surreal offering from Radio 4 came in 1997, when the station offered a six-episode run to four young comedians who had just won their first Perrier Award at the Edinburgh Fringe – The League of Gentlemen. Mark Gatiss, Jeremy Dyson, Steve Pemberton and Reece Shearsmith duly penned *On the Town with The League of Gentlemen* for the station. A black comedy, often edging into the comedy horror genre, it quickly acquired a cult following, and the foursome were awarded a Sony Award for the radio series. They were launched into the mainstream when the series became a television show in 1999, and have been credited with the revival of the sketch show format in BBC comedy.

A forum for creativity and ingenuity, over its many decades of broadcasting, Radio 4 has championed the careers of so many of our best-loved comedians. It has consistently given the kind of opportunities for experimental performing that television is so much more hesitant at offering. As a result we have a thriving British comedy scene – a scene that Sarah is now very much a part of.

CHAPTER 16

Panel Show
Prowess

'Usually you get to the end of those long-record panel shows and you're thinking "Thank God I can take my massive knickers off!"'

Since Sarah had made the decision to become a stand-up comedian, each year that passed had brought her greater recognition. 2010 was no exception.

Between her new radio show, and the tireless work she was doing on scripting and shaping her new summer Fringe show, Sarah was also securing her position as 'the guest to have' on every panel show of note. Between her second and third Fringe runs, she appeared on a whopping 13 popular programmes – and unbeknown to Sarah, it would be excellent practice for her very own show, which would begin in 2011.

Less than a month after Edinburgh 2009, she joined Dara O'Briain as a panellist on his hit show *Mock The Week*, alongside Hugh Dennis, Frankie Boyle, Andy Parsons, Russell Howard and David Mitchell. When the audience heard Dara announce her name, they cheered.

In the first round, the guests had to guess what the question would be, for the answer, '175 billion'. Each guest gave a fairly safe answer and had a few laughs. But Sarah didn't pull any punches, and sweetly said: 'Is it, how many hairs you'd have to pull from Susan Boyle's face to make her attractive?'

As the only female in an all-male line up, even the guys were shocked and their mouths fell open in surprise. Sarah just giggled as Dara shook his head and said: 'Not even we would do such jokes...' Sarah replied: 'Well it's like a part-time job keeping up with my beard...' But following her shocking remark, the comedians took no time at all to lower themselves to her level and from then on the laughs came thick and fast.

In the stand-up improvisation round, Sarah stole the show. When the subject of relationships came up, she walked to the centre stage microphone and said: 'I've been with my boyfriend now for a few years and it's going really well. But we've started sort of spicing things up in the bedroom – we've recently tried dirty talk. Neither of us had done it before and we're both a bit too nice and neither of us drink, so it was never going to go well. But we thought we'd give it a go and I said I'd start off... I didn't really know what you're supposed to say and I went, "Oh, erm, I've been a bad girl, I'm sorry about that". And he said: "Apology accepted."'

The audience laughed at her deadpan delivery, but she wasn't finished yet...

'Recently we've been getting a bit more practice and he started off and he said, "you've been such a bad girl, that I think I'm going to have to punch you..." He's gone a bit too far there hasn't he? But I'd actually misheard him, what he'd actually said was "punish you", which apparently is perfectly acceptable in terms of sexy lingo. But he hadn't really thought it through, because I said, "What kind of punishment did you have in mind?" He said: "Take the bins out."'

It was classic Sarah and the audience loved it. She was proving herself to be a versatile performer – both on stage and on screen.

Her first guest spot of 2010 was in January, when she was invited back to join the cast of *Mock The Week*. This time she joined her radio co-star Chris Addison and Hugh Dennis to form one team, while on the other was Andy Parsons, John Bishop and Russell Howard.

Sarah looked very different to when she had appeared on the show just a few months before. Her hair was now a honeyed blonde and she was wearing a bright red and purple dress that suited her complexion. Again she was part of an all-male, all-star line-up, and again, she more than held her own.

In the improvisation section of the competition, Sarah was given the subject of home life, where she covered a by now familiar topic. 'My home life doesn't involve children,' she said. 'I don't really like children and most of my friends don't have kids, and if you ask any woman who doesn't, what would worry them about having kids, the answer is always childbirth; because, from what I understand of childbirth, it changes your downstairs quite a bit. I quite like my downstairs, thanks very much. I certainly don't want an extension. But it's bound to change though isn't it? Because you're forcing a person out of there... I've never forced a person out of there – I've forced a couple in...'

As usual, Sarah had lowered the tone, much to the delight of the audience. And she wasn't finished. 'But I was in a shop recently and this little boy came running over to me and put his hand in mine and shouted, "mammy!" I thought, "I sometimes forget my keys but I think I'd remember that". And then his dad came over and I thought, "I wonder if this is the best chat-up line ever and he's gonna come over and say: 'No, no, that's not your mammy, remember – your mammy left us because my willy's too big.'"'

The audience cackled with laughter and Sarah did a neat little curtsey. She and Chris Addison shared the points for best improv, and double high-fived to celebrate.

Two weeks later she made her debut on *Argumental*, another comedy panel game show. At the time, the show was being hosted by John Sergeant, whose post-journalistic career was on the rise after a surprising appearance on dance show *Strictly Come Dancing*. A show in which the two teams have to argue over various controversial topics, it involves a representative from each team taking it in turns to argue for and against a subject. The audience then gets to vote over who they think has put forward the best case. In the red corner Marcus Brigstocke was joined by Jimmy Carr, while in the blue corner, Rufus Hound was teamed with Sarah.

The first topic of discussion was: 'If a dolphin has to die so

I can have a tuna sandwich then so be it.' Sarah was up first, arguing for the statement, which must have been very difficult for the animal-lover. Hound was extremely enthusiastic about having Sarah on his team and whooped and clapped with gusto as she walked to the centre stage to deliver her speech.

'I think I can address the ladies and gentlemen of the audience with a fact,' she began. 'Dolphins can't actually cure terminal illness. In fact it almost has the opposite effect: 85 per cent of children who had terminal illness and have been put in a pool to swim with dolphins, die within 48 hours of the experience.'

It was a risky subject to riff off, but Sarah had never shied away from the controversial. Hound solemnly nodded in agreement as the audience tentatively laughed.

'What really has happened is that once they've had the experience, which is apparently one of the best things you can ever experience, they've gone, "It's quite poor that."'

Enthused by the growing laughter, Sarah continued: 'I think it's almost about the fact that dolphins have better PR than tuna, don't they? They do, they have a better image. No Athena poster ever came out of a tuna majestically playing, did it? No, it was always dolphins and whales… But there is a new foundation for people, that has been brought about for people who don't have as much money but still have children who are dying. It's like a budget foundation. Instead of swimming with dolphins, what you do is have a bath with a tuna.'

Jimmy Carr looked puzzled as he waited for the punchline. 'It's called Bathing with Tuna and it's from the Take a Fish

Foundation…' The applause was loud and enthusiastic as she returned to her seat.

Brigstocke's response to Sarah's argument lay on much safer ground. 'You wouldn't eat crisps if a kitten had to die… you don't need dolphins to die for you to eat a tuna sandwich – killing dolphins serves no porpoise.'

As the votes were cast, it seemed that maybe her jokes had been a little too risky, as Marcus won the round. But it demonstrated how fearless Sarah was on stage, and introduced a whole new audience to her darker side – a side you would never know existed from her sweetly feminine appearance.

A month later, Sarah was invited on a brand new show called *The Bubble*. Already successful in Israel, Poland, Denmark and Sweden, the British version was the first to feature celebrities and was hosted by David Mitchell. It would prove an interesting experience.

Sarah was taken to a remote country house in the East Midlands, where she was joined by Clive Anderson, Andy Hamilton and two production staff members. Her mobile phone was confiscated and she was denied access to any newspapers, radio broadcasts, television shows or the Internet. For four days she lived in isolation with the other comics, before being taken straight to a studio set to take part in a quiz.

Presented with both real and fake news stories, the contestants then had to decided which were real. Both ITV News and Sky News gamely assisted in the filming of the fake stories. It was the first time that Sarah had been described as 'a celebrity', and it was a very positive sign of her growing status in the media.

Filmed in a reality TV style, it was also the first time Sarah's fans could catch a glimpse of what she was like when she wasn't performing on stage. 'We had a very jolly time,' said Clive Anderson when the gang returned from isolation. Sarah said that she'd been hoping times would have moved forward while she'd been cut off from the world. 'I was hoping things would be a bit more futuristic. You know, hover-boards and silver outfits and tablets instead of meals, but from what I've seen so far it doesn't seem to have happened.'

Sarah had to decide which was true out of three stories – 'Shopkeepers banned from holding naked Mondays', 'Chickens murder a fox', and 'David Cameron has a spray tan'. Sarah decided that the shopkeeper story was the real one, perhaps out of wishful thinking. But she was incorrect. Chickens had indeed exacted a fatal form of revenge on their coop intruder.

In the next round Sarah was delighted to see a picture of a gorilla in a bikini, which had apparently been spotted on planet Mars. The trio had to decide whether it was the real newspaper story, or whether it was 'Prince Philip snapped relieving himself behind a tree', or 'BBC's pre-election debate to be hosted by Fern Britton'.

Hamilton and Anderson began teasing her about her 'obsession' with animals in clothes, which they had apparently discovered while living together over the previous few days.

However much she would have liked it to be true, Sarah didn't believe the gorilla story, and instead plumped for the royal tale. But she was wrong again – a photograph had indeed been taken that appeared to show a gorilla on Mars.

Sarah appreciated her time in isolation – particularly the wonderful food that had been cooked for her. 'The food was really good in the house,' she said. 'And I'm all about microwave dinners normally, so I have got a lot closer to my target weight…which is just massive.'

Clive Anderson had taught her and Andy how to play bridge, which had been a novel experience. She said: 'Apparently you don't even shout "Bridge" at any point, which is rubbish!' But, although Sarah had obviously enjoyed herself, I doubt we'll be seeing her in the *Big Brother* House any time soon…

Soon after, Sarah jetted off to spend another month in Australia for the Melbourne International Comedy Festival, and once again she was well received. But once back on UK soil, Sarah wasted no time in getting back on the panel show circuit.

In early May, she filmed an episode of the hilarious show *Would I Lie To You?* It would be broadcast in August, while she was performing at the Fringe. Presented by Welsh treasure Rob Brydon, the show involved two teams of comedians each taking it in turns to reveal fascinating and previously unknown facts about themselves – not all of which were true. It was then up to the other panellists to decide if the tales were fact or fiction.

On David Mitchell's team, Sarah found herself teamed with the legendary Ronnie Corbett, competing against Lee Mack, Holly Walsh and Julian Clary. Sarah told the opposing team: 'I once spent an entire day on the ASDA shuttle bus, just to have a day out.'

Everyone fired questions at her to try and discover if she was telling the truth. 'How long did you spend on the ASDA shuttle bus?' asked Lee Mack.

'Three hours,' replied Sarah confidently.

'What branch were you going to?' asked Holly Walsh.

'It was the Boldon ASDA,' Sarah said without hesitating.

'Did you get on the bus thinking you were going to go shopping and then thought, "this is fun I'll stay on", or did you plan to get on the bus as a jaunt?' Holly went on.

Again, Sarah was quick to respond. 'I got on because I thought it would take me home, but it didn't go anywhere near my house. So I just stayed on and then got back off at ASDA.'

For Sarah, it sounded plausible – she has admitted to being scatty in the past and has mentioned ASDA in her stand-up a number of times.

'Yes it's true,' revealed Brydon. 'There's always one slightly strange person on those buses – you know, that everyone's slightly scared of. In this case, it was Sarah.'

Two weeks later she was once again on our screens as a guest on Frank Skinner's new series, *Opinionated*. A studio-based, light-hearted talk show, it focused on news events of the previous week, and involved a large amount of audience participation.

This particular aspect of comedy is something that Sarah has always been very adept at. Sarah first appeared in episode three of the new show, but she proved so positive with the audience that she was quickly invited back for two more guest spots over the next month.

Also in May, she appeared once more on *You Have Been*

Watching, alongside American comic Reginald D Hunter, Charlie Brooker and Peter Serafinowicz. After being shown a clip from *Junior Apprentice*, involving baby-faced business boys and girls trying to prove their worth to a stony-faced Sir Alan Sugar, Sarah took the opportunity to tell everyone a story about her first job. As usual, she managed to bring the house down by significantly lowering the tone of the conversation.

'I used to work at WH Smith when I was 16 as a Saturday kid,' she said. 'It was when they still sold porn. The price would never come up when you did the wand thing over the barcode, and I had to look amongst the boobs for it, at sixteen – and the blokes always went, 'It's £2.50', under their breath...'

'Lovely,' remarked Brooker.

Next, each of the contestants were asked to design their own camping product, to compete with the junior apprentice team's design of a travelling storage unit. Serafinowicz invented a 'bug sucker', while Hunter decided on some yellow-tinted sunglasses, designed to fool you into thinking it's sunny when it's not. But Sarah proved she would never be the outdoorsy type, when she designed a hi-vis jacket especially for camping at music festivals. 'It's got a key to your car, so you can go home when it starts getting s**t,' she explained, pointing to a picture she'd drawn to illustrate her invention. 'There's an iPod in case the music that's on is not very good, and a fold-out hotel, so that you don't have to go camping at all...'

It's safe to say Sir Alan would have fired her instantly, but Brooker gave Sarah the points for the round.

The panel also took a look at one of Sarah's favourite shows, *The Biggest Loser*, which takes dangerously overweight people and sends them to an extreme exercise boot camp. Sarah was quick to praise it. 'I really like it, I find that they really empower them, because they're sort of teaching them how to think, and how to get the hunger – pardon the expression – so they can do it themselves. And also it makes me feel really skinny…'

After going on to discuss the size of a dinosaur's man parts, the title of model Tyra Banks' new novel and Susan Boyle's newest reality TV rival (America's 'NuBo'), Sarah was announced the winner of the show.

Next for Sarah was a TV appearance that many would say was no surprise. With her confident pro-female attitude it was only really a matter of time before she was invited on the ITV lunchtime chat show *Loose Women*, as she was exactly the kind of potty-mouthed and cheeky female that its presenters – Andrea McLean, Zoe Tyler, Carol McGiffin and Jane MacDonald would enjoy having a cuppa and a giggle with. Sarah's first visit to the *Loose Women* studio duly came in July 2010.

It was worlds apart from her usual style of TV appearance, in which she usually competed with a panel of men. But with her gutter mouth and frank sex talk, she appeared to fit in right away. The producers were rightly impressed with her ease in front of a live audience and began to discuss having Sarah on board as a presenter.

It was another sign of her versatility. At home on both live and pre-recorded shows, equally comfortable chatting with a panel of strong-willed and arguably sex-obsessed women and competing for laughs with an all-male line-up – Sarah seemed to be able to do it all, even while writing a new show and preparing for yet another Edinburgh appearance.

Her work ethic in the first seven months of 2010 was certainly formidable. But it was positively restful compared to what she had planned for the rest of the year. More guest spots on *Have I Got News For You*, *8 Out of 10 Cats*, *Odd One In* and *Argumental*, would have to be fitted in around an extremely tight schedule – because Sarah was about to go on her first tour, with her new show, *Chatterbox*.

CHAPTER 17

Chatterbox

'You do have to be aware that you might be flavour of the month, but that a new flavour could come along. So I think it's all about making sure I'm good at things and making sure I get better at things. And I think that's how you get longevity in the industry.'

Ever since her return from the Fringe in 2009, Sarah had been hard at work on her new show – and by February 2010 she was ready to preview it.

Taking place early each year, The Leicester Comedy Festival is one of Sarah's important writing deadlines. She always makes sure that she has a recognisable new act to showcase there, so that she can start honing her material in time for the August Fringe. 'Leicester is very important to my gig,' she told their local newspaper when she arrived to perform. 'If you've seen it in Leicester and like it, you're responsible for my future finished show, and this festival has a clever and sharp audience.'

The festival director, Geoff Rowe, agreed – he told the same newspaper that the city had worked hard to ensure the festival was a comfortable space for acts to try new material.

Calling it *Work in Progress*, Sarah knew its first outing would be 'rough and ready'. 'A joke can seem funny in your house but you never know how it's going to work in front of an audience,' she said. She added that she thought about five out of ten of her jokes would work, but that 'hopefully by the end of the festival I could be at seven, fingers crossed.'

It was always a nerve-racking but exciting time for Sarah. Gauging audience reaction, mentally putting ticks or crosses against all of her jokes – she told the audience not to go easy on her. 'I'll be there with my cup of tea in one hand, list of jokes in the other and nerves of steel,' she said.

A few days later she was at The Mandela Hall in Belfast, in front of another test audience. This time, her boyfriend Gary was on the same bill. The promotional material described her as 'one of the top female comics in the business', and she was well received.

Over the next few months, in between her television and radio appearances, Sarah continued to perform her new work regularly. As late as June she still had a tape recorder at her side, and her notes in hand, when she got on stage at the Hyena Lounge Comedy Club in York.

Gary was with her once again, also testing out his new material. 'You shouldn't take notes into an exam, but no one feels the need to shout 'cheat' when Edinburgh-bound comedians so brazenly carry crib cards on to the Basement stage,' wrote one reviewer of the show. 'One of the Fringe benefits of the upcoming jamboree in Scotland is the chance to see headline acts discovering so bluntly whether their new material stands up,' they quipped.

Gary had made the tick or cross test part of his show – by reading his famous one-liners from cards, before either discarding them in the 'bin of shame', dropping them happily into the IKEA 'bag of quite good', or dumping them in a separate 'maybe' pile.

Sarah was particularly nervous about this year's new show, because she would be following it up with her first proper solo tour in the autumn, which had already sold out. In an astonishing act of trust – there weren't even any reviews of the show yet – her fan base was now so large that thousands of people were willing to take a chance and buy a ticket.

Sarah met the surge in demand by adding more dates to her tour, and one by one they all sold out too. But at least her 'work in progress' now had a name: *Chatterbox*. A chatterbox is exactly what Sarah is – a fast talker and funny with it. The name stemmed from the nickname her teachers had once given her at school, but one reviewer wryly observed a different meaning to the name. 'Boy can she chatter, even about her, um, box, as nothing seems too personal to be off-limits for this mischievous storyteller with the hidden whiplash behind the genial glint,' said her York preview review.

In July, days before the Fringe would kick off, Dominic Cavendish from *The Telegraph* met with the chatterbox herself for an interview. He commented: 'Listening to her in full flow, as she arrives at our Soho meeting place after racing down from her adoptive hometown, Manchester, I experience the same mixture of awe and envy you might get when watching someone speed-type...'

She had just had her first proposal of marriage from a fan, which had brightened her hectic day. 'I got a proposal on Twitter today,' she had said breathlessly as she sat down for the interview. 'That's not normal is it? At least he did put at the message, "This is weird, isn't it?" Yes!'

As Cavendish noted, it was an ironic moment for Sarah, seeing as it was divorce that had propelled her onto the stand-up circuit. But it was part of the immense build-up Sarah was experiencing for her Edinburgh show.

Soon after, Sarah packed her bags and moved to her temporary Edinburgh home for the month-long run. This year she was far too high profile for the small Pleasance Courtyard hut she had twice before performed in. Instead she was booked into The Stand Comedy Club for her entire run. The Stand is the only place at the festival that is used for comedy all year round and has live acts seven days a week. Queues regularly stretch far outside the club, and it is the fourth largest venue at the Fringe Festival, with a nightly capacity of 160.

It also has another unique selling point for performers: 'This is going to sound really pathetic, but there's a toilet backstage. It really matters to me that there's a toilet backstage,' she said. 'How many times have you had to queue with your audience to have a wee before your show? And if the queue's a bit long that you start worrying that you'll be late for your own show.

'I'm really flattered that The Stand thought I was good enough to be in that room,' she humbly told Sian Bevan, journalist at *The Skinny*, an independent cultural journalism website – days before the festival. 'I've always loved The Stand as a venue, and it just feels like a family. The fact that they keep the staff so long is such a testament to how good an employer they are. I've been to The Stand since I started, just doing five spots and so on, and they've always treated me well. They're very good at progressing comics. If you do well then they'll offer you 10 minutes next time where other promoters just aren't like that. And they're very pro-women in an amazingly non-patronising way; where some do it to tick boxes, they do it because they like having women on the bill.'

Despite the fact that it was by now, a common occurrence, Sarah had been astonished to find out that the run had sold out long before she was due to travel up to the Scottish capital.

'I'm just astonished by my ticket sales. It's so rare to go to Edinburgh knowing if anybody's going to come. Anybody. Literally anybody. You go up there and there might be four people in one day, the next day there might be none. So the fact that I've sold out the whole run is ridiculous. And also puts more pressure on to make sure that my show's really good because there's actually going to be people to see it. I just love it.'

Sarah was by now used to the hectic nature of the festival and over the years had made a lot of friends in the comedy world. So the Fringe was not only a profile-heightening, profit-making performance exercise, it was also a chance to catch up with her friends over a cuppa. 'I love being up there,' she told Bevan. 'I love turning a corner and there's someone you know. Like, most of my friends are up there. How good is it, when you want to have a cup of tea with that person, instead of saying, "well I'm in London in a fortnight", just saying, "are you free for lunch today?" Excellent.'

Sarah was quietly confident about the run, and her outstanding ticket sales were only partly responsible – her name was by now well-known all over the country, and thanks to her many and varied TV appearances, she was fast becoming Britain's funniest lady. But although she was enjoying her new-found acclaim, she did have one eye on the more negative side of fame. 'I think I'm more confident generally but you have to keep that in check so you don't become a dick. It's round the corner. I'm round the corner from becoming a dick and I keep poking my head round and saying: "I don't wanna go there, don't wanna go there!"

'So I have got people… who are ready to say: "yeah, we need to have a word". So I hope I'm not a dick, but clearly the ticket sales have given me confidence. But then, the ticket sales come from telly performances so it's sort of indirectly given me confidence. It's all been a bit hard to take in, because it has been a fairly ridiculous year.'

Sarah was right; it had been an incredible year for her. But it was about to get even better – because *Chatterbox* was an instant success.

'The only criticism Sarah ever received at school was that she was a chatterbox,' read her promo material. 'She still is. And now it's her job. She hopes the same fate didn't befall the school bike. Come and spend an hour in her charming company as she brings you up to speed on how to celebrate your fortieth, how to pick the best pudding and talks you through the five stages of tired. It's like having cups of tea with a dirty cow.'

Her new material ranged from the usual self-mockery to the shockingly filthy. She revealed her comic self-disgust at once spending £102 in a chocolate shop on herself, before pointing out her boyfriend's shortcomings by describing the time he got Accessorize and Claire's Accessories confused on an ill-fated birthday shopping trip. As for the shockingly filthy, her joke about having tiny tropical fish join you in the bath for added relaxation needs to be heard to be believed...

She was clearly still taking inspiration from her parents' darkly comedic moments. 'I took me dad, mam and me sister out for a nice meal just before Christmas,' she told the audience. 'And midway through the meal, me mam said: "When me and your dad go, we're going together"... I said: "Are you talking about a suicide pact?" And she went: "No we're not gonna call it that." So I sort of did the "what the f**k" face at my sister. And she quite calmly said: "As long as they leave me a letter explaining it cause I'm not gonna go to prison for them."

'It was just getting steadily worse, so I looked at me dad because my dad's the voice of reason in our family, I looked to my dad and said: "What do you think about this?" And he went: "First I've heard of it..."'

The reviews were more impressive than Sarah could have dreamed. Julian Hall wrote for *The Independent*: 'Sarah Millican's performance tonight is one of the most consistent and accomplished I have ever seen at the Fringe. A packed audience at the Stand, a venue favoured by many established comics as somewhere more "grown-up", forget the meaning of the word "listless" as the chirpy Geordie gossips her way through an hour of skillful observations on her domestic foibles.'

He observed that Sarah was no longer relying so much on the audience for her material, but added that she still maintained a close connection to them through her subject matter, notching up brownie points for avoiding clichés while implanting images that would resonate with anyone – like the guilty pleasure of wandering around your flat naked even if it means your neighbours rush out to buy curtains.

The Guardian's Brian Logan noted that Sarah invariably clings to the material she is most comfortable, but commented: 'If it ain't broke, don't fix it… I'd tell Millican to change the record but she'd probably fart while doing so, then tell a filthy joke about it.'

He also remarked that although observational comedy may have been being mocked by comics elsewhere on the Fringe – including by Kevin Eldon in the same venue – Sarah had strong faith in the laughter of recognition, especially with her jokes on weight issues.

'It's all very jolly – but that's because Millican isn't sending up the self-indulgent/self-loathing paradigm of woman-hood, she's celebrating it. The upshot is a show that invites us all to laugh at things as they are, and not imagine anything. At least in Millican's case, observational material seems to spring from a fascination with the commonplace, and a genuine desire to share it. And – purely mechanically – she's a great joke teller, topping off her tales of a divorcee and daughter's life with bullet-proof laugh lines…and cartoonish expressions of dismay.'

As she neared the end of *Chatterbox*'s Fringe run, there was more good news for the comic – and consequently her fans too. Sarah had signed a deal with 4DVD – Channel Four's distribution company – to release her forthcoming *Chatterbox* tour on DVD.

It was a bold move on behalf of the company and showed the enormous faith they had in Millican's appeal. Liz Hadley, A&R manager for 4DVD, said: 'Female comics have not traditionally performed as well as their male counterparts on DVD. We believe Sarah will break the mould. We've had huge success launching new comedians on DVD over the last few years and we're confident we will replicate this success with Sarah. We're very excited to be working with her.'

They were prophetic words. Sarah's DVD would prove the ultimate stocking filler the following year, and break records for its sales.

But as Sarah neared the end of her third Fringe run, she began to understandably get tired and as a result felt a little depressed. 'I was just hitting a wall of tired,' she told one interviewer a few weeks after the run. 'When I was little I used to cry and my mum would go: "Why are you crying?" and I'd go: "I don't know!" and she'd say: "Are you tired?" and I'd say: "No, something's sore!" so she'd say "What's sore?" and I'd say: "I don't know" and she'd say: "Are you just tired?" and I'd say: "I think so!" So I had a couple of those.'

But just when Sarah thought she would drop from exhaustion, she was nominated for a festival award, which she was both pleased and apprehensive about. 'It's brilliant,' she explained. 'But now instead of having lovely people in your audience you've got three judges in. Compared to most people's lives it's really not a problem, it's just that the festival is four or five days too long. I think for next year we need to get it changed. You know the bit where I start crying? Let's stop then.'

She had missed out on a gong the year before, despite a hugely successful show. Now, in the face of her tiredness, she was pleased to discover she had been shortlisted for the main event – the Foster's Award (formerly the Perrier Award).

On the night, the prize went to Russell Kane, who had been shortlisted twice previously but had never won before. The result was announced by comedy star Al Murray, who had himself won the award in 1999.

Kane leapt up on stage to collect the £10,000 prize for his show, *Smokescreens and Castles*, leaving fellow nominees Josie Long, Greg Davies, Bo Burnham and Sarah Millican waiting in the wings.

It was no reason to be upset. Sarah had delighted all her audiences and packed out The Stand every single night. It had been yet another phenomenally successful Fringe experience and she must have been rightly proud.

But at the end of the run Sarah didn't have much time to bask in the glory of her success. A month later she was off on tour, where she would stay until December. But those initial 25 dates weren't anywhere near enough to fulfil demand. Month by month her management added more and more dates the following spring, bringing her total to an incredible 120 performances. It was an epic achievement for a first tour. 'Now is a good time to tell you I'm much ruder than on the telly,' she told each new audience. And they delighted in her giggling brand of homely filth.

On one of the dates, *The Liverpool Echo* highlighted the many notices that were taped around the Philharmonic Hall's foyer – warning that the show 'may contain adult themes and content'. And although they admitted it posed difficulties for the reviewer (the *Echo* is a family paper) they praised the show highly. 'While the smut-o-meter is turned to high, it's all done with such warmth and conspiratorial incredulity that it would be mightily difficult for anyone to be really offended.'

'The bad news is it's already sold out,' wrote the *Manchester Evening News*. 'Some years belong to certain comedians and [our] money is on the fact that from beneath the pile of hilarious boys that made stand-up an arena draw last year, will emerge one funny female – Sarah Millican.'

It was a whirlwind experience for the Geordie, who was steadily playing to bigger and bigger crowds, up and down the British Isles. But she was unfazed, as she told one Irish newspaper: 'It's not about bigger shows, but more about ticket sales. If you have a 400-seater venue but you've only sold nine tickets – that's what fazes me. A full room is a joy to play; we erred on the side of caution at first and booked just 25 days, so I'm pleased it's been so successful.'

And although it must have been an exhausting time, Sarah loved being on tour, surrounded by thousands of people, all laughing along with her. 'The travelling side can be tiring,' she confided in one reporter once it was over. 'But the shows are always great fun. It's the best part about the job, performing live. Although the travelling is tricky. I'm looking forward to the invention of magic shoes. Click my heels and I'm in Milton Keynes. The audiences were great, I was very lucky.'

CHAPTER 18

Fringe Benefits

'My whole year revolves around the Fringe. It's like nothing else – I can't imagine not doing it.'

The Edinburgh Festival Fringe is the largest arts festival in the world. If you can crack it there, as the phrase goes, you can crack it anywhere. Nowhere else on the planet has such a wide variety of performance available for audiences to see at any one time.

It is a theatre and comedy lover's dream.

Anyone who has been there will know that the array of acts on any day in August is almost overwhelming. Besides all the shows in recognised venues, it is impossible to walk down the street in the centre of Scotland's capital without constantly stumbling across impromptu performance after performance.

It offers an absolute cornucopia of talent, an excess of entertainment and more laughs, drama or experimentation than would be available on any TV channel in the world for probably an entire year.

These days, the figures are mind blowing. In 2012, there were 42,096 performances of 2,695 shows. An estimated 22,457 performers took part and 1,857,202 tickets were issued for shows, events and exhibitions in 279 venues across the city. That number didn't include the tens of thousands attending the 814 free, non-ticketed events of the Fringe, from tented comedy to street theatre.

It is highly unusual for any actor or performer not to want to perform there at least once in their lives. For most it is an annual event where they have the chance to meet up with or just observe former fellow cast members, rivals, or friends performing their latest work – or just in passing in the street.

For comedians, Edinburgh has become a critical return destination on their road map to success. There is not a single comedian working on television today who has not at some point appeared at the Edinburgh Fringe. Most comedians regard it as the fulcrum of their year, the point around which they anchor the unveiling of new material and the springboard from which to launch new tours.

When Sarah Millican took her first show to Edinburgh in 2008, she did so knowing that if she went down well, it would give her the impetus and justification she needed to carry on.

But the Edinburgh Fringe doesn't just provide performers with the confidence they need. It also provides amazing exposure, the sort that is impossible to achieve without being a regular on TV. For a budding comedian on their way up, the Edinburgh Fringe is the one event that is a must-attend with absolutely no excuses.

This status hasn't come about overnight. It is the result of a long history that in many ways reflects the vast changes in popular entertainment in Britain over the last 70 years.

Like many of the biggest festivals, the Fringe started in 1947 almost by accident. The city's leaders had decided the Scottish capital should host a major international performing arts festival to put Edinburgh on the map – and to start to look forward following the end of World War Two.

Their view coincided with the search by a man called Rudolf Bing, the general manager of the Glyndebourne Opera, for a city where he could organise a major cultural event. Bing joined forces with the city's leaders to put together a programme of arts and music that they called the Edinburgh International Festival, which was designed to 'provide a platform for the flowering of the human spirit.'

It was all very highbrow. While there was supposed to be something for everyone, the International Festival emphasised traditional types of performance like serious theatre and classical music over others.

For some people it was a little too intellectual. With the festival being tightly curated, there was limited opportunity for young, up-and-coming acts to get on the bill. In various parts of Scotland and England, eight separate theatre groups were slightly annoyed that such major acts were the only ones allowed to appear in the city and decided they would take advantage of the influx of people to see if they could get an audience too.

Their appearance was low-key, but successful. In the first year, they attracted big enough audiences and impressed people sufficiently to encourage others to come back the year after with a similar number of performances on the periphery of the main International Festival. It was during the 1948 festival that the event received its name, when Scottish critic Robert Kemp, who had turned up to review some of the events, wrote in one of his articles: 'Round the Fringe of the official Festival drama, there seems to be more private enterprise than before…I am afraid some of us are not going to get home in the evenings!'

What he was referring to was the tendency of the Fringe to stage more shows at night. Whereas the majority of the International Festival events took place during the day, the Fringe shows played to audiences wanting something to do when night began to fall. To entertain them at a time we now regard as the norm – perhaps with a drink in their hand rather than in the traditionally rather stiff-shirt environment of a concert hall or grand theatre.

It was a way of doing things that would later add to the festival's appeal as the place to go to be entertained in a more light-hearted fashion, without needing to adhere to the conventions of the day.

In the first few years, all the acts that turned up for the Fringe did so completely independently of each other. There was no co-ordination, no programming and no curation of those that took part. Groups from Cambridge, Oxford and Durham Universities came to join their colleagues from the equivalent Scottish learning establishments.

Many began to see this less-organised aspect of the Fringe

as one of its strong points. Acts that turned up to take part did not have the luxury of pre-publicity and marketing. They were forced to perform to the top of their abilities in order to get the crowds in, or they would end up as commercial failures. It was a case of 'entertain or die'. Anyone who attended did not have the advantage of knowing that an act had been chosen for its previous record, but they could be sure the actors and theatre producers would be trying their hardest to impress people. It was a Darwinian ethos that echoed through the ages to today, with acts surviving purely because of their ability to put bums on seats.

Originally, the groups that turned up tended to put on fairly traditional theatre. In 1947, Shakespeare was performed, alongside more avant-garde offerings such as Strindberg and T S Eliot. But, as time went on, the Fringe began to become increasingly an outlet for more experimental or original work.

It became a place where theatre writers and directors could try out new work to see whether it was likely to get an audience if it went elsewhere. Many of the shows began to be more lighthearted, with increasing numbers of revues appearing on the bill.

In 1951, the first signs that some sort of organisation would soon start to evolve came when Edinburgh University students opened a drop-in centre for Fringe performers offering cheap food and a bed for the night. By 1954, that had coalesced into an agreement among some of the groups taking part to hold a meeting before the start of the festival to discuss working together. At first, it was agreed that they would establish a joint box office, arrange publicity and produce a joint programme. In that year, 13 groups took part, but not all of them agreed to take part in the joint arrangements.

In 1958, the Festival Fringe Society was created, making the term Fringe official, and setting the boundaries for the events that were not covered by the International Festival. Its constitution was written in line with the ethos that had brought the first eight groups together in 1947: that there should be no vetting of or restrictions on any person or group wanting to take part. It was a principle that was to stay at the heart of the festival right up to the present day and one that would ultimately lead to its success.

In 1959, the year after the society was formed, 19 groups took part. By 1962, 34 were on the bill and Edinburgh University was already complaining it couldn't cope with the numbers involved.

It was around this time that performers who would later go on to make their names in television, began appearing. With its atmosphere of freedom and experimentation, the Fringe provided many of those who later became Britain's most famous and distinguished writers and actors the chance to try out something that hadn't been seen before.

One of the most famous was not actually in the Fringe at all. *Beyond The Fringe*, which appeared in 1960, was a stage revue show starring Dudley Moore, Peter Cook, Jonathan Miller and Alan Bennett. Despite its name, or possibly as revealed in its name, it was in fact part of the International Festival. Its mix of sketches about current affairs and British society and willingness to cock a snook at the establishment, is regarded as having heralded a wave of political satire that much later came to dominate the world of light entertainment. *Have I Got News For You* can trace its lineage right back to the revues of which Beyond The Fringe was the most famous early version.

In the late 1950s, Derek Jacobi appeared in a sixth-form production of *Hamlet*, playing the lead role. The first performance of Tom Stoppard's play *Rosencrantz and Guildenstern are Dead* also took place at the Fringe in 1966.

In the 1950s, 1960s and 1970s, an increasing number of student groups began to use the evenings at the Fringe venues to perform revue shows, giving them a chance to supplement the amount they were earning from the more serious theatre they would perform in the daytime. Student groups might perform a Shakespeare play during the day and then put on a more humorous show later that night, to help fund the cost of staying in the city.

The Monty Python team members were among those who took part in shows of this type in the 1960s. Some appeared as members of Cambridge University's Footlights groups that became regular visitors to the Fringe; others with the Footlights' Oxford University equivalent. The Fringe was a rite of passage for young talented performer and writers who could cut their teeth in front of a receptive audience and became a testing ground for many of those who later went on to become the mainstay of British TV comedy of the 70s, 80s and 90s.

Tim Brooke-Taylor, Graeme Garden, Bill Oddie, Rowan Atkinson and Douglas Adams, were among some of those from Cambridge University who took to the stage along with the Python members during that period.

With such talent and originality on show, the Fringe began to expand rapidly. Under the direction of Alison Moffat between 1976 and 1981, the number of companies performing rose from 182 to 494, making it at that point already the biggest arts festival in the world. Its expansion was driven by its attractiveness to performers of genres that, up until that time, had had few outlets for the kind of material they wanted to perform.

As well as revue shows, the Edinburgh Fringe increasingly became a home for the what became known as the one-man-show, which allowed every actor with an idea they were keen to develop, the chance to turn it into a show and put it on for an audience willing to see something new and untested.

In 1981, a Cambridge Footlights revue called *The Cellar Tapes*, featuring Stephen Fry, Hugh Laurie, Emma Thompson and Tony Slattery, with extra material by Sandi Toksvig among others, went down a storm, winning the inaugural Perrier Award. The award, for the best show in the Fringe, had been set up to support young and up and coming talent. It provided the spur needed to draw more comedy acts to the Fringe and soon all of the country's funniest people were doing their best to be crowned the best act there.

Later winners included a litany of comedians who went on to be top-rated stars. Those who later won the Perrier Award included Armstrong and Miller, Jeremy Hardy, Sean Hughes, Frank Skinner, Steve Coogan, Lee Evans, Alan Davies, Chris Addison, Dylan Moran, The League of Gentlemen, Al Murray, Richard Ayoade's Garth Marenghi, and Daniel Kitson. In 1995, Jenny Éclair became the first and only female winner for *Prozac and Tantrums*. In 2005, the Perrier Awards changed their name, later becoming the Edinburgh Comedy Awards.

Throughout that time, although the festival continued to expand, the number of traditional venues didn't increase significantly. To cope with the rise in the number of acts, a solution was found that became another facet of what many people enjoy about the Fringe – the reuse of all types of venue throughout the day for a wide variety of acts.

During a typical day at the Fringe, all the major venues will see several performers putting on different types of show. In addition, an extraordinary array of ordinary establishments, ranging from pubs, to small halls, to tents, to basements, will be commandeered and turned into places where shows can be put on. Whereas, in the 1950s and 1960s, there would typically be only one group per hall, today a single performing space would be used by up to seven different shows per day.

As a result of the rise of stand-up comedy, which had gone from being performed in a few select venues in the early 1980s to pubs across the country by the late 1990s, solo comedians were increasingly encouraged to play the Fringe to see if their acts could compete with shows featuring several performers. Tents and marquees, put up especially for the four-week run, began to rival pubs and small halls as the places where people could see high quality acts.

In 2008, when Sarah performed *Sarah Millican's Not Nice*, comedy finally overtook drama as the most-performed type of performance genre at the Fringe. Before that point, drama had been the dominant art form.

While there are still hundreds of serious dramas available to see, most people who now go to the Fringe expect to see something that will make them laugh. The number of comedy acts reflects that desire and many of the biggest shows are seen by thousands of people throughout August.

Today, the Fringe has totally eclipsed the International Festival in size and scale. But in creating such a gathering of people interested in performance and arts, the Fringe has become a magnet for those involved in other arts so that the Fringe and International Festivals now share Edinburgh with five other festivals in August every year. There is an art festival, the Royal Military Tattoo, a book festival, a film festival and a television festival all taking place around the same time.

Comedians who perform at Edinburgh now find themselves rubbing shoulders with not just artists and composers, but with TV producers and production company executives – exactly the sort of people they need to meet if they want to make the leap from stand-up to radio or TV.

Lynne Parker, the founder of Funny Women, and promoter of women's comedy in general, has said Edinburgh is unrivalled in providing a platform for people like Sarah when they are on their way up. She told the *British Comedy Guide* website: 'It is expensive, time-consuming and sometimes disheartening but there are lots of reasons to showcase yourself at Edinburgh, which is the toughest kind of "trade fair" imaginable with an unrelenting public to attract and amuse.

'Getting recognition by winning an award of any kind does help as long as you milk it. The Foster's Edinburgh

Awards is the big ticket. Having a successful sell-out show at the Fringe can help put your name on the map, as much as being nominated for the Foster's Edinburgh Comedy Awards. Some acts go back there year after year without even a whiff of an award but still pack in the audiences and gain massive exposure that leads to other work.

'Miranda Hart was performing in a small venue at the Pleasance when I first went to the Fringe in 2003 – this was her test bed for the material, which has become the mainstay of her hugely successful BBC series, *Miranda*. She performed until she got noticed – trying out her ideas on Fringe audiences and honing her craft as a writer and performer.

'The Fringe is rich pickings for talent scouts looking for a range of women to cast in any number of roles, funny or straight acting. The chutzpah it takes to write, produce and present your own show in the world's largest arts festival is not for the faint hearted. Most acts, not just women, work for years before their big break and the real money comes in from TV and DVD deals, commercial voiceovers, acting roles and sell out tours.'

In the last five years the Fringe has gone stratospheric. In 2008, the Fringe featured 31,320 performances of 2,088 shows in 247 venues. That means in just four years, it has added 600 shows and more than 10,000 performances.

With such a huge range of people taking to the stage and so many jokes told, the competition to make an impact is extremely intense. But the rewards for those who are successful are immense.

As well as the overall prize in the Edinburgh Comedy Awards, (formerly the Perrier Awards), there is now an award for 'best joke', which often gets as much coverage as any other story from the event. Sarah regularly gets nominated for the award.

Sarah has acknowledged the importance of the Fringe as a honing exercise to make her shows as good as possible. But she says it also helps her improve over time so that every time she comes back, each year is better than the last.

She told the *Daily Record*: 'What I like is it shows progression. That's all you ever want, to just be learning and getting better. It means if the show is rubbish thousands of people will hate you instead of hundreds, so you have to make sure it is doubly good. I don't want to let anyone down. Tickets are expensive for everybody, you just want to make sure people get their money's worth.'

But as well as what it offers her as a performer, like many other comedians, Sarah loves what the Fringe offers for punters as well – the chance to see other shows and experience some top-notch laughs.

While at the festival one year, she told fellow comedian Richard Herring during one of his podcasts: 'It was one in the morning and two little kids came in they said they had tickets to see Daniel Kitson, in my opinion the greatest comedian the UK has produced, and these kids said they couldn't go, and did we want the tickets, and of course we did. We got there and it was amazing.

'But during the show, it's a testament to how good Daniel Kitson is, someone behind us threw up on my friend's back, fully all over her back. Five people around us got wet wipes out and tissues and just cleaned her up and we stayed. That was how much we wanted to see Daniel Kitson.'

In several interviews, she says she regularly circles up to 80 shows because there are so many she wants to see. Despite that, she usually only manages to see between 10 and 15.

Sarah admits that with all the pressure to do well, Edinburgh can be a stressful place for a performer. With so many performers taking to the stage, not all will enjoy large audiences. Even within the month that shows are put on, audiences for the same act can fluctuate wildly. She admitted to the *Edinburgh Festival Guide* in 2011, such pressure and stress has left her crying without knowing why, by the time the third week comes around.

In Edinburgh, even the biggest and best comedians can have no idea whether anyone will turn up. But despite her fears, Sarah has always been the darling of the Fringe – and as her star continues to rise, it's almost guaranteed she always will be.

CHAPTER 19

Performing for Royalty

'It's an honour to be performing at the Royal Variety performance – I'm preparing for a very churny belly on the day.'

By December 2010, Sarah was ready to enjoy a welcome break from her exhausting *Chatterbox* tour. She'd hardly been home since July, and thoroughly deserved some much-needed down time, as well as a long overdue catch up with her friends and family.

But before she could put her feet up, Sarah first had to head to London for a night – because she had just received the best early Christmas gift ever: an invite to perform at The Royal Variety Performance. A gala evening held annually in Britain, the show consists of family entertainment including comedy, singing, dancing, magic and a whole host of other acts. Organised on behalf of the Entertainment Artistes Benevolent Fund, various senior members of the royal family put on their gladrags to attend, and the show is always televised and shown to millions of viewers.

First held in 1912, the variety show is now a British institution, which many see as a Christmas tradition, seeing as it is always held in late November or early December. Sarah felt honoured to be invited to perform, especially when she learned Prince Charles would be in the audience at London's swish Palladium Theatre. Along with his wife Camilla, he would also undoubtedly be in fine spirits – as his son Prince William had just proposed to his long-term girlfriend, Kate Middleton.

The show would be an incredible evening to be part of, and has had a rich and interesting history of performances. When The Beatles performed there in 1963, John Lennon made a statement that has since passed into legend. 'For our last number I'd like to ask your help,' he said. 'Will the people in the cheaper seats clap your hands? And the rest of you, if you'll just rattle your jewellery…'

Controversially, Stephen K Amos told the 2007 audience that he'd like a show on TV, but that the BBC's diversity policy meant Lenny Henry would have to die first. Ouch. And HRH herself only knows what The Queen made of Lady Gaga's 2009 performance… The eccentric pop starlet wore a full-length red latex dress, with a 20ft train, while suspended 30ft in the air – alongside her piano.

So, along with a place in the history books, royal approval beckoned… Sarah was incredibly excited and so were her family, who she immediately rang and invited to the night. 'To be able to bring those who have supported my daft career for years to the Palladium, feels like a career milestone,' she told local newspaper *The Press and Journal*. 'I'm preparing for a very churny belly on the day. Four of my family are making the trip down and my mam is buying a new outfit "to meet the Queen in". I'm not sure if she's realised it's not the Queen and even if it was, she doesn't shake the hands of the whole audience.'

But as much as her mum was looking forward to the possibility of touching royalty, Sarah seemed more excited about meeting her music heroes – heartthrobs Take That, who would also be performing on the night. 'I'm a massive fan and actually squealed when I heard they were on,' she told the paper.

Even though she had been performing to thousands over the previous few months, nerves suddenly began to get the better of her. 'The performance is nerve-racking. As soon as it's over, I'll then get nervous about the meet and greet. Then I'll get nervous about the after-show party. Then I'll get nervous about missing the train the next day,' she gabbled.

Sarah wasn't the only performer excited about the glittering night, which would also be marking its centenary year. Michael McIntyre, who was set to host the event, was also overjoyed. He joked: 'It's a dream come true to be introducing the likes of Take That, Cheryl Cole and Prince Charles's own personal booking, NDubz.'

And Jack Whitehall was looking forward to the event because it meant he could finally make up for a missed opportunity in his teens. 'Prince Charles came to my school once when I was 16, but there wasn't time to tell him any jokes,' he said. 'Now I have the opportunity to. Maybe it's fate.'

Fellow comic Micky Flanagan wasn't worried about the

extravaganza, saying he had a foolproof back-up plan if his act bombed on stage. 'If things don't work out at the comedy, I might have a word with Charles to see if I can get the contract for doing the windows at the palace,' he said, cheerfully.

For tenor Russell Watson, performing at the show was especially poignant – because he had battled a brain tumour in the nine years since his last Variety Performance. 'As an entertainer there are few greater moments than a performance on the Royal Variety,' he said. 'After my health problems of the last few years it's an even more significant career moment for me.'

Singer Rumer was also on the bill – she would be taking to the stage with jazz star Jamie Cullum. And Kylie Minogue, Susan Boyle and Kinks singer Ray Davies were also scheduled to appear. Acrobatic act Spelbound also had high hopes for the night. The *Britain's Got Talent* winners had competed against thousands of other acts to earn their place on the stage, and said it was the greatest honour they'd ever had.

But the night proved to be a controversial one before it even began. As Sarah mingled backstage with the other acts, Prince Charles and Duchess of Cornwall, Camilla were making their way to the Palladium Hall. Halfway there, disaster struck. A mob had gathered in London, to protest at a recent hike in university fees, and the royal couple's car soon found itself at the centre of a terrifying attack. While they were trapped inside, the angry gathering began throwing things at the car, and managed to smash a window before it could move on safely.

It was a frightening start to the evening, and no one would have blamed them if they'd gone right home and had a stiff brandy. But they showed great fortitude when they finally arrived, smiling, to take their seats in the royal box. It was up to the performers to entertain the poor couple and make the night memorable in a more positive way. They certainly succeeded.

While real royalty was in the audience, it was the duty of pop royalty to open and close the event. Kylie kicked off the night with her song *Better than Today*, and Sarah's personal favourites, Take That, were on top form as they closed the night with their latest hit, *The Flood*, surrounded by close to a hundred semi-naked male dancers.

'Heaven knows what the Queen would have made of it had she been in attendance,' wrote *The Stage*, which claimed the night was one of the strongest in recent history.

'Each year the artists in the line-up are carefully chosen for their ability to be entertaining, yet inoffensive,' wrote *The Mirror*. So Sarah would have to pick her material for the night very carefully – and tone down her prolific swearing and dirty talk.

Finally it was time for Sarah's royal debut. 'It's the comedian everyone's chatting about,' came the announcement. 'It's Sarah Millican!' She wore a broad grin and a pretty black dress as she walked confidently onto the stage. 'Well hello,' she began, before quipping: 'Ooh, somebody's just wooed. That's quite terrifying. My mum must be in…'

Sarah wasted no time in garnering some laughs from the audience, as she launched right into a gag about her father. She knew it would be a safe choice. After all, it was a joke about Philip that had got her first ever laugh. 'I drove here today and I've only been driving for three years,' she began, 'And when I passed me test, me dad's quite a practical man, and he said: "There's three things you always have to have in the boot of your car – you need a blanket, you need a shovel and you need a flask…" And he's right, because whenever I've killed a man I'm always parched.'

It immediately became clear that although Sarah was minding her 'swearies', she certainly had no plans to sugar coat her black comedy – and she had absolutely no need to, because the laughs came instantly.

Sarah continued… 'I live on my own. I do like living on my own but I always wonder if I'm on my own and somebody breaks in – what do I do? What do I hit them with? You've got to think of these things… I talked to a couple of my friends and I asked the first one and she said: "I don't really know." And I said: "Well what would you normally have to hand?" She replied: "Empty bottles?"'

After another round of laughter, Sarah really got into the swing of things. 'I told her: "I don't think you'd really notice if somebody broke in." – "I don't care who you are",' she pretended to slur, "shut the door on your way out, I can feel a bloody draft!"'

'But I asked my other friend: "What would you hit someone with?" She said: "I've got a rounders bat down the side of my bed, for protection."' Sarah paused while she put on a look of surprise, before saying, 'But she's been told by a policeman that that's not allowed, because it's classified as an offensive weapon. The only way she's allowed a rounders bat down the side of her bed is if it's accompanied by something it would normally accompany – so now she's got a rounders bat, and a rounders ball as well. And I'm the same, because I've got a massive knife and a massive fork – so if someone breaks in with a big lump of steak, I'm champion!'

The hall reverberated with clapping and laughter, and though Sarah wouldn't have seen it from far below on stage, Charles and Camilla were chuckling away too. Maybe Sarah's gag about protecting yourself against violent intruders had seemed appropriate after all the couple had been through that night…

Sarah went on for another 10 minutes before she finished with a sweetly funny story she had been saving for a while. As the audience listened, entranced, she told them about the time she had been missing Gary in Australia, and he'd misunderstood her when she said he was too far away. 'He moved the webcam, and I didn't have the heart to tell him I meant geographically…'

After thanking the audience for their cheers of appreciation, Sarah bowed and waved. Then she left the stage, pleased that it had gone so well. She had made royalty laugh, and now she was off to mingle with the best of the British entertainment industry: a group to which, by royal seal of approval, she now officially belonged.

When the show was screened on BBC One soon after, Sarah got to see the royal reaction to her performance. And the viewing figures reflected the quality of the talent on the night, with an amazing 9.6 million viewers tuning in to watch the extravaganza. A whole new audience had been introduced to Sarah Millican.

CHAPTER 20

The Loose Woman

'It's all very well to be a feminist, but it's nice to know you've got good knockers.'

In late December, Sarah Millican appeared on *Loose Women* for the second time, but it would by no means be her last. Because it was on this episode of the daytime chat show that she announced she would be joining the show's famous panel in January 2011 – just a short month away.

'I'm thrilled to be joining an esteemed panel of loose ladies,' she told the audience. 'From someone that was a prude as a teenager, it's nice to finally become a loose woman! I get my own mug with my name on as well! I'm told it's already been ordered – it's just a mug but I'm really excited.' Sarah went on to explain that when she'd texted a friend to say she was officially a 'Loose Woman', they thought she'd split up with her boyfriend, Gary.

Rightly pleased about her new job – which came with a rumoured £200,000 salary – Sarah immediately took to Twitter to share her good news, and was soon inundated with congratulations.

The day after filming the episode, she tweeted: 'The ladies were very welcoming yesterday. Feel like part of the team already.' That team included fellow northerner Denise Welch, Carol McGiffin, Coleen Nolan and Sherrie Hewson, who were led by show anchors Kate Thornton and Andrea McLean.

At first glance, it's easy to think that Sarah would be right at home on the controversial show, which would give her a forum to discuss the hottest topics of the day.

Loose Women had first aired in 1999 on ITV and was first presented by Kaye Adams and Nadia Sawalha. In the years that have followed, the panel has consisted of a rotating group of females from various professions in the entertainment and journalism industries, including actresses, singers, authors, presenters, journalists and reporters.

It is mainly presented by women over the age of 30, a fact which presenter Denise Welch says is down to the fact that older women are more willing to have personal conversations. 'The great thing is that it's the one show where you have to be older to be on it,' she has said. 'We've tried younger presenters and unfortunately they've either not had a life or aren't ready to talk about it. With us, all our dirty linen has not only been aired in public, it's been washed and put back in the drawers.'

And the presenters have done a substantial amount of airing on the show too. Coleen Nolan joined the cast after her split from husband Shane Ritchie, and has openly spoken about the problems in her marriage during her airtime. Denise Welch used the show to admit her split from husband of 24 years, Tim Healy. After pictures of her with another man had appeared in the national papers, Welch openly wept on air as she told viewers how their relationship had ended some time before, before being comforted by her fellow panellists.

Andrea McLean had recently announced her own break-up on the show, saying: 'For those of you who may not know, my husband Steve and I have separated and split up… I wanted to bring it up today to thank everyone for their huge support.' Her fellow presenters discussed the split with their usual candour. 'You do have to recognise when it's time to go,' said Jane MacDonald. 'Staying together for the children is not necessarily the right thing,' admitted Andrea.

It was the kind of conversation that would resonate with a huge swathe of the television audience, and is a prime example of why the show has thrived for so many years.

Early on it was an instant hit with viewers, as it broached typically taboo subjects such as sex in a forthright and open manner. Open and honest about their feelings, the presenters are seen as role models for the modern woman – strong, independent and not afraid to speak their mind. As one producer explained to a trade magazine, the show is popular with housewives, pensioners, students and young mums. They discuss mainly female concerns – relationships, children, sex, sexuality, age, beauty, and the hosts' own many and varied personal issues.

Despite this, the show is very 'laddish' in its content, with its presenters often boasting about their heavy drinking and nighttime exploits. Interviews with male guests are usually conducted with a healthy dose of sexual innuendo – something Sarah is an expert at.

In 2010, the women interviewed lothario Russell Brand. Denise Welch welcomed him by lifting up her top to reveal a corset emblazoned with his favourite football team's logo. Then Carol McGiffin told him that after reading his autobiography – which graphically reveals the extent of his sexual conquests – she had fantasised so much about him that she actually believed they had 'done it'. 'Was he bendy?' asked another panellist? 'He was very bendy and dirty,' she replied, with a coy smile.

In the wake of the Tiger Woods affair scandal, the Loose Women discussed the issue in their own imitable style. 'How much does sex occupy your thoughts?' Andrea asked the panellists. 'I was a bit of a sex maniac, I was a bit of a terrible teenage slut. I am a very sexual person,' offered Carol McGiffin. At first, it wasn't difficult to imagine how Sarah would fit in with the style of the conversations. Just as Sarah conducts her shows like a friendly chat with your favourite aunty, the Loose Women entertain by sitting around with a cuppa, chatting about the topics of the day.

Its supporters immediately hailed it as a triumph for feminism, and it quickly racked up a string of impressive awards. In the past it has been nominated for Best Daytime Show at the Royal Television Society Awards, and Best Topical Magazine Programme and Best Talkshow respectively at the National Television Awards in 2011 and 2012. The TV Quick and TV Choice Awards have announced Loose Women the Best Daytime Show four times in a row – in 2007, 2008, 2009 and 2010, while the Television and Radio Industries Club also gave it an award for Best TV Daytime Programme in 2009.

But the show has seen its fair share of controversies. In 2008 doyenne of comedy Joan Rivers appeared on the show, and apparently completely missed the fact that the show was live and not pre-recorded. As a result when discussing the actor Russell Crowe, she said: 'Get ready to bleep this: he's a f*****g s**t…'

The audience laughed hysterically, but anchor Jackie Brambles rushed to apologise for the outburst, before cutting to a commercial break. Doing the break, it was decided that Rivers not rejoin the show for the remainder of the segment. Rivers found the whole thing very funny. 'I said: "I apologise." Everyone apologised. It was hilariously funny.' It was the first time in her 40-year career that she had ever been asked to leave a show, and she was 'thrilled'.

But despite its public and critical acclaim, not everyone is so impressed with its chatty format. Also in 2008, *The Guardian* branded the show as hateful and offensive to both men and women, and called it a case of feminism having gone too far. And in 2010, *The Daily Mail*'s Jan Moir declared outrage at the show's National Television Award win, saying: 'How was *Loose Women* voted best factual TV show when it is fronted by a gaggle of sexual incontinents?'

The show certainly divided public opinion, which is something that Sarah's similarly open and frank style of feminism has never done. Unlike the Loose Women, she has never been criticised for her approach to female concerns –

only applauded. And, while the presenters are often photographed out on the town, drinking, a throwback to the ladette culture of the nineties, Sarah is not one to booze.

By the time Sarah arrived on the panel, the show had been on air for a decade and ratings had started to fall. Many national newspapers began claiming that Sarah, along with fellow new presenter Janet Street-Porter, had been brought in as a result of the slump. If so, it was a clever move. While Sarah could chat away on any subject, and still offer her humorous opinions on sex and relationships, she was much less controversial than some of the show's other hosts and appealed to a broader audience.

She was certainly popular on the show and pulled no punches with her comments. When on one show Kate Thornton asked the girls if they worried about morning breath after waking up next to a guy, Sarah was blunt. 'Well, I'm not like a big slapper, so...' 'Unlike us two?' cut in McGiffin, referring to herself and Denise Welch. Sarah commented, wryly: 'Well I wasn't going to say it, but if you volunteer the information...'

But when the rest of the women went on to crudely discuss the matter in more detail, Sarah just looked a bit bored. And when she did join in it was to gently mock the other women.

After Thornton described how she sometimes woke up early to apply her make-up before her bedfellow noticed, Sarah said: 'Do you fan your hair out on the pillow as well?' Sarah just seemed surprised – and a little bit disappointed – at the effort Kate described putting into creating an illusion of perfection for a man.

She also sometimes struggled to join in on the rowdy

conversations. When psychologists in Hawaii announced that 'dawdlers' weren't just annoying, they actually had an illness – Pedestrian Aggressiveness Syndrome – the Loose Women took the opportunity to discuss the subject. 'I didn't even think they had pavements in Hawaii, I thought they just surfed and wore grass skirts,' said Denise, attempting some humour.

As she and the others discussed the issue, getting increasingly loud, Sarah could hardly get a word in. When she finally began to speak, she got the audience laughing instantly and even got a round of applause. But it had been a struggle. One viewer was unimpressed. 'You have Sarah Millican on the show and you are trying humour and not just letting her make all the jokes?'

All in all, it seemed that perhaps it wasn't the best place for Sarah's many talents. As she had illustrated in her stand-up comedy, she was a great believer in equality between the sexes, and didn't believe in changing herself to please others. She didn't believe that to be a strong woman meant she had to be loud and dominant.

She has an unexpected take on feminism; for example, she believes Page 3 is a celebration of women's natural beauty. 'It is celebrating women as opposed to saying: "Oh my God, she went out without any make-up – isn't she disgusting,"' she said in a 2012 interview. Sarah was more concerned about the scrutiny and criticism of women in magazines, which she had been disappointed by in recent years.

'I stopped buying women's mags as they made me feel really bad about how I should be and that if I was 'this' I would be happier, which is s***e. You feel judged and it's also damaging for women. They read that and then they believe that's how people should be, when it should be that people are how they are and if they are happy then that's great. I find it damaging and horrible. I think I shouldn't feel bad. I look in the mirror objectively and I think, "It's all right, it's not amazing, it's not s***e, it's in the middle, like most of us".' It was an intelligent and thought-provoking observation, as well as a classic example of her well-reasoned opinions.

So it was no surprise that when the Loose Women aired the infamous Andy Gray and Richard Keys conversation to provoke a discussion, Sarah was balanced and typically blunt about her thoughts on the matter. Immediately after the recording was played, the audience drew a collectively sharp intake of breath at the shocking display of sexism by the two commentators, which had been recorded in an off-air moment during a football match.

But before anyone could say anything, Sarah said: 'I think what you've got to remember first of all is it was a private conversation. I'm not excusing it – I'm saying at least that that shouldn't have been made public anyway. We've all said things behind closed doors, haven't we? It's like the Gordon Brown thing when he still had his mike on in the car – you've got to remember it's a private conversation, I'm not excusing it, but they were never intending that to be heard by anybody.'

In some way Sarah became the voice of reason for the show. She offered a different kind of insight to its viewers, many of whom agreed with her measured and honest opinions, which were delivered along with some cracking one-liners. But sadly, ratings continued to fall.

When Coleen Nolan left the show in March, she was swiftly followed by Kate Thornton and Zoe Tyler, prompting viewers to come to the conclusion that *Loose Women* was in dire straits.

The Daily Mail reported that a mere 700,000 viewers were tuning in to watch the ITV show by June 2010 – half of BBC One's low budget time-slot rival *Bargain Hunt*.

Two months later it appeared Sarah had a decision to make. Her other commitments – including other TV appearances, her new show and tour and the scripting and filming of her own TV show – were taking up more and more of her time.

She began negotiations with the studio bosses, who had decided on a huge revamp of the show's format, which viewers were starting to call 'stale'. Carol Vorderman and Sally Lindsay were asked to join the show, in an attempt to breathe new life into it. Should she stay with an ailing programme? Or should she leave to concentrate on her own rising stardom?

The answer was obvious. On 3 August 2011, she appeared for the last time as a presenter on the show.

CHAPTER 21

On the Sofa with
P Diddy

'I couldn't hold it in for five years, no...'

In early 2011, Sarah made a television appearance that the celebrity world would be talking about for years to come. It was also the moment that TV bosses began to animatedly discuss Sarah's possible future as the host of her own show.

On 21 January, she was invited to appear on Graham Norton's fabulous and ever so slightly filthy, self-titled BBC One chat show, alongside P Diddy and Vince Vaughn. It must have seemed an unlikely trio – a Geordie comic, a ridiculously rich rapper and a Hollywood actor. But the combination would eventually prove compelling television.

Sarah was dwarfed as she sat between the two towering A-listers, but she was remarkably unfazed by their celebrity status. She listened politely as they each talked about their careers and recent successes. Then Norton turned to ask her a question and Sarah began to speak about her boyfriend and their relationship. P Diddy looked bored and hid behind his huge sunglasses, while Vaughn nodded and smiled, trying to understand her thick accent.

'We try doing date nights,' Sarah told them all. 'To get things… you know… moving. We went out for a lovely curry, put a DVD on, but then half way through the film we got a bit… you know… frisky – things started getting a little bit hot.'

Vaughn looked amused and raised his eyebrows at Norton, while Diddy just sat back and continued trying to look cool.

'We'd obviously forgotten that we'd had a curry a couple of hours before that,' she went on, as Norton began to look a bit grossed out. He obviously thought he knew where Sarah was going with her story, but the truth was he had no idea how far she would take her tale.

'Nevertheless he went "downstairs",' she went on, making a fairly obvious insinuation.

At this point, Diddy almost pricked up his ears. Surely she didn't mean what he thought she meant? Sarah clarified, 'I don't mean in case I wanted a glass of water…'

The audience giggled, and Vaughn, a little bit embarrassed, said: 'Yeah, we know what you mean. Was this pre-shower, post shower, during shower?'

'After shower, I'm not a pervert,' Sarah shot back, as Diddy stayed silent, trying to rise above the dirty chat. 'So we're keeping it fresh,' nodded Vaughn, gamely joining in.

'Yes, and, er, he went "downstairs", and er, it was fun. It was all going so well and I realised I could – I'm sorry, there's no nice way of saying this, I apologise in advance – I could feel a fart brewing…'

Diddy's cool exterior melted instantly. His mouth fell open and his eyes nearly popped out of his head. He actually couldn't believe the woman sat next to him was discussing farting during sex on television.

Norton began to rock with laughter, pointing at the stunned rapper. 'Your face!' he gasped through his giggles. Sarah started laughing too as finally Diddy cracked a small smile. 'Now who's learning?' she told him cheekily, before carrying on with her tale – with Diddy and Vaughn now a very captive audience.

'I didn't really know what to do, so I did a similar thing to in the film *Rainman* – I started going, "Uh oh, uh oh"… And he just carried on, because as he told me afterwards, he thought I was doing an impression of Beyonce.'

The audience began to applaud wildly, and even Diddy gave up posing sternly and began to chuckle. 'Did you manage to hold it in till after it was over?' Vaughn asked, clearly egging her on.

'I managed to hold it in, you'll be pleased to know. We've got safe words and stuff now – it's good to have safe words. Even if it's, "I need to fart!" It can be blunt, it doesn't need to be coded.'

'But the other thing is,' Vaughn added, feigning seriousness, 'You guys have obviously gotten close if you are that comfortable with each other – but there is still room to grow when you "let it go"…'

'Oh I mean absolutely,' Sarah said. 'That's the next stage I think.' Vaughn and Sarah made a good double act as they continued to discuss the virtues of farting as intimacy. 'Maybe save it, for if you wanna give him that gift?' he asked.

Sarah nodded. 'Maybe if it's an anniversary or something?'

'Don't do it with every man, save it for someone special?' added the actor.

'Oh absolutely, that's a good tip. Thank you,' replied Sarah.

Norton looked on in amazement as Diddy finally entered the conversation, probably wary of the fact that he had been silent for so long. 'I have a saying that you can't really trust a woman till she's farted in front of you,' he offered.

'That's a great saying,' said Sarah. 'You could get badges with that on. They'd probably sell on your website.'

It was impossible to tell whether Diddy knew that Sarah was teasing him, but he added: 'If she can hide a fart, you don't know what else she can hide. I'll tell you where it comes from: 'When you've been with a girl for five, six, seven years, and I'm like: "You don't fart?" And I know she farts…'

Sarah nodded encouragingly as he continued: 'If she can hide a fart from me, what else is she hiding from me?'

'You go through phases, don't you?' Sarah said, still teasing the mega star. 'Where you don't do it in front of each other and then you do it.'

'Yeah but I've been with her for five years though, you know,' said Diddy. Sarah put on a look of shock in preparation for her punchline: 'No, I couldn't hold it in for five years,' she said, shaking her head.

It was a masterful appearance. Diddy and Vaughn had come on the show to plug a new album and film, and had no idea they would be taken down to Sarah's laddish level. It must have come as a shock to them both, as they clearly had no prior knowledge of who the blonde bespectacled women between them was.

A lot of people would have been a little star struck, but not Sarah. She shocked and surprised the world-famous pair, and practically took over hosting duties from Norton as she drew them into her story. Essentially, Sarah got Mr Cool himself – P Diddy – to talk about farts on TV. It was a triumph, and one that certainly got her noticed by the show's execs.

'Americans aren't very rude on their telly,' she explained to *The Mirror* soon after. 'You'd never get them talking about that kind of stuff on Letterman. I just decided to talk to P Diddy like he was normal. That was a big turning point, as a lot of people who weren't aware of me, became aware of me. The experience was ridiculous but I loved it.'

The paper went on to report that a well-placed TV source had told them: 'BBC bosses were impressed by the way Sarah handled being on the show. She was sat between P Diddy and Vince Vaughn and yet was still the most entertaining guest that night.' It was high praise indeed.

Two days later, Sarah travelled to London's O2 Centre for the British Comedy Awards. It was the first time she had been nominated for an award at the prestigious ceremony, and for Sarah, it proved just how seriously she was being taken by the industry.

Celebrating the best of the entertainment industry from the previous year, the British Comedy Awards has been recognising comic talent since 1990. Jonathan Ross has presented the ceremony since 1991, only missing a year in 2008 following the Russell Brand/Andrew Sachs radio disaster.

Sarah had, in fact, been nominated for two awards: Best Female TV Comic and Best Female Breakthrough Comedy Artist. The comedy world had been rightly impressed with her recent TV appearances and stand-up shows, especially since she was a relative newcomer to the scene.

Sadly, on the night, Sarah was beaten to both awards. Jo Brand walked away with Best Female TV Comic, while Breakthrough Artist went to Sam Spiro. It was an entertaining evening, but Sarah would be forgiven for feeling a little disappointed at the loss. However, she was in high spirits when she appeared on *Loose Women* a few days later to discuss the event. In fact, she burst out laughing when she told her fellow panellists that she didn't win either award.

Carol McGiffin was sympathetic and told her she'd been 'robbed'. 'Yes, yes, that's the response, carry on,' Sarah said warmly, before explaining how she had reacted to the loss on the night. 'They want to see your response when you've lost, and they bring a camera right up to your face, so I ate a creme egg whole – cause that's my equivalent of like downing a whole glass of wine!' Everyone laughed as she re-enacted stuffing her face with the chocolate treat. 'Oh yeah, I'm really happy for her…'

But although it must have been a disappointment, Sarah was far too busy to be down for very long. As usual she was working hard on her new show, which she would perform at Edinburgh in the summer, and she was regularly appearing on *Loose Women*, and a variety of other panel shows.

In March, Sarah gave her fans a rare serious glimpse into her past, when she was invited to talk about her favourite reads for BBC Two's *My Life in Books*. She was suffering slightly from a cold as she sat next to former *EastEnders* baddie Larry Lamb and talked about the books that she felt marked out the most important moments in her life.

She reminisced about her school days, with a little help from her first choice, *Daphne's Book*, by Mary Downing Hahn. 'It's about a little girl with glasses, who struggles to make friends,' she explained to the show's host, Anne Robinson. 'It was only when I was asked to choose my five books that I realised how incredibly autobiographical it was. It's about a little girl who struggles to make friends cause she's quite bookish, and she's forced to make friends with another little girl when they do a school project. The other girl's quite popular and they both learn things about each other.'

Robinson said: 'It wasn't exactly your childhood though was it? Because they were in America and you were in Newcastle…'

'Yeah but nerds look like nerds across the world, don't they?' Sarah replied a little sadly, though she got a laugh from the audience.

Robinson showed the audience a picture of Sarah as a child, beaming in a school photograph. With her huge glasses, tight curls and dungarees, she was a very cute 'nerd' indeed.

Another choice for Sarah was the book she had read after her divorce – *Coach Yourself: It's Your Life: What Are You Going To Do With It?* by Anthony Grant and Jane Greene.

'It's unashamedly self-help – heroically self-help,' said Robinson. 'Yes but it's quite aggressive,' said Sarah. 'I think that's why it caught my eye, it wasn't namby pamby. I think

I was probably looking for inspiration, just wandering around in a bookshop…'

Sarah never actually finished the book, a fact she said proves that it had done its job – by making her enact changes in her life almost instantly. When she picked it up on the shelf to prepare for the interview she found a post-it note on page 18 – that was as far as she had got.

But she had dipped in and out of it at other points, and had chosen a particular passage to read out to the audience – one of the life-changing tales that she had been inspired by. 'Angela became a professional actress at the age of 50,' she read. 'She managed to break into an overcrowded, insecure and uncertain profession, long after most people would have even thought of it. At 49 she auditioned for the Royal Academy of Dramatic Arts, and with a little help from friends and acquaintances, she had her first professional job at 50. She went on to have a successful career on stage and TV, appearing in London's West End with Alan Alder.'

When Sarah finished reading, she was smiling. Robinson began to mock the book, but Sarah was firm. 'It depends whether you see it as inspirational – whether your glass is half empty, or half full, Anne, which I expect you're the former… It's about realising that you can do anything.'

It was obviously a very personal realisation, and one that had changed her life significantly. By sharing the book with others, she hoped to herself inspire people to go out and do great things. 'I like to be inspired. Even though I've got a really nice life now, I think you can always make it a little bit better,' she told Anne, to justify why she would recommend the book over all her other choices.

Sarah's three other choices were *The Vagina Monologues*, by Eve Ensler, *The Weeping Tree* by Audrey Reimann, and *Forever*, by teen favourite Judy Blume. If you'll forgive the pun, her book choices spoke 'volumes' about her personality. The show was a rare insight into the serious and intelligent woman who ultimately lies behind her funny and seemingly bullet-proof exterior.

Barely a week later, Sarah was back to her hilarious self, travelling all over the country for the second half of her sell-out *Chatterbox* tour. Reviews began to appear again in local papers everywhere, praising the show but disappointing those who hadn't booked well in advance. 'She plays Warrington tonight,' said the *Liverpool Echo*, 'but if you haven't got a ticket then bad luck, because that show is deservedly sold out too.'

At the Bloomsbury Theatre in London, Sarah made room for some extra special guests – the TV crew who were filming her for the forthcoming *Chatterbox Live* DVD.

'When I go out for the evening, I like to know when it'll be over and I can finally take my bra off,' she told the London audience, before mocking herself for having a full-blown 'cake shelf', where most women's 'muffin top' should be.

'The quips and revelations made the evening fly by and soon it was half past 10, when Sarah could break out of her prison and take that bra off,' joked the *Bournemouth Echo* in their review of her performance at The Tivoli Theatre.

Up and down the country *Chatterbox* was a success. And in London – where she regularly went to film her panel show spots, she continued to be well received. In April she appeared on *Opinionated* again, this time with Ross Noble.

In June she debuted on ITV's *Odd One In*, with Stephen Mulhern, and in July she began appearing regularly on *8 Out of 10 Cats*.

Sarah also got to put the lessons she had learnt from her first marriage to good use on *The Marriage Ref*, a new show on ITV. Hosted by Dermot O'Leary, it featured a panel of celebrities refereeing arguments between couples.

Sarah gave advice to Elena from Chingford, whose husband Tony was sick of her trying to make him eat vegetables; Chris from Cardiff who'd had enough of his wife Gillian's obsession with buying bedding; and Sonia from County Durham who was desperate for her hubby Shaun's obsession with the Chuckle Brothers to end. It must have been an odd show for her to work on, considering she had long since lived alone – precisely to ward off any such minor arguments. But it meant she was brilliantly impartial, and she featured in four of the show's seven episodes.

It was a lot of work, especially since Sarah was preparing for yet another Fringe Festival. But as ever, she was diligent and hard-working, giving her best every time she appeared on stage or screen. Her work ethic was phenomenal – and it was soon to be highly rewarded.

CHAPTER 22

A Thoroughly Modern Millican

*'I love my life and I never imagined it would get as good as this.
I get paid to make people laugh – how good is that?'*

Sarah's *Chatterbox* tour had been such an outright success
that her growing fan base must have been waiting,
telephones in hand and fingers on keyboards, for her to
announce a second one.

Because when it was announced she would be going on the
road a month after the forthcoming 2011 Fringe, once again
the tickets were sold out in hours. Initially a 100-date run,
the speed at which its tickets were sold was phenomenal,
especially on her home turf in Newcastle. Within 40
minutes of them going on sale, everyone was gone, and
organisers immediately added a tenth night at the local Tyne
Theatre, in a vain attempt to keep up with demand.

It was a record-breaking run at the theatre. No comedian

had ever sold out 10 nights there and Sarah was chuffed to bits. 'It's ridiculous isn't it?' she told the *Newcastle Chronicle*. 'I just thought it was clearly something some people had done but I'm pleased to find out it's a record. I'm just pointlessly adding more dates to my record, just to make it harder to beat,' she joked.

It was a lot of pressure for the comic, especially since the show – *Thoroughly Modern Millican* – hadn't even had the Fringe seal of approval yet. But she'd had the same fears about *Chatterbox*, and they had since proven spectacularly unfounded.

This year, Sarah was really looking forward to Edinburgh. It would mean she would stay put for a month, which was unusual for the travelling gagster, plus she would be able to spend lots of time with Gary and her friends.

In 2011, Sarah shared her digs with fellow Fringe comediennes Juliet Meyers and Sally-Anne Hayward. Meyers was in town for her show, *I am Spartacus*, at The Assembly Rooms, while award-winning Hayward was performing her lunchtime show, *Don't Judge Me*.

Both comics have a very similar style to Millican, so it was easy to see how the trio had become firm friends over the years. Hayward in particular was a fellow master of observational humour, focusing on dead-end jobs, annoying parents and the joys of living alone.

Sarah packed up her slippers and her favourite mug and travelled to Edinburgh for the mammoth month-long festival. On her first night, Sarah and her flatmates had sausage and mash for tea – a tradition that had started a few years before and now had become a ritual.

The town was already buzzing about her and she was being touted as one of the biggest names at the festival, which strangely surprised her. 'People say, "you are one of the big hitters this year", but all it really means is a lot of the really big names aren't going,' she told *The Daily Record*, who immediately said she was doing herself a huge disservice by the comment.

They weren't wrong. Yet again Sarah had sold out her Fringe run, a feat made even more impressive by the fact that she would this year be appearing at The Assembly Hall.

For *Chatterbox* she had been at The Stand, an impressive location that held 150 audience members. Now, just a year later, she was at The Assembly Hall – which seats an incredible 840 people each night.

It wasn't the biggest venue she would ever play, but it was a definite rise up the pecking order. And she'd even had to add four more dates at the Edinburgh Conference Centre, to keep up with the voracious appetite for her stand-up. 'It feels nice to know I've got an audience because very few people going to Edinburgh know that,' she told *The Record*. 'What I like is it shows progression. I won Best Newcomer, then had my difficult second album, which actually went well and got good reviews, and then for my third show last year I was up for the main award, which felt like I had gone from being good for being new to just being good. That's all you ever want, to just be learning and getting better.

'It means if the show is rubbish thousands of people will hate you, instead of hundreds, so you have to make sure it's doubly good. I don't want to let anyone down. I want them to go away thinking, "that was great, I really enjoyed it".'

If comedy was the new rock and roll, then Sarah was definitely morphing into Mick Jagger. There was no longer any doubt: she was famous. But she still couldn't quite get her head around it. 'I still find it a bit odd,' she revealed. 'People have always been really nice and supportive and I appreciate it but I am not a massively tactile person. I don't want to get a wipe out after I shake somebody's hand but I also don't want to hug every single person I meet. So it's trying to get a balance between that. It doesn't feel normal and I don't know if it ever should.' Arriving on stage each night to a dramatic *X Factor*-style theme tune, it felt like Sarah was musically proclaiming this disbelief at her new celebrity status.

Loosely based on Sarah's self-proclaimed 'risk-averse nature', *Thoroughly Modern Millican* centered around a childhood memory of going to the funfair. Some people are go-getting bumper cars, she claimed, while others are more cautious dodgems. 'Exciting is when you start a new tea towel,' she quipped, after telling the audience she believed she was firmly in the dodgem camp. 'Live life to the full, that's what it's all about!' she said, rousingly – before undercutting herself with a perfectly timed: 'No it isn't.'

She discussed drugs, saying she'd never taken them and preferred a Twix or a cake. 'I did have an apple the other day,' she said with an air of mock adventure, reinforcing her well-cultivated image of an exercise-shy cake-lover.

Her friendly inquisitive style was still very much in evidence, suggesting that fame most definitely hadn't gone to her head. Revealing more intimate secrets of her domestic life, she asked the audience for some of theirs in return –

such as any obsessive quirks they might have. One woman admitted that she had checked under the bed ever since watching a particular episode of a crime drama. 'What would you do if you found a man under your bed?' she asked the woman, and listened to the whispered response. It was comedy gold and she repeated it to the audience: 'Oh, you're a lesbian so you don't know?'

Once more, Gary didn't get off lightly, as she discussed his snoring and sexual practices. The audience laughed hysterically when she confessed that the custard jug at her local carvery had got her juices flowing on one of their dates. 'Get in the car,' she'd breathlessly told Delaney. 'And bring the custard…'

The show was unremittingly saucy but rarely crude, a fact that made some of her more risky jokes infinitely more palatable. 'I like swearing,' she admitted at the beginning of each show. 'And anyone who doesn't like it can f**k off.'

One of the other questions she asked the audience was: 'What's the strangest thing you've ever used to wipe you bum with?'

'A sock,' shouted one person.

'A sandwich!' admitted another.

'A pantyliner,' came another offering.

'That was my only period joke and it wasn't even mine,' she giggled.

'I love you!' shouted one man in the audience. She asked him to repeat what he'd said, and added: 'I heard it the first time, I'm just really needy…'

It was another great show, although many found Millican's decision that she is a dodgem oddly incongruous with her history. After all, it had been a brave decision to quit her job and focus on a career in comedy. She couldn't have predicted the success she would have but she chose to take the risk anyway – much more of a bumper car mentality than a meek and mild dodgem.

'With Cheryl Cole no longer crying perfect tears on *The X Factor*, the path is clear for Millican to become the nation's Tyne sweetheart,' wrote *The Metro*. '*Thoroughly Modern Millican* is another filthy-minded and frequently hilarious ramble through personal and relationship foibles that trades heavily on her natural warmth and ability to tease confessions out of the audience… In Millican's own words, it's "champion".'

'The theme for Sarah Millican's latest show is a gift for critics – it's all about how she's risk-averse,' wrote comedy website *Chortle*. 'Because her comedy is rarely, if ever, going to take a chance, being based so firmly in homely, comfortable domesticity. Equally, there's no gamble in buying a ticket; you can be guaranteed a solid hour of charming anecdotes, easily identifiable situations, and the odd pun, all accompanied with a saucy self-deprecation. It's that certainty that means in just four short years she's become one of the biggest acts on the Fringe.

'This adept offering is perfect for the dodgems; a trusted and proven hour sure to generate if not "uncontrollable" smiles, but plenty of grins and the odd hearty chuckle. Leave the bumper cars to fling themselves to the more obscure corners of the Fringe, and the very real possibility of disappointment you will never get with Millican.'

With the rave reviews rolling in once more, Sarah relaxed

into her fourth Fringe experience. She found new places to have late night pots of tea with her friends and larked around with her flatmates. She even punched one of them in the head and explained: 'She was wearing a hard hat we found at our flat.' She sang *Summer Nights* in the cobbled streets while stone cold sober one night, and watched as much of the other comedy offerings as she could, picking out Michael J Dolan and Tim Key as being among the most memorable.

Having Gary around was both a joy and nerve-racking. She had laughed uncontrollably when he stole a poster of her without realising someone had drawn a moustache on it, but was nervous when performing in front of him – especially since her *Would I Lie To You* pal Ronnie Corbett was in the audience that night too.

One a rare day off Sarah found herself co-hosting the *Radio 2 Arts Show* with Penny Smith, for a special edition being broadcast live from a tent at the Fringe. Penny was pleased to have Sarah – such a great fan of the festival – with her on the show and it was a chance for Sarah to talk about what headlining at the festival really meant for her.

'My whole year revolved around the Fringe,' she told Penny. 'I have sleepless nights in September because I haven't thought of a title for the next one. Then in February I do my first preview and then I work constantly – doing other things – but on trying to make my show as good as it possibly can be. Then you come up here, you stick your head above the parapet and you hope that people might like it. It's like nothing else, I absolutely love it. I can't imagine not doing it.'

The duo chatted incessantly, obviously enjoying each other's company, before getting back to the topic of the day. 'We're not doing very well, are we,' laughed Penny. 'We haven't talked about Edinburgh and what we're doing. We are interviewing loads of fantastic people.'

They made a great pair, chatting to Tim Vine, actor Julian Sands and beatboxer Shlomo. Shlomo may have become a phenomenon in the human beatboxing world, but he was still amazed by Millican's incredible horn impression, which he asked her to teach him.

As the Fringe came to an end, it was once more time to announce the festival's winners. Strangely, Sarah missed out on a main nomination – but she was honoured to have one of her gags voted into the top 10 best jokes of the Fringe, an accolade awarded by digital channel Dave.

Comedian Nick Helm won the prize overall, while veteran entertainer Paul Daniels won the wooden spoon award for the worst joke of the festival, with: 'I said to a fella: "Is there a B&Q in Henley?" He said, "No, there's an H, an E, an N, an L and a Y".' It was a dubious honour, but Daniels seemed pleased.

The top 10 were:

Nick Helm: 'I needed a password eight characters long so I picked Snow White and the Seven Dwarves.'

Tim Vine: 'Crime in multi-storey car parks. That is wrong on so many different levels.'

Hannibal Buress: 'People say "I'm taking it one day at a time". You know what? So is everybody. That's how time works.'

Tim Key: 'Drive-Thru McDonalds was more expensive than I thought... once you've hired the car...'

Matt Kirshen: 'I was playing chess with my friend and he said, "Let's make this interesting". So we stopped playing chess.'

Sarah Millican: 'My mother told me, you don't have to put anything in your mouth you don't want to. Then she made me eat broccoli, which felt like double standards.'

Alan Sharp: 'I was in a band which we called The Prevention, because we hoped people would say we were better than The Cure.'

Mark Watson: 'Someone asked me recently – what would I rather give up, food or sex. Neither! I'm not falling for that one again, wife.'

Andrew Lawrence: 'I admire these phone hackers. I think they have a lot of patience. I can't even be bothered to check my OWN voicemails.'

DeAnne Smith: 'My friend died doing what he loved ... Heroin.'

When the festival was over, Gary drove Sarah and her luggage back home to Manchester. She was exhausted, and grateful to have booked a few weeks off before she was set to embark on her exciting second tour. But she was also a little sad. She wouldn't perform at Edinburgh again for another two years, as she had decided to miss the festival in 2012.

Sarah was planning to give herself a well-earned break from the summer extravaganza, to give herself time to concentrate on other aspects of her comedy career. 'I might grow some tomatoes and paint a wall,' she told journalist Emma McAlpine. 'I'm calling it nesting. Even though I won't be having any kids, I'll be building a nest.'

She still however, planned to go up to the Edinburgh Festival to support all her comedy friends. 'I'll still go and take people out for lunch who are crying because there's a lot of upset. A lot of people on the brink of... something. If you can just run in with your arms and a hug you might save their show that night. Or their sanity!'

For the first two days back at home she didn't leave the house. 'I'm focusing on relaxing and catching up on sleep,' she wrote in her blog. 'I've only had one bath... and no showers. I disgust myself. F**k knows when I'll put a bra on again. I've spent a lot of time in a nightie that makes me look like Bubbles DeVere. It's so comfy, if a little tent like.'

She arranged a few lunches out with friends and enjoyed having nothing in particular to do, which was a rare treat. She discovered new local cafes, nurtured an addiction to *The Great British Bake Off*, and did a few domestic chores, like buying a bedside lamp so that she could enjoy reading Tina Fey's new biography. 'I've slept a ridiculous amount, eaten the same dinner four days in a row, and eaten twice at the same restaurant where sausage and mash is listed as a starter,' she wrote, before realising a week later that she still hadn't unpacked her Edinburgh suitcase.

'That is one of the joys of living alone,' she mused. 'No one but me to climb over the massive open suitcase in the hallway and I can even do it in the dark now. Some people would consider it lazy to not have unpacked yet, but compare it to the fact that my fake mini Christmas tree is still in the spare room, fully erect, fully decorated including lights, so that when December comes I can just plug it back in. Lazy, or Brilliant?'

Sarah also took a few days to go on a mini break with Gary. 'We can sing our silly songs and just be daft with each other. Planning days around meals and never wearing a watch. That's my kind of holiday,' she wrote in anticipation of the break away.

In September 2011 Sarah embarked on her tour of *Thoroughly Modern Millican*. She was conscious that it would be a long stint, especially since she kept adding dates to keep up with demand. She wouldn't finish until the following May, but this time she at least had a tour manager. 'Last year it was just me driving everywhere, so it's been really nice to have some company,' she told one journalist. 'He makes sure all the lighting's right so I can concentrate on the show. I would say it's like having my dad there but he's the same age as me!'

In an interview with *The Sun*, she revealed that she darkened the room during the gigs to encourage the audience to share their sex-related secrets. 'I always make sure the room is really dark so I can't see them, which makes them happier to join in when I ask them to talk about sex,' she explained. 'Because it's dark they know I won't recognise them in the street afterwards, so I can't run after them saying: "You're a bit of a slag, aren't you love?"'

It was clear that an awful lot of hard work went into her 90-minute shows, which involved a lot of improvisational comedy as well as her scripted gags. But she still had time to feature on a few panel shows on her rare days off. In October she appeared once more on *Would I Lie to You*, and this time revealed a very personal story about touring life. The other guests – David Mitchell, Bill Oddie and Frank Skinner – would have to decide if it was true.

'I once wet myself in a car, and then blamed it on my friend's dog,' she told everyone.

'I'm willing to believe it,' said host Mitchell, before asking why she had done it. 'Because I needed a wee in a car,' Sarah said bluntly, giving nothing away.

Rob Brydon admitted that he had once urinated into a litre bottle of Volvic on the Severn Bridge, while Skinner agreed he'd had a similar experience. 'The problem was I had a bottle of water, and I had to drink the water,' said Brydon. 'My body was saying, "no, no more water!" It was a terrible cyclical thing, no sooner had I got it down it was out again.'

'So basically apart from me this is a commonplace occurrence,' joked Mitchell. 'Essentially, lavatories are just for me.'

Sarah explained that she'd had to take the car for valeting soon after, and it was there that she blamed the strange odour on the dog.

Skinner was unconvinced. 'I think Sarah is the kind of strong, independent woman who would step out of the car, stride over to the hard shoulder, and just go,' he said.

But Bill Oddie said he believed the tale, and he was absolutely right. It was hardly surprising – the amount of time Sarah spent on the road while she was touring meant that she must have been caught short once or twice in her life.

The day after the episode aired, the BBC made an announcement. 'Award-winning comedian Sarah Millican has landed her own series on BBC Two,' read the statement. '*The Sarah Millican Television Show* will be a mix of Sarah's unique and brilliant stand-up, with some special guests along the way.'

The six-part series would be filmed in front of a live studio audience at the new BBC Northern hub, MediaCityUK, early the next year. Based in Salford, it was appropriately close to her Manchester home.

The show would be a joint venture between Sarah's newly formed production company – Chopsy Productions – and So Television, Graham Norton's successful business.

Her brief sofa time with P Diddy had been very lucrative indeed… 'I am thrilled to be making a series for BBC Two,' Sarah said in her own statement. 'So thrilled that I do little claps every time I think about it.'

Alan Tyler, BBC executive for entertainment commissioning, added: 'Sarah Millican and So Television feels like a bit of a dream team. Sarah is one of the UK's funniest comedians and we are delighted to bring her first TV series to audiences on BBC Two. She is a truly unique combination of wit, warmth and killer punch lines. Sarah is in great hands with So Television who are one the foremost entertainment producers in the UK.'

It was the moment Sarah – and her thousands of fans – had been waiting for. She would be hosting her own show, even though she would have to wait until March before it would air. For her fans it must have felt like a lifetime. For Sarah, she must have wondered how on earth she would fit it into her bursting schedule. But as her father had often told her, there's no such word as 'can't'.

CHAPTER 23

The Queen of Comedy Rocks with Laughter

'I hope those bullies have all got their tellies on now…'

In December Sarah took time out from her tour to travel to the LG Arena in Birmingham, and perform a one-off stand-up routine at the Rock with Laughter event. Put on annually in the Midlands, it combines top comedy acts and live music for a show that many Midlanders view as their Christmas tradition.

There were plenty of jokes and toe-tapping tunes for the 14,000 members of the audience, and Sarah was perfect for the line-up – *The Guardian* had once written of her: 'She can make a room rock with laughter…'

Sarah's pal Graham Norton was responsible for introducing all the acts, which included Jimmy Carr, Dara O'Briain, 10cc, singer Gabrielle and 90s crooner Marti Pellow. Sarah covered an array of subjects, from Twitter and exercise DVDs, to her almost obsessive love of Twix bars, while Dara shared his hilarious experiences of being a stay-at-home dad.

But the show was interrupted half way through, by a live link up to an entirely different event happening in London on the same night: The British Comedy Awards. Sarah had been nominated for King or Queen of Comedy, but after missing out on an award last year, she didn't think for a second that she would win. So when Dara O'Briain approached her backstage with the massive award in his hand – followed by a camera crew – she was overwhelmed.

She had beaten off stiff competition for the award, with nominees including Miranda Hart, Jo Brand, David Mitchell, Graham Norton and Jack Whitehall. The winner had been voted for by the public, which made it extra special for Sarah. She may have been shocked, but her colleagues in Birmingham weren't surprised in the least.

After a year that had seen her complete a nationwide sell-out tour, embark upon another, secure her own BBC2 show and become a regular face on the UK's top comedy TV shows, Sarah had ascended to become one of the nation's best-loved comedians.

A few moments earlier, Barbara Windsor and Danny Baker had got on stage at the comedy awards to announce the winner. The audience had looked around, trying to spot the nominees, to catch a glimpse of their surprised face when they won.

'This year's king or queen of comedy is…' Danny had said, opening the envelope for Barbara to read the winner: 'Ah, the people have a new queen – Sarah Millican!' The audience whooped and clapped, as camera footage of a very surprised looking Sarah appeared on the screen. She was close to tears and fanned her face with her hands to fend them off. 'Cry, cry for God's sake,' teased Dara, while handing her the award. Jimmy Carr suddenly appeared by Sarah's side, looking confused – he had no idea what was going on. 'She's won Queen of Comedy,' Dara explained, before turning to the camera and joking: 'Which is funny because both Jimmy and I blew her off stage tonight.'

Sarah giggled before fighting Dara for the microphone. 'Cor, thanks very much,' she said, when she'd finally wrestled it off him. 'Thank you to everybody,' she said, trying to regain her composure. 'Thank you to my agent, my family and my boyfriend and to everybody who voted for me, I'm so thrilled, and I've just had to put my cup of tea down and I'm going to cry any minute, thank you very much.'

It was clear it was a crowning moment for the hard-working comic. In a mere seven years she had embarked on and risen to the top of a brand new career – one that is notoriously difficult to even survive in. As the applause rang out, Sarah tried to take it all in. She had made it.

The following day, her smile was beaming out from every newspaper and her phone was ringing off the hook with interview requests. Her Twitter and Facebook pages were flooded with praise.

But as well as the kind congratulations from well-wishers, Sarah was shocked to also receive some startling abuse from a group of online haters. It was her first real experience of the 'trolls' who spread venom and misery indiscriminately all over the web, and she was not impressed. But the thick-skinned Geordie took it all in her stride, treating the trolls in exactly the same way she had tackled her bullies as a child.

She told her Facebook followers: 'Just a little note to say I've done some tidying on this page. 99 per cent of you who post are lovely and polite, but for the remainder, if you want to bitch about me, I will delete and block you. My page, my rules. Ta ta for now.'

Two days later she was still being targeted, and decided to use humour to cope with the nastiness. 'Have started blocking the daily trolls while having a sh*t. Seems appropriate.' It was an example of Sarah's unsinkable attitude. Her rapid rise to fame has been a way of standing up to the nasty, the treacherous and the faithless; to tell them that she can live without them, outgrow them and eclipse them.

The world was now laughing with her, not at her. If childhood bullies, a heart-breaking ex-husband and the tough world of stand-up couldn't destroy her, there was absolutely no way a few bitter, anonymous cowards would even break her stride.

Besides, Sarah had far too much to celebrate. She'd just received word that sales for her *Chatterbox* DVD had passed the 150,000 mark, smashing the previously held record for a female comic's DVD sales.

It was an astonishing achievement, made more so by the fact that it had only been on sale for a month. It had been released in late November, alongside a whopping 35 other stand-up comedy DVDs, all competing for a share of the lucrative Christmas market. The record had been set a decade earlier by French and Saunders, and since then no other female had even come close to breaking it.

The French and Saunders' follow-up DVD *Still Alive* sold 38,089 copies in 2008, Pam Ayres sold 25,544 copies of her DVD in 2007, while Victoria Wood had shifted a massive 48,339 copies of her Royal Albert Hall show in 2002. But Sarah's DVD – which went on to sell more than 250,000 copies in total – had literally flown off the shelves at a rate of over four every minute.

'It feels incredible to be at the heart of a major development for women in comedy,' Sarah said. Her agent, Hannah Chambers, added: 'We are extremely proud of Sarah and what she's achieved. It bodes well for other female comedians in the market and Sarah's success has certainly paved the way.'

And distributor 4DVD's product manager Jessica Scott said: 'We are over the moon that Sarah has achieved this incredible feat. Given her infectious sense of humour and her down-to-earth delivery however, we are not surprised. Sarah really seems to have captured the nation's hearts this year, as demonstrated not only by these record-breaking sales but by her being crowned The Queen of Comedy at the British Comedy Awards. Here's to another record-breaking year in 2012!'

Back on the road in the run-up to Christmas, Sarah continued her epic second tour, fuelled by the echoing laughter she heard in every venue. But as she explained to the *Newcastle Journal*, she was most looking forward to the 10 record-breaking dates she was booked for three months later at the Tyne Theatre.

Despite her recent fame, Sarah would always be a 'home girl'. Her new life was, she admitted, exciting and she would give it her all – but her family was more important than anything. 'Wherever my case is, is my home at the moment,' Sarah told journalist Gordon Barr. 'I leave it on the floor half packed, take out dirty underwear, put in clean underwear, that's it. But where my family is and my roots are, is still in the north east. I still love going back. If I'm in a café or train and I hear my accent, I love that, it makes me feel all warm and gooey inside. As soon as I hear someone talking "propa Geordie" I absolutely love it. It's where my family are so it's where my heart is. I visit them as much as I can. We sit in the house and we drink cups of tea and we put the world to rights. That's my favourite time – all together in the house where I was brought up, just chewing the fat. I love it. Absolutely.'

Despite being on tour, Sarah was also focusing on her forthcoming new show: 'It is a bit of stand-up, audience stuff and some guests. A bit of a mish-mash of those,' she explained. 'My main priority is that it is consistently funny for half an hour. It is exciting and slightly terrifying at the same time. You have to really put your all into it and make sure it is as good as it can possibly be, for if something like that fails, then I think it is harder to come back.'

Only time would tell what kind of reception she could expect from her hosting debut…

CHAPTER 24

The Sarah Millican Television Programme

'It just has to be really, really funny. I get uncomfortable if no one is laughing. I don't like it if there's not a punchline every 15 or 20 seconds.'

In January 2012 Sarah began filming the first series of *The Sarah Millican Television Programme*. It was an exciting time, especially since her boyfriend, Gary, was working with her too – he would eventually get a writing credit on the show. But she would have to wait two months to see what Britain made of it.

In the meantime, she went on the road again for the last remaining dates of her show, which would finish in May. During that time she also appeared on *Celebrity Deal Or No Deal*, raising an impressive £20,000 for her chosen charity, Macmillan Cancer Support. It was nerve-racking – especially when the banker offered her £15 and a delicious looking banoffee pie to walk away from a chance at the top prize. The banana and cream treat has always been Sarah's favourite, and it took a lot of willpower to turn the offer down!

Finally, on 8 March, the first episode of her own show was broadcast. Fans anxiously tuned in to BBC2, excited about what the half-hour slot would bring. But Sarah was worried. 'Everything's going too well,' she had told one reporter on the morning on the show. 'I'm sure there will be a power cut at 9.55pm and no one will see it.'

At 10pm – after no sign of electrical failure – Sarah's face was beamed onto television screens up and down the country…

'Hello and welcome to the *Sarah Millican Television Programme* – a show that dines at the buffet of TV while choosing to ignore the salad bar,' she began. 'I absolutely love telly and it's taught me all I know. I learnt loads about antiques from watching *The Antiques Roadshow*. I like it when they find out how much their grandmother's vase is worth and they pretend they'd never sell it. "Ooh, no, I'd never sell this vase, it reminds me too much of my nana. Hold on – twenty grand? For that much I'd even wash her ashes out of it…"'

She was sitting on a very comfy looking yellow sofa and was sporting a short blonde bob – shorter than her fans had ever seen before. And although she had to be very careful not to swear, or be too crude – a difficult task, considering the adult content of most of her stand-up – her milder jokes were still very funny.

The theme for the first episode was *Wildlife and Sex*, and with that in mind she had wildlife buff Chris Packham and sexpert Tracey Cox join her for the show – plus a very special extra guest star.

'When I was a bairn,' she told the audience, 'I was obsessed with wildlife programmes. I once asked my mum: "Did dad climb on your back to make me?" Watching wildlife programmes with family can be tricky, especially older members. The sex stuff, plus the bit where the older members of the herd is pushed out to die alone, while the younger members carry on. Bet you're glad we're not elephants, eh nana?'

The audience was pleased to be treated to a fair bit of Millican stand-up before the guests were announced. It was, after all, the reason people were watching the show. 'A 4ft child can fit into the mouth of a hippopotamus. I'm guessing whoever found that out isn't allowed to babysit anymore…'

She then headed into more risky territory, declaring that she had recently discovered that some people like animals a bit more than others: 'A survey said that 275,000 Swiss people have had sex with an animal. Which makes you wonder whether those cowbells are a rudimentary rape alarm.'

She asked the audience which animal they would most like to have sex with, and while one woman chose a lion, Sarah once more shared her love for gorillas. 'I was in Bristol Zoo last year and one definitely gave me the eye,' she said. 'I wish I knew more about animals. What I need is an expert… Please welcome a man who can tell us exactly what bears do in the woods – Chris Packham…'

Packham – the star of popular show *Springwatch* – joined her on stage, where Sarah immediately asked him: 'Why do you do *Springwatch* every year? Isn't it mostly the same?'

Packham laughed and admitted he wished he could change things up by having a tiger on the show, before joining Sarah in the proverbial gutter by saying he sometimes went a little bit 'moist' at the sight of a bird. 'I prefer the feel of feathers to say, fur, or…' '…skin?' interrupted Millican, giggling.

Packham was good fun, partly down to Sarah's wonderful interviewing technique, which she had previously used on stage to involve her audience in her stand-up routines. She got him to open up about his bird 'fetish', and his love of spiders – but when Packham said that he thought there were far too many domestic cats in the UK, Sarah was almost speechless. 'But what about all those people who put their clips on YouTube?' she asked, dismayed.

She showed Packham a series of close-up pictures of body hair, and asked him to decide whether they were man or monkey. His knowledge was impressive and he got all but one right.

The show progressed nicely. It was funny, informative and entertaining – all the main hallmarks of a good chat show. She'd even managed to talk about bestiality on TV – a dubious achievement.

'So it seems to me that dating and wildlife both involve eating, followed by shagging,' she said, once Packham had left the stage. 'The main difference being whether or not Bill Oddie is watching. Penguins mate for life but spend most of their life apart – this seems to be the secret; that and separate bathrooms. Whether I've needed it or not, there's always been someone in my life all too keen to dish out relationship advice. But to be fair to him, he's been married for 47 years.

He's not here, but we can talk to him now, via the magic of the Internet...'

Sarah announced her next guest to be her dad Philip, and he soon appeared on screen via Skype. For Sarah it was the perfect way to involve her family in her new comedy world. And she knew that Philip was funny – after all, he'd been making her laugh all her life.

Philip smiled and waved to the audience from the family home in South Shields, before recounting a story about how he had met Sarah's mum. 'Seemingly, this is what she told me,' he said in his broad Geordie accent. 'When she first saw us, I had a sticky plaster just above my nose, on my forehead, and she thought I'd been in a fight. And that I had a nice bum.'

It was immediately obvious where Sarah got her particular sense of humour from, and the audience chuckled. 'Too much information,' said Sarah. 'Had you actually been in a fight?' Philip said he hadn't and explained: 'It was a sticky plaster covering a huge, burst zit.'

'Oh, what a lovely story,' Sarah said sarcastically.

She asked her dad to share some dating advice and Philip told the audience that he had always shared his ambitions in life with his wife.

So what were his ambitions? 'All the mod cons,' he revealed. 'Televisions, dishwashers, washing machines – you name it we'd get it. Also, we'd have children...' 'I was wondering when I was going to come in,' Sarah quipped. 'After the washing machine, obviously.'

Philip was a definite hit, which was no surprise. After being the subject of so many of Sarah's jokes, he was infamous with her fans, and it was a rare treat to actually 'meet' him.

Next Sarah chatted to Tracey Cox, the famous sex expert, and admitted she wasn't very good at flirting. With that in mind, Sarah had set up a fake cocktail party on the stage, with various actors milling around, ready for her to try out some of Cox's techniques on.

'You match your flirting to the type of guy that you're going to be flirting with,' Cox explained. 'Let's start with that gentleman.' She pointed to an older, sophisticated looking gent. 'He's sort of been around the block, so he's used to picking up signals. He's kind of sexy, so you can be sexy and sophisticated with him.'

'Okay,' said Sarah, readying herself. 'I'm going in.' She sidled up to the silver fox, elbowing one woman out of the way in the process.

'So what I'd like you to do is what's called a neck display,' coached Tracey. 'Pull your top down, showing your shoulder – it gives him a hint of what you would look like naked.' She tried to keep a straight face as Sarah exaggerated the move for comic effect. 'And then sort of like pretend to massage your neck a bit, this sort of makes your breasts look perky,' she said, before giggling.

Sarah obviously couldn't quite get the hang of it, because the man immediately walked off. And after a few more attempts at following Cox's instructions, Sarah gave up. 'You know what, I've got a really nice boyfriend and I got him by just being myself so I think I'll stick with that,' she said, to a huge round of applause. Following that, there was just enough time to thank the audience and say goodbye, before Sarah's first ever show was over…

Over the course of the next six episodes, Sarah

mischievously ribbed her guests and gently mocked almost every TV show she had ever watched.

When Noel Edmonds appeared on one episode she had to rein in the gags because he was laughing so hard at her jokes. 'For the first four questions he just laughed,' she told *The Sun*. 'I kept thinking: "Get him to say something, please". I was asking him about his beard and boxes but I had to keep a couple of questions hanging as he was just laughing. I thought: "Well this is very flattering, but we aren't going to get a good interview out of it."

She left property guru Kirstie Allsop speechless when she questioned the nature of her relationship with co-host Phil Spencer – 'Everybody thinks they are a couple, so I asked if she had ever thought, "F**k it, I'll have a go on it?" She sort of implied that it had crossed her mind...'

In the episode *Crime and Medical*, *Crimewatch*'s Rav Wilding taught Sarah how to use different things in her handbag as weapons. 'It was funny, but also useful. If you've got experts on, you might as well get a bit of useful information out of them as well as taking the mick.'

Which is exactly what she did with *Embarrassing Bodies* host, Dr Pixie McKenna, when she got her to try and explain some x-rays for the audience. Alongside the usual keys and bullets, Dr Pixie was shocked when she was shown an x-ray that showed a Buzz Lightyear doll, stuck up a man's bottom. 'I'm sure, it wasn't a Woody,' Sarah joked, leaving the good doctor speechless.

She was remarkably relaxed on each episode, considering it was her first time hosting a show. But she admitted it helped to have the audience there. She told *The Telegraph*: 'I think it's just the place I feel most at home and I understand that's a really odd thing to say. It's still nerve-racking, still terrifying for the first few minutes until I get a few big laughs under my belt, but then, I'm much more relaxed than I am off-stage. I love talking to the audience, because those are the bits that make me feel alive, like a proper comedian as opposed to a funny writer.'

It also helped to have her Dad appear each week. 'It's the most relaxed part of the show, as I know he's got my back,' she told *The Sun*. 'It's like a tea break in the middle of a panic. I know that he is funny, so he can hold the fort for a couple of minutes while I relax. When you've had a proper job in an industry where it can be dangerous, like down the pit, you don't think being on telly is scary.'

The resulting viewing figures were impressive, with Sarah (and her dad) averaging an audience of just over 1.75 million viewers per episode.

Critics were positive. One stated that Philip was definitely a bonus on the show and observed that they must be the first father and daughter comedy act in television history. Lucy Mangan, writing for *The Guardian*, said: 'I laughed many times during *The Sarah Millican Television Programme*. At first glance, Millican's is a warm, unthreatening world of gentle comedy about nanas, nighties and nature programmes but, in fact, she's an iron fist in a Marigold glove. Her deadpan asides and sudden glances to camera have a touch of Eric Morecambe and her sudden shut-downs... are things of simple beauty impossible to reproduce in print.' Lucy went on to claim she thought the format wasn't quite right yet, but: 'Once it is, hopefully television will become Millican's world and we can live in it.'

Bernadette McNulty wrote a review of the show in *The Telegraph* that summed Sarah up perfectly: 'Sarah Millican belongs to the new breed of comedians who come across as reasonably sane. By laughing at her you don't feel like you are funding any dangerous manias, personality imbalances or drink and drug problems as you do with many compulsive jokers.

'She looks like your sweet friend who has an immaculate home and always brushes her hair, but gets the laughs coming when she opens her mouth and, in that sing-song South Shields accent, says something unequivocally filthy.

'Tellingly, the guests sit behind a desk while Millican nestles among Orla Kiely cushions. But there's nothing soft about her. She's also not above a bit of gurning at the camera in the great tradition of Les Dawson. All these are hopeful signs she may not be a one-joke pony.'

Almost immediately after the first series ended, BBC2 commissioned work to begin on a second. Sarah took to Twitter to share the news, saying: 'Thrilled to report that *The Sarah Millican Television Programme* will be back for a second series.*runs around clapping and jumping*'.

She quickly released a formal statement to the media, detailing how much she had enjoyed the first series and saying that she couldn't wait to get cracking on the second, which would be broadcast in January 2013.

Everyone wanted to know whether Philip would be returning to the show, as he had collected quite a fan base following his string of appearances. 'People are constantly asking me if my dad is coming back on the next series – he is,' she told *The Mirror*. 'Before we had even told him… he had bought new shirts. Then he rang and said, "I'm not saying I want to do it, but if you want me, I've got me shirts."'

The show was the success that Sarah had hoped it would be and she promptly went on holiday to celebrate. In April, she travelled with a group of friends to the lakes in Cumbria, where she stayed in a cosy cottage.

It's actually something she admits she does regularly. 'I spend such a lot of time touring,' she says. 'So every few months I try to get away for a few days with a couple of girlfriends who are also comedians. After so many nights in hotels, a holiday is about being able to get up in the middle of the night and make some toast.'

A month later she decided to go further afield – this time with her big sister to New York. Sarah was grateful when Victoria took control of the overseas holiday. 'She took my passport and kept it safe,' she told *The Sunday Times*. 'It was like being a child again. Our day would begin when she knocked on my door and said, "You look comfy". I don't always get when people are being complimentary, but I know that "comfy" is not a compliment. Apart from that she was a good travel companion.'

Sarah was a definite 'dodgem' on the trip. 'I have this image of myself as someone who shuns all those touristy things and ventures off the beaten track,' she explained. 'With this in mind, I saw lots of shows, went up the Empire State Building and did the open-top bus tour. That's how adventurous I actually am.'

When she returned, she announced that she had been

offered yet more work – this time as a TV columnist for the *Radio Times*. Editor Ben Preston was thrilled to have her on his team. 'Sarah is that rare thing, a comedian who is genuinely warm and optimistic about life, wonderfully funny and a gifted writer. And she knows – and loves – her telly, too.'

By now her workload must have been gruelling, but her ambition – and ultimately her capability at handling it all – was no surprise. Sarah had always been a hard worker, and now she was at the top, she knew she had to keep working hard to stay there. Even if it meant she would be writing a TV show, filming, touring and now penning a column, all at the same time.

Nonetheless, it must have been both a relief and a disappointment not to be appearing at Edinburgh in the summer. It meant that Sarah could truly enjoy the experience, and she made the most of it by going to see a wide range of shows, including those of her friends Joe Lycett, Juliet Meyers and Sally-Anne Hayward.

In October, Sarah announced that a recording of her *Thoroughly Modern Millican* tour – which took in a collective audience of over 200,000 – would be released as a DVD in time for Christmas. Sarah loved the idea that a lot of her new fans would have only seen her toned-down TV persona, and would be unprepared for her much naughtier stage act. 'People will think, "Oh, we'll put it on after Christmas dinner with Nana and the bairns",' she said. 'Then they'll put it on and very quickly pause it and put the bairns to bed so they can watch it with Nana who, let's face it, knows exactly what I'm talking about.'

As 2012 drew to a close, Sarah had a lot to be happy about. With her best-selling DVD, a record-breaking tour and countless popular TV show appearances, she had everything she'd ever hoped for and so much more. She had even just bought her first house, and had moved Chief Brody in just in time for Christmas.

2013 was destined to be another very good year.

CHAPTER 25

Comedy Gold

'It's always nice when you work hard and it pays off. It hasn't really changed me, it hasn't really changed my life very much.'

The year 2012 was a year like no other for British comedians. It smashed records that in years gone by would have seemed inconceivable.

During that year it was revealed that Michael McIntyre, who only six years before had been £30,000 in debt, was the biggest-selling comic in the world. Suddenly, a Brit who told jokes for a living was earning mega bucks, outstripping even the Americans. His ticket sales from his UK gigs in 2012 equated to £21 million worth – just £1 million less than the Rolling Stones, and they had embarked on a worldwide tour. His earnings were only beaten by those of the biggest names in music in the world – Madonna and Bruce Springsteen among others.

It was unprecedented that a Brit who made their living from standing on stage and telling jokes was doing so well. Headlines that had started appearing a few years before, said it all – Stand-up Comedy was the new Rock 'n' Roll.

Michael's success did not come out of the blue. Comedians had been steadily seeing more and more success during the previous couple of years. In the 2011 figures of earnings in the entertainment industry, McIntyre was up there, but he was far from alone in earning the kind of money that most people only dream of.

In 2011, the highest-earning comic was Peter Kay, who raked in more than £20 million from ticket sales and DVDs. Also in that year, there was a surprise addition to the top 10 highest paid gag tellers – a woman. At number six was Sarah Millican, the first time a woman was ever thought to have been in the top 10 British earners for comedy in recorded history.

In 2011, according to *The Sun*, Sarah earned £1.46 million, just behind Russell Howard at £3.26 million, John Bishop at £4.98 million, Alan Carr at £5.99 million and Lee Evans at £12.9 million, as well as Peter Kay.

She might have had some way to go before she earned the same as Kay and Michael McIntyre, but her figures for 2012 were expected to be even higher. She is living in an age in which comedy gold is exactly that; an age in which, if you can make enough people laugh, you are made for life. An idea that up until recently would have been so unbelievable, it would have sent the comedians of yesteryear to the funny farm.

It is not the first time that comedy has been massive – the sort of draw that has them packing in the stands at venues around the country. As far back as the 1930s, comedians like Max Miller were huge.

The reason many people believe it happened then and it's happening now is because when times are tough – as they are in a recession – people turn to something that makes them feel better, and there is nothing better than making people laugh to cheer them up when they are down.

According to psychologists, it is a natural reaction to our need to cope with life when it gets difficult. Media expert Dr Matt Kerry told *The Sun*: 'When life is grim, we need back-to-basics comedy. The best humour is directed at the self. It's an acknowledgment of your own misery... but you're laughing at it!'

Max Miller was just one of dozens of acts which filled the theatres of the 1930s when the dole queues stretched round the block following the Wall Street Crash and the onset of the depression. At times in the 30s, the unemployment rate in parts of Britain was at 45 per cent.

But, conversely, the queues didn't just stretch round the outside of the dole office; they stretched round the theatres. Many people paid over what little they earned for a chance to watch as their so-called betters, the upper classes, being lampooned for getting them in the mess they found themselves in. They couldn't actually do anything to them, so they paid to watch others making fun of the hooray Henrys and the Bertie Woosters of the world around them who it appeared were responsible for causing their economic woes.

But then, unlike now, Max was one of the few who ended what had been a successful stage career well. Others who had also been massive during the years of plenty, when people had been clamouring to see them perform, ended their days in poverty, the few fat years failing to make up for the many leans ones later.

One act which was highly successful in the music hall era of the 1930s and early 1950s was a duo called The Western Brothers, who had audiences rolling in the aisles with their impressions of a parade of posh men. Theatregoers who went to see them couldn't stop laughing at their impressions of the upper classes, the ones they felt were at fault for the state of the country. It didn't last. The Western Brothers both died in relative poverty, one spending his final six years running a kiosk at Weybridge station.

When the next major recession happened, in the 1970s, comedy again hit highs it hadn't seen in years. The audiences for TV shows featuring Morecambe and Wise and the Two Ronnies were again testimony to the fact that people in economic down times are looking to have a laugh.

At that time, a handful of top comics became millionaires thanks to the power of television, but very few made enough to retire as happy as their acts made those who came to watch them.

Fast-forward another 30 years to the worst recession since the end of World War Two. When everyone else is having difficulty making ends meet, the top comics in the land are raking it in like never before; and this time, unlike in the 1930s or even the 1970s, they are making so much, many of them could retire tomorrow.

For stand-up comedians, the figures are mind-blowing. During his 2012 *Showtime!* tour, Michael McIntyre sold

600,000 seats at his 71 venues, with 10 sold-out nights at the gigantic O2 Arena in London's Docklands. Along with McIntyre in the comedy gallery of stellar earners of the last few years were also Ricky Gervais, who was paid so much he ended up in the *Sunday Times Rich List* with an estimated fortune of £35 million, Rowan Atkinson, who still rakes in money annually from the Mr Bean franchise to add to his £71 million fortune, and Peter Kay, whose amazing annual earnings also put him in the list at £40 million.

Less stellar, but still with stratospheric earning power, according to *The Sun*, were Steve Coogan, who made £5 million in 2010; Jimmy Carr, who also earned £5 million; Frankie Boyle (£4.5 million); Russell Brand (£4 million) and Eddie Izzard (£4 million).

In 2010, when these men were earning amazing amounts and the recession was in full swing, 24 comedians earned more than £1 million a year. The highest-paid female comic was Jenny Éclair at £600,000. In that year, Sarah Millican earned £250,000.

Many would say they deserve it. It takes many years of hard graft, trawling up and down the country, staying in miserable hotels or hostels, earning pennies, if anything, by performing in dingy pub back rooms, before most comedians get anywhere, assuming they actually do.

The average amount paid to a stand-up comic who isn't doing an arena tour or putting out a DVD is about £100 a gig. Many when they are starting out work for free. Even if they are successful enough to manage a headline tour, most would be lucky if they make more than about £40,000 a year.

The line between getting by and earning huge amounts is a fine one. It is one that many comedians feel they have a right to exploit when the opportunity comes along, as, in the past, history has shown how easy it can be for it all to slip away. But it was also this issue that led Sarah to sail closest to the sort of PR disaster that has got some other high-earning comedians badly stung.

After watching one of Sarah's gigs in Wolverhampton, a fan posted on her Facebook page that she had really enjoyed the show and if Sarah wanted to know which one she was, she said she was the one in the front row who had been videoing it.

Sarah was horrified that material people had to pay to see could end up on Youtube or somewhere else. She promptly responded by accusing the fan of theft and told her that if she was going to be so 'disrespectful', she was not going to be welcome at her gigs in future.

The subsequent row that erupted in response to her comments ended up in the newspapers and led to her being branded disrespectful herself for 'bad-mouthing' those who 'enabled' her 'to lead the life' she lived.

In the end, apart from upsetting a few fans, she largely escaped major harm to her name. Most people appreciate that comedians have to safeguard their routines if they are to continue to make a living.

The huge amounts that many comedians earn, however, is leaving them increasingly open to attack. In 2012, one of the mega earners, Jimmy Carr, was forced to backtrack after it emerged that most of his annual earnings was funnelled through a tax avoidance scheme designed to prevent him and others from paying most of it to the Inland Revenue's replacement HMRC.

It was a hot issue, as within the deepest moments of the downturn, the chief secretary to the Treasury, Danny Alexander, had branded tax avoiders lower than the worst kind of benefit scroungers. After it emerged that Carr was paying less than one per cent on his earnings, he was forced into making a grovelling apology.

It wasn't over then either, as his participation was mentioned every time the company that had set up the scheme cropped up in the news thereafter. It might not have mattered if he hadn't had a pop at tax avoiders Barclays a few months before, but he had. It was a case of those who make jokes at others expense, shouldn't be caught doing what they were making jokes about. It throws into perspective the difficulty comedians have of remaining relevant enough to continue being funny, yet taking advantage of the good times to make sure that they don't end up running a kiosk in Weybridge.

There are some who believe that all this success is a sign that a bubble is about to burst; that the good times are about to come to an end. Part of the justification for that belief stems from one of the things that has driven the rise of stand-up comedy in the last 10 years and put the comedians on the pedestal they now balance precariously on – the panel show.

After Edinburgh, the chance to appear on a panel show has for the last 15 years been the golden ticket to a comedian's success. Starting with shows like *Whose Line Is It Anyway*, *Have I Got News For You* and *They Think It's All Over* in the

1990s, dozens of comedians have been able make the move from stand-up in pubs, clubs and theatres to the mass market of television by appearing on such shows.

Because of their format, in which a series of comedians appear on a 'panel', making gags in turn about a particular subject, the TV producers who make them require a steady stream of people who can provide quick-fire laughs. In the process the comedians turn themselves into a walking advert for their own material, which, instead of requiring word of mouth from those who might have been to their show to recommend it to others, is suddenly being seen directly by millions.

In the 15 years or so since they were created, panel shows have gone from being rare but successful formulas, to one of the dominant types of programming on TV. Almost all of those who have appeared on such shows have gone on to make a lot of money. Even though they may only make a few hundred pounds from each appearance, being a regular guest on *QI*, *8 Out of 10 Cats* or *Argumental*, among others, creates an instant audience eager to hear what a comic has to say live on stage.

It is this profusion of panel format programmes that some believe will be the death of stand-up on TV. Although people still want to laugh, they will only continue to find it funny if they haven't seen or heard the gag before. With so many shows trotting out the same formula, some believe that this over exposure will end up with many people losing interest.

Another victim of the dangers of earning too much, with the recession as a probable influence, was Jonathan Ross.

Not that long ago he was tied to the BBC with a golden handcuffs deal said to be worth £6 million.

Although he was not a comedian, his shows often had a comedy element and he regularly teamed up with comics on the shows he presented. One of those was Russell Brand, who he joined on Brand's Radio Two late-night show back in 2008. When the pair thought it would be hilarious to ring up the grandfather of one of Brand's litany of conquests, *Fawlty Towers* actor Andrew Sachs, and brag down the phone, they hadn't bargained on the level of vitriol that would be unleashed.

Both lost their jobs, Ross having to take an extended period of leave from TV in Britain and Brand having to head across the Atlantic to find someone prepared to employ him regardless of his reputation.

While many found what the stars did unacceptable, the fact that they were both paid large amounts of money at the public expense almost certainly contributed to the rage felt. It was yet another sign that people were starting to feel that while comedians may be entitled to earn a reasonable amount of money to stave off poverty in later life, if they started to mock those who paid their wages, they had better watch out.

It wasn't a new phenomenon. In 1970s America, during the country's last bad recession, comedians were king. The stand-ups of the time, like Robin Williams, Richard Pryor and Bill Cosby, were among the first to make the move from the theatre to film and television. Many others began appearing on mainstream TV, on late night shows like *The Tonight Show* or *Saturday Night Live*. While these programmes were incredibly popular when they first started, eventually the audience began to tire of seeing the same old formats and increasingly similar jokes.

The comedians listed above made millions in the 1970s and 80s. With a handful making so much, soon, everyone was wondering if they could make a fortune as a stand-up. The number of comics rose and the quality of joke telling dropped. As the 1990s dawned, TV viewers who were starting to suffer the effects of that decade's recession began to yearn for something new. Seeing those who were making them laugh earn huge amounts of money began to stick in some throats. Others just weren't being funny enough. As a result, earnings began to fall.

American comics are back on ridiculous earnings, but even they have seen the amount they can earn fall again in the last few years. In 2009, Jerry Seinfeld earned $85 million (£55 million), partly off the back of his final TV series deal. In the same year, Chris Rock earned $40 million (£25 million). All in the US top 10 earned $10 million (£6.5 million) or more, including two ventriloquists.

Just a year later, the uncertainty of it all was demonstrated by how much the figures had changed. In 2010, the highest-paid comic was another ventriloquist, Jeff Dunham, whose DVDs and film appearances earned him $22.5 million (£13 million).

Most of those in the top 10 were able to take advantage of the money offered by roles in Hollywood films. With such a huge audience for laughs in the States, the fees they could earn from appearances were at the top end of anything even Michael McIntyre could earn. The tenth placed comedian, for example, Bill Engvall, could earn $100,000 per gig. But, perhaps showing how things had started to change, in 2010, Jerry Seinfeld didn't even get into the top 10, and the overall amount earned was well down on the previous year.

But, in the meantime, Sarah Millican has been on a high and taking advantage of the fact that comedy is currently literally gold. And, perhaps true to her upwardly mobile working class roots, she is adamant that she will be not one of those left working in a kiosk at the end of her career.

Shortly after the incident with the videoing fan, she made no bones about the fact that it was essential to preserve the source of her income, to make sure she didn't end up with nothing worthwhile to say.

She told *The Independent*: 'If I write a joke and it works, and it works consistently, that is gold to me. One hundred thousand people have bought tickets to see me on tour and if any of them see that and go, "Oh, I've heard this..." it's spoilt a night out. It's not just me saying, "it's my material, leave it alone".'

Talking about the huge amounts she stood to earn in the modern era she said: 'I'm aware that it does reap very good rewards, but I'm not embarrassed by that. The British newspapers' fascination with money is slightly vulgar – that rather than going, "well done, you picked yourself up from nothing and you've really made something of yourself and you worked really hard almost constantly for four or five years and drove 50,000 miles a year", which would be the American way – the British way is, "how the hell have you got that much money?" It's quite jealous and dismissive of the work.'

But, again true to her humble background, she is equally determined that she will not be changed by her new-found fortune. She told Jonathan Ross on his show: 'It's always nice when you work hard and it pays off. It hasn't really changed me, it hasn't really changed my life very much. I still shop in the same places and I still eat the same things, I think I need to upgrade a little bit, like, [but] I don't go to designer clothes shops and things like that.'

Demonstrating such typically down-to-earth northern ways of thinking, it is unlikely she'll suffer the same fate as those from an earlier depression – who ended their days struggling to make ends meet.

CHAPTER 26

Home Bird and Beyond

'I could never write an autobiography. There's nothing left – it's all on stage…'

When the second series of *The Sarah Millican Television Show* aired in January 2013, it was swiftly followed by an announcement that a third was on its way.

Sarah was now a fully-fledged television star, a comedian who could command an audience of nearly a quarter of a million on tour, and a proud cat owner. She had achieved her ambition with a steely determination – a fire in her belly that had begun seven years before when her first husband walked out on her, and had since been stoked each time she heard a crowd laugh at her witty jokes.

In late 2012 she announced her third tour, *Home Bird*, a

mammoth 86-date tour that stretched as far into the future as May 2014 and sold out, just like all her others.

So what was next for the potty-mouthed Geordie? Certainly not Hollywood, where she says they wouldn't understand a word she says. 'They'd be saying: she's lovely, but is she foreign?'

Instead Sarah's ambitions were much simpler. 'To still be doing this in 30 years' time, that's all I want, just to be constantly getting better. I just want to be constantly improving. I want to be able to play the Albert Hall and nail that, but then be able to nail a gig that's got four people in a pub who haven't paid to be there, and there's snooker and slot machines in the background… You want to make those four people wee themselves as much as the people in the Albert Hall, you know? Just to be able to turn your hand to any room and make it work. I think I'm a long way off, I think most comics are a long way off, there's only a handful that can do it. But that's the ultimate aim.'

Her other aim was to get a Nando's For Life card. 'A few high-profile comedians have got one,' she has said, dreamily. 'You can have free Nando's whenever you like, up to five people each time.'

But despite her incredible achievements Sarah has been grittily realistic about the future and never takes anything for granted – it's one of the reasons she has been so successful.

She embarked on her new comedy career with no room in her mind for failure. She worked day and night until she achieved critical acclaim, and she has approached each milestone since with the same work ethic. For Sarah, every award and every positive review was never enough. It simply spurred her on to do bigger and better things.

And if it all ended – this magnificent, glittering career she has made for herself? 'I'm very good in a call centre, so if this all goes to pot I'll just try and get back into that,' she says. 'With this soft Geordie accent I could probably get a job in the complaints department. I'm pretty good at calming people down.'

Even then it was doubtful you'd ever hear Sarah's voice on the line again, and things were only going to get better for her, personally and professionally, in 2013.

CHAPTER 27

The Best Is Yet to Come...

'I used to laugh really quietly, but I've grown in confidence. Now I don't wait for permission anymore; I just laugh.'

Sunday 12 May and the rain was taking centre stage at the 2013 BAFTA awards at the London Royal Festival Hall. The crème de la crème of television actors, reality stars, national treasures and well-known TV presenters gaily trotted up the red carpet, smiles plastered as they signed autographs, spoke to journalists and posed for the paparazzi whilst dodging the puddles. And Sarah was no exception. She was delighted to have been nominated for a BAFTA in the Best Entertainment Performance category alongside Ant and Dec, Alan Carr and Graham Norton and was excited about hitting the red carpet. 'I was thrilled. If winning is chips and gravy then being nominated is still chips,' she told the *Radio Times*. 'Lovely, lovely chips.'

She was certainly giddy with nerves as she waved to fans and spotted 'amazing people, the best in the business – writers I'd admired, actors I'd cried to and comedians who'd made me laugh so much I got a headache' - before taking part an interview with Heatworld.

'Where is your lovely dress from?' asked journalist Lucie Cave. 'Er, it's from the Trafford Centre,' giggled a nervous Sarah. 'To be honest, I'm not worried about what I am wearing, I am more worried about presenting an award. I have a job to do,' she told them. Little did Sarah realise that her dress was soon going to be what everyone was talking about. In the run up to the big event, Sarah and a pal had visited John Lewis to choose an outfit for the special ceremony. 'Fancy designer shops are out for me as I'm a size 18, sometimes 20 and I therefore do not count as a woman to them,' she later revealed in the *Radio Times*.

After Sarah tried on five dresses, she chose the one that she and her friend had 'oohed' at and that was that. She found it slightly bewildering that so many press had asked her who she was wearing but didn't think anything else of it. She had a fabulous time at the awards. She might have lost out to Alan Carr, but she did get to meet long-term TV hero, Matt LeBlanc. However, it wasn't until she was in a taxi on the way home that she realised what a hoo-ha her outfit choice had caused to the opinionated public.

'I went on Twitter and it was like a pin to my excitable red balloon,' she explained, in a touching feature for the *Radio Times* after the event. 'Literally thousands of messages from people criticising my appearance. I was fat and ugly as per usual. My dress, (the one that caused oohs in the department store fitting room) was destroyed by the masses. I cried and cried in the car on the way home. The next day I was in the newspapers pilloried for what I was wearing. I was discussed and pulled apart on *Lorraine*.'

In this heartfelt account of her experience that night, Sarah went on to explain that she wanted to apologise. 'Sorry because I thought I had been invited to such an illustrious event because I am good at my job. Putting on clothes is such a small part of my day. They may well have been criticising me for brushing my teeth differently to them.'

And the comedian wasn't going to let this vile abuse get her down and she vowed to herself the following day, when her upset turned to anger, that if she was invited to the BAFTAs again the following year she would wear that same dress. 'I felt wonderful in that dress, surely that's all that counts?' she asked readers. When she appeared on Radio 4's *Desert Island Discs* the following year she talked about the more modern form of bullying that exists on social media. 'The public, fans, nice people, realise how unimportant it is,' she told Kirsty Young. 'I was thrilled to be there [at the BAFTAs] it was so flattering. And then to be pulled apart for something so unimportant seems really odd. If I saw somebody wearing something and I thought, "oh that's brave", I wouldn't go up and tell her. And that's what Twitter and Facebook are. It's tapping somebody on the shoulder and saying; "Oh you look rubbish, you shouldn't be wearing that, you're too fat for that, you're too ugly for that." Of course that hurts.'

The following year, she did indeed get an invite back the prestigious awards as *The Sarah Millican Television*

Programme was nominated again in the same category. Sadly, she was performing her stand-up show in Buxton at the time of the ceremony so wasn't able to attend. But that didn't stop her making a point. When fellow comic Jason Manford tweeted her to ask if she was going to keep her pledge of wearing the same dress, she posted a photo of herself in the that same frock with the caption 'BAFTA dress on and almost showtime in Buxton.' The public and media loved her gutsy attitude with Metro listing '6 reasons why Sarah Millican is simply brilliant (and her BAFTA bullies should run away and hide)'.

Sarah later revealed that she had received an extraordinary response from the audience that night with the tweet, 'Well, I'm glad I didn't buy a new dress,' and then later, 'And an extra special thanks to those in my audience in Buxton last night. Your response when I walked out in my BAFTA dress choked me up.' It was a statement of power, a two-fingers-up at the fashionistas of the world who bullied and insulted her and she won. Not only was she making a statement to everyone that it shouldn't matter what you wear, it was a personal triumph for the comedian who has never been and will never be dictated to over her appearance. 'Am I funny? Yes. Do you care what I have on? No. As long as I'm covered, as long as nothing's hanging out unless I want it to hang out. I think that's enough,' was her simple yet powerful reply to the bullies.

But there was an extra special accessory she was supporting with her BAFTA dress the second time she wore it, a sparkling wedding ring! Having previously summed up her relationship with Gary Delaney, who she had been dating since 2006, by saying 'we're having a lovely time but don't believe in forever,' she announced to her fans on Twitter in a New Year message at the beginning of 2014 that they had tied the knot over the festive season.

In a post on January 3, she said; 'Thrilled to announce that @garydelaney and I got married last weekend. We are loved up and beaming. X.' It didn't take long for the messages of congratulations to come pouring through the social networking site and Sarah was inundated with well wishes. '@sarahmillican75 @garyDelaney many congratulations, little bit hurt, not gonna lie ;) x' exclaimed TV presenter Philip Schofield. Overwhelmed by the amount of congratulatory messages she had received, she put out a touching tweet from her and new hubby. 'Thanks for all the lovely messages from friends and fans alike. Bunch of smashers, you are. X'

The wedding was a simple yet personal affair and Sarah revealed some of the details of the big day when she took part in *Desert Island Discs* later that year. She told radio host Kirsty Young that, as she wasn't particularly religious, there weren't any hymns that she particularly liked so she decided to choose something less traditional – Paul McCartney's 'Frog Chorus'. As an avid listener of *Desert Island Discs*, she told Kirsty she had got the idea when she listened to actress Kathy Burke on the show. 'There was a Frank Sinatra song and it was in the order of service of a wedding she was at and it said it in the service sheet "everybody sing with gusto" and I remember listening to that and thinking how lovely, to just go "we love this song, we want all of our friends and family to sing it." How awesome would that be? So when we were planning the wedding and thinking what could we pick that everybody would sing, Gary started playing this [the Frog Chorus] so I started to laugh. Then he said, "listen to the lyrics" and I started to cry so we played this at our wedding and the whole congregation sang all the noises. We made sure all the noises were in the order of service as well and this is what we walked out of the wedding to.'

She had come a long way from her interviews in which she insisted she would never marry again, which proves how much she has grown in strength – as a person ready to face that commitment but not desire it so intently it is the be all and end all. 'I don't think a piece of paper changes your relationship,' she had previously told the Mirror Online. 'If it makes it more acceptable to others, others should butt out. I like the security of knowing I'll never be out on my ear again. I'm a whole person – I never wanted to be part of a couple in that 'my other half' sort of way' .

There was no long honeymoon in the sun however as fellow comic Gary had to embark on the 2014 leg of his *Purist* tour. The wedding was the perfect ending for the couple who had moved in together earlier in 2013 after she admitted on Alan Carr's *Chatty Man* that after seven years of living apart, the couple had finally decided to co-habit. It wasn't a decision she had rushed in to, certainly, we know her aversion to living with someone under the same roof and the strain that can put on a relationship but, as she joked, she was sick of always being the one taking the bins out. 'It's big stuff, we've been together for seven years. For so long I killed my own spiders and now somebody else kills the spiders. I just got sick of taking the bins out,' she told Alan. Sarah had been living in a rented flat up until 2012, in the heart of Manchester and during her relationship with Gary, commuting 80 miles to visit him in Birmingham which was also an endless source of gags in her routines.

But now they were living together and, as the *Daily Mail* exposed at the beginning of May, Sarah wasn't 'slumming' it in a flat anymore, she and Gary (and her two cats, Lieutenant Ripley and Chief Brody) were living in a five-bedroomed, gated mansion in Cheshire. Bought for £1.3 million in the leafy fringes of Mere, the comic's new abode had a library, conservatory and enough garage space for four cars and, according to accounts with the company that run her affairs, SM Comedy, she had earned more than £2 million since 2011. And that was only increasing. But as her mam explained to her, talking about how much you earn, even if you are a millionaire, is not cool. 'My mam is right, you should never ask how much people earn,' she told the *Daily Mirror*. 'No one wanted to know how much I was earning when I was on £9,500 at the Jobcentre.'

So within a year the couple had moved in and got hitched, and to round off a fairly wonderful 2013 even further, Sarah had featured on a prestigious list of names of the 100 most powerful women in the United Kingdom by *Woman's Hour* on Radio 4. And now she had gained further cred by snubbing the BAFTAs and wearing, shock horror, the same dress that had been vilified the previous year. This wasn't just about the dress though, Sarah knew there was so much support for her when she exposed herself about how she felt after being criticised for something she wore. This was about empowering women to be themselves and not be affected by what others think. From a situation that left her crying in the back of the car on the way home, her experience at the BAFTAs was now going to be the trigger to push her to start up her own feminist website. And that is exactly what she did. In September 2014, Standard Issue was launched and alongside journalists Mickey Noonan, Hannah Dunleavy and comedian Kiri Pritchard, the online magazine was to be a sharp, witty, irreverent magazine that championed women. 'Standard Issue will never tell you who to be, what to wear or how to look. We believe that every woman should feel empowered to be themselves. It's relatable, like a long lunch with a group of brilliant friends and it tells it like it is,' informed Sarah.

Mickey Noonan, the editor of the site also explained that the this was about reclaiming back the Internet in support of women – not being hostile towards them. 'We wanted to see what would happen if we made a magazine our way. No celebrity tittle-tattle, no photoshopping, no calorie counting, no cellulite circling. A lot of media is keen to put women into boxes but we need to do our own thing and not be told that women are only interested in certain topics.' It was a magazine for women, by women about everything and it was a big success in that Sarah and the team created something unique and didn't pander to society's narrow definition of what women are interested in. In 2016 it seemed like it was going from strength to strength with Sarah saying; 'Of all the things I've done, it's the one I'm most proud to be part of. We're creating a healthy alternative to what is generally out there.' Sadly, it wasn't making enough money to cover the costs and the team were forced to axe the website two years after it launched. 'It's sad and we're gutted,' explained Mickey in March 2017. 'But Sarah and the editorial team our amazing roster of writers and illustrators created something absolutely excellent and vital. Standard Issue came, we saw, we kicked ass. And we made thousands upon thousands of you excellent people feel great about as you got in touch and told us so.' But the team weren't going to give up and Standard Issue developed to become a magazine-style podcast with the same content but on a different platform.

As her *Home Bird* tour came to an end in 2014, Sarah was due some time off and settled into domestic life – although not as easily as she anticipated. Especially the day-to-day spousal annoyances! 'When my husband has finished in the bathroom, I go in to powder my shit and the floor is like a leisure centre changing room: all wet and pants. The sinks are swimming. He says it's just water; it will just evaporate. He is right, but still. TUT,' she reported to her Standard Issue magazine. 'And having had some time off this year and no one told me I was funny every day – I had to get used to that.'

But it was back to business in March 2015 when she announced that she would be embarking on a new tour. It would be her longest one yet, starting in October, and called *Outsider*. She would be playing 176 dates around the UK plus 9 in Australia. Having just been named the hardest-working comedian in the UK from her *Home Bird* tour in which she travelled 14,718 miles, Sarah was out to prove she was ready for even more dates, even more laughs and ready to travel half way around the world for her fans.

Outsider took its name, like Sarah's other tours, from a subject about her. She explained the reasoning behind this to comedy site, Chortle. 'You have to pick your title quite early. I always pick a title that's about me. The first one was *Sarah Millican's Not Nice*, then *Typical Woman*, *Chatterbox*, *Thoroughly Modern Millican* and then *Home Bird* and now *Outsider*. So they're all about me. *Outsider* is about slightly meatier subjects. About feeling like you don't belong – which is a feeling that's commonplace, I think. We should all talk about that experience and that feeling because then we'd belong to this big group of people who don't belong. But it's not a heavy duty show. I also wanted to talk about moving to the country. It worked out well: if you use the word 'outsider' it can mean either I like being outsider – which I never really did before – or not belonging. Are comedians outsiders? Yes, we're not misfits, but maybe a little bit odd, a little bit 'outsidery', often observing other people having fun rather than being in the middle of it.'

Outsider began its run at Stockton ARC on 15 October before she travelled up and down the country for the rest of the year and early into 2016, before flying Down Under to perform in Melbourne, Brisbane, Perth and Sydney in early April. Then it was back to the UK for the final leg with the final shows in late September. It was her biggest and best tour yet and the critics and audiences alike loved it. Asked by Chortle about any superstitions or rituals she undertakes before heading out on stage, Sarah admitted the most important thing was to empty her bladder! 'I wee right up to the last minute and sometimes have multiple wees. So much so that my tour manager will tell me when it's 'wee time'. Not, "the audience are all in and we're ready to go," but two minutes before that he'll come in and say, "Wee time!" Some people like to be full of wee because it keeps them on their toes, but all I'd do is talk about wee. I have occasionally farted on stage too. And one time I was talking about farting in the show and I did fart on stage and you think, "God, I hope there's an orchestra pit", the front row are close enough to not know what they're letting themselves in for. It's a whole different level of experience, all of their senses are going to be rocking that night. And I always check my nose because if somebody's got a bogey hanging you can't concentrate on what they're saying.'

The promotion for *Outsider* was typically tongue-in-cheek, saying; 'In the past when you put Sarah Millican outside, she asked things like: 'Why? Where is the taxi? Do I need a cardie?' and said things like: 'There'll be wasps. I've got nothing to sit on. Is that poo?' But things have changed. Now she has outside slippers. She can tell a chaffinch from a tit (hey). But she still can't tell if it's an owl or her husband's asthma. Sarah Millican is venturing outside. Bring a cardie.'

And just how does Sarah prepare for such a mammoth tour? It isn't just a case of relying on her skills as a writer and hoping for the best. Before she even began *Outsider*, she undertook a mini tour to make sure she had the material just perfect. 'At the beginning it's like, 'is it good? Will they laugh?' I do quite a lot of warm-up gigs, then progress to 'Sarah Millican and Friends' nights where I do an hour with other comics as well, then an hour solid with support and then two 45 minute sets with a break in the middle,' she told in an interview on The Phil Marriott Podcast. 'A tour is a long time coming before you get to the start so it's a bit of a relief when you're on the treadmill. And it is a treadmill because it's hard work. It's not hard work like being a nurse – I'm well aware of that – but it's hard work. I keep saying treadmill like I know what it's like, I've never been on a treadmill!'

All the hard work certainly paid off. Her tour was sold out in record time – including a whopping 11 dates at the Tyne Theatre and Opera House in Newcastle – and fans and critics alike were vocal in their praise for the new material. 'Her audience loves her,' reported *The Guardian*. 'There is no-one better at mining laughs from smut and confidential sex talk. Occasionally the show's gaze rises above the belt, notably in the sequence addressing Millican's relocation to the country. More compelling are later routines on her body image issues and on receiving fan mail from a girl who bullied her at school. But we are never far from another crack about warm dog poo or Millican's piles. She might have moved geographically, but Millican's not budging an inch comedically.'

The Telegraph were equally praising of her 90 minute set, reviewed when she performed in front of 3500 fans at the Hammersmith Eventim Apollo. 'Millican used to be able to capitalise on the comedic contrast between her demure, butter-wouldn't-melt appearance and the weapons-grade filth of some of her material. That's more difficult to pull off now she is so well-known but a spectacularly off-colour gag about pensioners and oral sex still manages to draw delighted shrieks from the fans.'

Sarah was in her element. She loved doing her shows, she loved meeting people and she didn't see the year-long tour as hard work at all – even though her voice sometimes suffered. 'I am relieved it went really well, we sold lots of tickets, had lots of full rooms and saw lots of lovely theatres,' she told Chronicle Online. 'We only had one show that we had to cancel one where I lost my voice and we had to move it to another date but that's quite impressive really, in a whole year, to have only had to cancel one. I worry about my voice. When I am talking for 2 hours for 5 or 6 nights a week for a year, it's terrifying thinking you could lose your voice. Without it, I am nothing! I saw a coach who gave me some exercise which I do every day to make sure I still have a voice.'

And there were no mishaps or embarrassing moments on stage either, you know, walking out with toilet paper stuck to her shoe or something! 'I have a tour manager who I hope would tell me if my skirt was tucked into my knickers. And I also wear leggings, I think it's dangerous territory to have bare legs. I look alright I think, I don't want people to laugh at the wrong things!'

Her audience had shifted too and perhaps in the past where she attracted an older, female audience, the people that came to see her on tour varied greatly. 'People always assume my audience is entirely female but that's not the case at all, I would say generally it's about 50/50 or 60/40 women. Couples come and multi-generational groups come - like a girl, her mam and her grandma and then the young one worries what their grandma will think but Grandma actually knows more what I'm talking about! Gender isn't always relevant in my show, I know a lot of blokes who have done things that I have done. And my audience aren't really drinkers either,' she told HMV.com. 'They get mad if there isn't any ice cream, but booze not so much. They are more tea drinkers, they'll bring a flask from home.'

The tour was a massive success and there was further good news in November when the *Outsider* DVD was released and went straight to the top of the charts, knocking Billy Connolly's *High Horse Live* into second place. So what did Sarah make of the tour? During her podcast interview with Phil Marriott she explained why she thought it was her best show yet – even though it was her longest. 'Am I tempted to do less dates in bigger venues? No, arenas aren't for me. They're OK if you move away from the mic stand but I don't. I love the theatres that we play and I love doing my job and I want to do it loads which is why I end up on tour for a year. It was longest one I've done but it was fun, it's my favourite thing to do. So if something is long, but you still love it, that's alright isn't it?'

Sarah was excited about promoting the DVD, which she saw as the final 'hurrah' of the tour and rounded off the show quite neatly. 'The show has been with me for quite a while,' she revealed to Phil. 'I write it in dribs and drabs and then I start working on it properly, then we get it ready and take it on tour for a year and now I get to show it on DVD to the people who've seen it and want to see it again or people who didn't get chance to come and see it. My tours are always about me, what I am up to now. Some comics this year have done 'the best of' shows but I can't really do that with mine as I work in quite a chronological order so when you come to see me it's more of an update on what my life is at the moment. It's like a really arrogant diary really.'

Like every aspect of her show, Sarah liked to get involved

in the construction of the DVD, having the final say on the extras that are included and where the filming takes place. 'The show was recorded in Brighton, it's a great venue. It has three different buildings, you work your way up as a comic from performing at the Pavillion, then the Corn Exchange and then you have the Dome and that is where we filmed it,' she told the *Chronicle Live*. 'You could arguably record the show anywhere you want to but I have played in Brighton for years and it's a really good place to hang out too. Between shoots we could go and walk the dog on the beach so from a selfish point of view, I wanted to pick somewhere I like. It's important that everything is as good as it can be. I like to be in control of things, in life and as well as the DVD. I'm a terrible back seat driver/pilot/doctor.'

With Christmas coming up, the tour now finished and the DVD promotion complete, Sarah was able to relax a bit and put her feet up. Well, sort of. She wasn't one to rest easily!

'I am having some time off after this tour, because my tours are always about me, I do have to live a bit otherwise I am just writing about staying in hotels and driving on motorways and nobody needs to hear that,' she also revealed to Phil. 'I am going to have a few months off work, live a bit, have a bit of a normal life I suppose. I am a bit of a workaholic though and I need someone to say to me, 'we are not allowing you to do any work!' I like my job. I am looking forward to Christmas although I'm not one of these people who puts up their Christmas tree mid November. When the shops shut on Christmas Eve and you think, well whatever we haven't got we'll just have to live without it – I quite like that bit. There is no pressure. At Christmas I do a thing on Twitter called 'join in' where we get everyone who is on their own and doesn't want to be, to use the hashtag of '#joinin' and they can all have a conversation with each other and it makes everyone a little less lonely. We've done it for 6 years, I love it.'

And what about the future? Well there is good news folks, Sarah is already in the middle of writing her next show. In fact, she started working on it during her *Outsider* tour because she when it comes to her work, she can't get enough. 'I have probably written half an hour of the next show already because I don't like that panic of when it comes to writing, sitting in front of a blank screen,' she told Chronicle Online. 'I do a low-level of writing constantly, I am always scribbling. It's going pretty well. I am taking it easy, working from home which counterbalances the fact that I haven't been at home for a while. Like people who work for 5 days and then have 2 days off, but I just do it in bigger chunks I suppose.'

Talking of big and chunky things… Sarah was, at the beginning of 2017, looking decidedly un-big and not chunky. Photos she posted to her Instagram account showed bowls of healthy snacks and eaten bowls of fruit that she titled her 'writing snacks'. Having previously always been happy to admit she had a good appetite and ate what she liked, she was now taking control of her diet and embarking on a new healthy lifestyle. Well, sort of. Her snaps of fruit were also punctuated with snaps of more, er, unhealthy snacks and Sarah admitted to the Mail Online that actually, despite media speculation to the contrary, she wasn't wasting away at all. 'They reported that I've managed a dramatic weight loss. I have never been fatter and I am happy. When I read it, I thought, "Oh, I have let everybody down!"'

So what is the biggest lesson she thinks she has learnt from being a comedian? Simple, really, she says: 'laughing can fix anything.' Or to elaborate a little more, she told Chortle. 'It can't 'fix' anything, but it can temporarily fix things. And while I love to make people laugh, I also love to laugh. Laughing is a massive release and relief. It's very good for you to laugh. If I'm the only person laughing in the room I don't give a shit. I can be howling and I don't care if other people aren't laughing because it's so subjective. I just laugh.'

And let's hope that never changes Sarah...